Classics of Political Thought for Today

An Introduction

Classics of Political Thought for Today

An Introduction

Colin Farrelly

Hackett Publishing Company, Inc.
Indianapolis/Cambridge

Copyright © 2024 by Hackett Publishing Company, Inc.

All rights reserved
Printed in the United States of America

27 26 25 24   1 2 3 4 5 6 7

For further information, please address
    Hackett Publishing Company, Inc.
    P.O. Box 44937
    Indianapolis, Indiana 46244-0937

    www.hackettpublishing.com

Cover design by Laura Clark
Interior design by Laura Clark
Composition by Aptara, Inc.

Library of Congress Control Number: 2024932615

ISBN-13: 978-1-64792-197-2 (pbk.)
ISBN-13: 978-1-64792-198-9 (PDF ebook)
ISBN-13: 978-1-64792-199-6 (epub)

The paper used in this publication meets the minimum requirements of American National Standard for Information Sciences—Permanence of Paper for Printed Library Materials, ANSI Z39.48–1984.

∞

Contents

	Preface	*ix*
1.	Introduction	1
2.	Plato, Justice, and Epistocracy	19
3.	Aristotle, Virtue Ethics, and Happiness	43
4.	Hobbes, Human Nature, and Anarchism	67
5.	Locke, Limited Government, and Toleration	93
6.	Rousseau, Inequality, and the General Will	123
7.	Conservative Political Thought	149
8.	Feminist Political Thought	177
9.	Black Political Thought	205
10.	Utilitarianism	233
11.	Marx and the Critique of Capitalism	263
12.	Conclusion	291
	Index	*309*

For my students, who always remind me of why it is important to foster intellectual curiosity, humility, and optimism

Preface

Writing a book that surveys and critically assesses the history of Western political philosophy is both a rewarding and also an intellectually demanding endeavor. Determining which thinkers to include/exclude, finding the optimal balance between outlining the details of the thinkers and political traditions canvassed versus exploring the critical insights and objections typically raised against those ideas, and framing the relevance and significance of thinkers long dead for the practical predicaments we face today can feel like daunting endeavors for any instructor who teaches a course on this subject. And that is because such intellectual tasks are indeed daunting endeavors! This book treats the ideas of the past as part of an ongoing conversation and debate with the present and the future concerning how we, both as individuals and collectively as societies, ought to live our lives.

The initial research for this book goes all the way back to my time as a graduate student at the University of Bristol, when, as a final year PhD student in philosophy in 1999, I taught my first lecture course, which was a whole semester just on Karl Marx. Since that time I have expanded the range of thinkers I have taught, teaching philosophy students at Aberdeen University, and then, switching from philosophy to political science departments, teaching at Birmingham University, Manchester University, Waterloo University, and Queen's University. I have been teaching at the latter since 2009. At Queen's University I teach a full-year course on the history of Western political philosophy/theory (I take "political philosophy" and "political theory" to be synonymous terms) to a few hundred students every year.

The discipline of political philosophy has evolved and changed significantly over my career. Both the thinkers we typically teach (historically it was all white males, with rare exceptions) and how they are taught have changed over the past quarter century. I am grateful to the thousands of students who have joined me on the intellectual journey of exploring and critically assessing the ideas of past political thinkers. This book is dedicated to my students.

The bulk of this book was written during the COVID-19 pandemic, when unprecedented public health measures were implemented in an effort to mitigate the spread of SARS-CoV-2. As the initial weeks of lockdown turned into months, followed by more months of continued restrictions on social interactions, I invested most of my energies into writing this book and teaching the course material in an online format. The pandemic amplified many of the themes debated in the history of Western political philosophy concerning the relationship between expertise and democratic governance, as well as the scope and limits of individual rights. At this same time, during the summer of 2020, the police killing of George Floyd, and the Black Lives Matter protests that followed, helped spur a broader societal debate about the persistence of racial inequality and the function of protests.

In the final months of writing this book I was living in Ankara, Türkiye, while on sabbatical from my home institution. I was teaching a course at Bilkent University when the devastating earthquake hit Türkiye and Syria in early February 2023, killing tens of thousands of people. The Turkish government then canceled all in-person classes in the country for the next two months, and my students and I returned to virtual teaching (which exhausted all of us during the pandemic). Türkiye is currently listed as a "hybrid-regime" by the *Economist*'s Democracy Index 2022 report. This means, ranking 103rd in the world by measures like "electoral process and pluralism," "political culture," and "civil liberties," Türkiye has both democratic and authoritarian elements. As I am writing this preface there is a Turkish presidential election next week. Spending time writing and teaching in a country where people, including university students, do not feel they can openly express their views about their own government and political culture helped remind me why it is so important to teach the topics covered in this book. The ideals of freedom, democracy, and equality are ones future generations must continue to engage with and refine.

In addition to the thousands of students who helped participate in the writing of this book, by their questions and comments in my lectures over nearly the past quarter century, I am very grateful to the members of the political philosophy reading group at Queen's University. In the fall of 2021 we had our first in-person meeting since the pandemic had started, and the group kindly read and commented on an earlier version of chapter 1 of this book, providing me with the opportunity to reconsider both the thinkers covered in the book and the manner in which the material would be covered. I am grateful to Sue Donaldson, Will Kymlicka, Meena Krishnamurthy, Margaret Moore, and Christine Sypnowich for the helpful comments and critical feedback on the initial conceptualization of this book. While perhaps no consensus could ever emerge among political philosophers concerning which thinkers should be taught, let alone how they should be taught, I have profited immensely from engaging with the members of the political philosophy reading group over many years.

Sandrine Bergès was kind enough to provide feedback on the chapter on feminist political thought, and reviewers of the initial book proposal offered helpful suggestions and insights on what the book should aspire to cover. I am also grateful to two referees who provided insightful suggestions for improvements and revisions on a complete draft version of the manuscript. My editor, Jeff Dean, provided extensive and substantive feedback on the complete manuscript, and he always offered helpful advice on how parts of the book could be tweaked or modified to better serve the general reader. Finally, my research assistants Jennifer Guiho and Yerin Chung provided excellent editorial assistance.

CHAPTER 1

Introduction

> The trained mind is the one that best grasps the degree of observation, forming of ideas, reasoning, and experimental testing required in any special case, and that profits the most, in future thinking, by mistakes made in the past.
>
> John Dewey, *How We Think* (1910)

Humanity faces many pressing societal predicaments in the twenty-first century. These problems include addressing climate change, globalization, and poverty; managing pandemics, population aging, and novel technologies (e.g., genome editing, artificial intelligence, etc.); and redressing historical and contemporary injustices (e.g., those pertaining to colonialism, slavery, and patriarchy). With so many pressing predicaments to address, one might be skeptical of the suggestion that engaging with the thinkers of the past can serve a critical pedagogical function for students in the humanities and social sciences today. "To tackle today's societal problems we must think cogently, creatively, and ambitiously," the skeptic might reasonably contend. "We need *forward-*, not backward-looking, thinking," our skeptic would assert.

I agree with the claim that the problems of today require cogent, creative, and ambitious forward-looking thinking. But I believe our skeptic is guilty of making a false dichotomy when they maintain that we must choose between the ideas of the past or those of the future, as if these two things are distinct and unrelated. Following John Dewey's sentiment in the epigraph above, I also believe the past can teach us many important lessons, such as revealing the mistakes we are prone to make in diagnosing our societal problems, as well as how best to confront them. This book is written from the conviction that critically engaging with the past thinkers addressed in this book can serve an important, twenty-first-century, pedagogical function. Fortunately for us, the ideas of the historical thinkers covered in this book—which range from the ancient Greeks and the social contract tradition, to conservatism, feminism, Black political thought, utilitarianism, and Marxism—offer a rich and varied treasure trove of cogent, creative, and ambitious (as well as fallible, erroneous, and short-sighted) political ideas. There is much we can learn from the way past thinkers grappled with what they saw as the pressing problems of their day.

The historical thinkers and topics surveyed in this book include Plato's critique of democracy, Aristotle's emphasis on the primacy of virtue and well-being (*eudaimonia*), the account of human nature posited by Thomas Hobbes in his justification for the state, Emma Goldman's defense of anarchism, John Locke's defense of the right to private property, Jean-Jacques Rousseau's diagnosis of inequality, Edmund Burke's condemnation of the French Revolution, Booker T. Washington's emphasis on self-improvement, Christine de Pizan's condemnation of misogyny, Mary Wollstonecraft's critique of the nature/nurture debate, Anna Cooper's analysis of how sexism and racism are intertwined, Frederick Douglass's condemnation of slavery, W. E. B. Du Bois's critical analysis of racial segregation, Martin Luther King Jr.'s defense of civil disobedience, Frantz Fanon's critique of colonialism, Jeremy Bentham's critique of the talk of "natural rights," John Stuart Mill's defense of free speech, and Karl Marx's critique of capitalism.

The diverse thinkers covered in this book were all societal *problem-solvers* of different types. They theorized about different societal predicaments—ranging from economic, political, racial, and gender inequality to state censorship, civil war, and revolution—problems that reflected the history, geography, and culture of their day. Attending to the details of the arguments advanced by this diverse range of problem-solvers can help us refine our own problem-solving "cognitive toolbox." Thus I invite the reader to engage with these thinkers not only to gain a better appreciation for history and what these political thinkers offered, but because doing so can help us refine the intellectual skills and insights needed to identify and help remedy the problems of today (and tomorrow).

What Is Political Philosophy?

There are different ways to approach the study of the history of political philosophy. *Historians* of political thought prioritize understanding the detailed historical specifics of past thinkers, such as religious and other cultural factors at play during an author's lifetime, or the original meaning of key ideas and concepts employed in their writings. Other scholars survey historical thinkers not for the purposes of getting clear about the details of history but to help bring *conceptual clarity* to political concepts like freedom, equality, and justice (which historical thinkers addressed in their writings). And still others canvass different political philosophers to provide some coherence to the study of *political ideologies* (e.g., liberalism, socialism, feminism, etc.). All of these approaches have their strengths and weaknesses. But the approach taken in this book tries to forge a distinct path from these well-trodden traditional approaches.

This book explicitly, and consciously, embraces a form of what Lynn Fendler calls a "strategically presentistic approach to historiography."[1] "Presentism" means an approach to studying the past which is grounded in the present (versus being primarily concerned with reconstructing the past), "using that vantage point as an opportunity to foster a critical understanding of our present circumstances."[2] This approach to educational historiography is "strategic" because the link between the past and the present is made for the explicit purpose of facilitating our (i.e., readers in the present context) intellectual insight and development, so that we are better equipped to be effective problem solvers for the challenges of today.[3]

---

1. Lynn Fendler, "The Upside of Presentism," *Paedagogica Historica* 44, no. 6 (2008), 677–90, 687.

2. Fendler, "Upside of Presentism," 678.

3. Fendler notes the following three appeals of a strategically presentisitic approach to the study of the past:
   - Epistemologically allow for the possibility that the present may be similar to and/or different from the past;
   - Methodologically allow for both discontinuity and continuity in history, permitting a critical perspective on extrahistorical mechanisms such as causality, linearity, or circularity;
   - Pedagogically recognize multiple interpretations of things in both the past and the present (677–78).

The thinkers surveyed in this book are not presented as conceptual "puzzle solvers" intent on outlining, in the abstract, what is entailed by political ideals like justice, freedom, and equality. Nor are these thinkers treated (at least not primarily) as proponents of easily identifiable and distinct "political ideologies" (e.g., socialism, feminism, liberalism, and conservatism). Instead, we engage with, and critically assess, these thinkers as practical "problem-solvers." The history of Western political philosophy is thus presented as a history of different attempts to solve different types of societal problems, problems that are still with us today in the twenty-first century.

The characterization of political philosophy as a particular type of "problem-solving" endeavor is of course a contentious and debatable claim. Political philosophers will provide diverse, even conflicting, answers to the question "What is political philosophy?" Leo Strauss, for example, had the following to say in answer to this question in 1957:

> Since political philosophy is a branch of philosophy, even the most provisional explanation of what political philosophy is, cannot dispense with an explanation, however provisional, of what philosophy is. Philosophy, as quest for wisdom, is quest for universal knowledge, for knowledge of the whole.... Political philosophy will then be the attempt to replace opinion about the nature of political things by knowledge of the nature of political things.... If political philosophy wishes to do justice to its subject matter, it must strive for genuine knowledge of these standards. Political philosophy is the attempt truly to know both the nature of political things and the right, or the good, political order.[4]

My characterization of the study of the history of political philosophy as the study of different types of "problem-solvers" has some partial

---

The survey of historical thinkers covered in this book aspires to achieve these three appeals, making links between today and the past when relevant, but also emphasizing the dissimilarities and discontinuities between the past and present, and finally acknowledging that multiple interpretations of these issues is both defensible and pedagogically beneficial.

4. Leo Strauss, "What Is Political Philosophy?," *Review of Politics* 19, no. 3 (1957): 343–68.

overlap with, and some strong divergence from, Strauss's popular understanding of the discipline. I think Strauss's characterization captures the primary concerns of certain political philosophers better than others. Classical thinkers like Plato and Aristotle, for example, fit well with Strauss's characterization, but thinkers like Bentham and Marx do not. More importantly, Strauss's characterization of the discipline as being primarily concerned with the nature of political things is ill suited for most of the political thinkers that have typically been (unjustifiably) excluded from the canon: Christine de Pizan, Emma Goldman, Mary Wollstonecraft, Booker T. Washington, Frederick Douglass, Anna Cooper, W. E. B. Du Bois, Frantz Fanon, and many others.

A more inclusive (from a historical perspective) characterization of the discipline is, I believe, one that makes more explicit the real-world urgency captured in the writings of these political thinkers, with respect to redressing the "knowledge gap" in our wisdom concerning different types of real-world, societal predicaments (not just a concern for universal knowledge about the nature of political things). Plato wanted to abate the harms of rule by the ignorant. Hobbes wanted to abate the risks of civil unrest and war. For Rousseau the concern was those inequalities that could erode the expression and realization of the general will. For feminists the primary concern is to abate patriarchy, while for critical race theorists it is abating racial inequality. Conservatives emphasize the importance of "the actual and tried" versus "the untried" in political life. And finally for liberals there is great urgency to limit state power to prevent unjustified state interference with individual liberty, whereas for Marx the primary practical task is to abate exploitation and alienation due to capitalism.

To equate political philosophy with the aspiration to know about the nature of political things and the good political order risks framing political philosophy as an ivory-tower academic exercise in a priori reasoning[5] rather than the exercise of experiential, practical reason designed to improve the quality of our collective political lives. I think the latter is a more apt characterization of the canon of political philosophy for the twenty-first century than Strauss's characterization. But I concede that

---

5. Or even worse, as a form of ideology that distracts our attention from the injustices and problems of the real world. See Charles Mills, "'Ideal Theory' as Ideology," *Hypatia* 20, no. 3 (2005): 165–84.

there are different opinions about this as the discipline is *pluralistic* in its methodology. But I hope the merits of my characterization of the discipline come to the fore when addressing the diverse range of thinkers I canvass and assess in this book.

To clarify the type of problem-solving that was addressed by the canonical thinkers covered in this book, it may be useful to make an illustrative analogy between medicine and political philosophy. Two essential skills are necessary for success in both medicine and political philosophy. The first essential skill is a *diagnostic skill*—to accurately identify pathology (in the case of medicine) and pressing societal ills (in the case of political philosophy). The second skill is a *prescriptive skill*—the insight and foresight to know how best to prevent or remedy the problems/challenges (health or societal) identified by the first epistemic skill.

The first step in any potential medical intervention is to accurately diagnosis what it is that ails a patient. Symptoms must be identified and categorized, along with findings from more precise diagnostic measures (e.g., biopsy), before ascertaining if pathology is the prognosis. Many things can go wrong with the human body and mind. A skilled healthcare clinician must first be able to discern what the cause of a health malady is. This diagnostic step is necessary before any sage prescription for treatment or therapy can be made. Once the health malady has been properly identified, medications, surgery, or some other treatment can be prescribed to treat or manage the health problem.

Like a skilled health-care clinician, a political philosopher will both engage in a diagnosis of societal ills and formulate some tentative prescriptions that could help prevent or improve the problematic state of affairs. Over the course of the history of Western civilization there have been a multitude of societal ills political philosophers have addressed. In ancient Athens Plato diagnosed what he took to be the problem inherent with democracy—namely, that it was a political system that placed power in the hands of the *demos* (majority) who were governed by their appetites and lacked the knowledge of what was truly good for society. Plato's remedy to the "rule of the ignorant" was to entrust power to "philosopher rulers," individuals whom Plato believed would not deviate from the quest to achieve the truth. Aristotle concerned himself with quality of character, maintaining that virtue involved an intermediate position between the extremes of having too much or too little of an emotion.

The societal unrest of civil war in seventeenth-century England was the pathology Hobbes concerned himself with, which led him to argue for the legitimacy of an absolute sovereign. The opulence and inequality of eighteenth-century France led Rousseau to prescribe the remedy of a democratic form of sovereignty (guided by the general will). In contrast, Wollstonecraft, Douglass, Cooper, and Du Bois all diagnosed significant inequalities (e.g., gender and racial) that must be redressed by challenging the hierarchies embedded in the status quo of the family, slavery, and segregation. Utilitarians like Bentham and Mill identified the problem of predicating laws on appeals to natural rights versus a concern for happiness, and championed democracy and limited government as concrete prescriptions that could help promote "the greatest happiness of the greater number." And perhaps the grandest of all "political health practitioners," Karl Marx, detailed the social ills of capitalism and the prescriptions of a postcapitalist way of life.

The Importance of History

History is relevant to our future because the past was once someone else's present, and today is the future that they theorized about. Others contemplated the social ills of their day and offered prescriptions to redress those shortcomings. Attending to the errors and omissions of past thinkers (e.g., such as the marginalization of the actual history of colonialism and slavery in social contract theory)[6] can help teach us about the importance of observation, intellectual humility, and creativity, making us more cognizant of our own biases, blind spots, and faulty assumptions. Conversely, acknowledging and celebrating the persistent efforts and innovative insights of past thinkers—whether it be Plato's critique of democracy, Wollstonecraft's diagnosis of the cause of gender inequality, Bentham's championing of the principle of utility, or Fanon's criticism of colonialism—can teach us about the value of insight, courage, dedication, and having an adaptive (problem-solving) mind.

---

6. Charles W. Mills, "Race and the Social Contract Tradition," *Social Identities* 6, no. 4 (2000): 441–62.

Our interpretation of the past is not static, nor will it (nor could it) ever yield a fixed consensus in terms of how to interpret it. The past is constantly being rewritten, as our understanding of both the past and present evolve and change. Writing over a century ago, the Spanish American philosopher George Santayana quipped, "History is always written wrong, and so always needs to be rewritten."[7] And nearly half a century after Santayana penned those words, the philosopher of education John Dewey made a similar point about interpreting history, maintaining that the story of the past is written by the agenda of the present:

> The slightest reflection shows that the conceptual material employed in writing history is that of the period in which a history is written. There is no material available for leading principles and hypotheses save that of the historic present. As culture changes, the conceptions that are dominant in a culture change. Of necessity new standpoints for viewing, appraising and ordering data arise. History is then rewritten.[8]

What both Santayana and Dewey recognized is that the past should not, and can never be, treated as "settled." Furthermore, they understood that the act of interpreting and making sense of the past has important significance for us in the "here and now." Rewriting our collective history, like rewriting one's own personal history, is a *transformative* act, one that permits a new identity to cohesively emerge. Storytelling is an integral part of the process of self-development, education, and growth. This is especially true when the history in question is the history of ideas. Ideas can be powerful catalysts for change, but they can also be powerful tools that entrench an exclusive and unequal status quo. This book concerns itself with a specific domain in the history of ideas, namely a number of influential political thinkers who have helped shape, for better or worse, the culture and sociopolitical institutions of Western civilization. This book is designed to

---

7. George Santayana, *"Reason and Science": The Life of Reason, or the Phases of Human Progress*, vol. 7, eds. Marianne Wokeck and Martin Coleman (Cambridge, MA: MIT Press, 2024), 26.

8. John Dewey, *Logic: The Theory of Inquiry* (New York: Holt, 1938), 232–33.

help inspire and aid the reader in the intellectual journey of engaging with, and critically assessing, classics of Western political philosophy.

The Foundational Question Guiding This Project

Before embarking on the intellectual journey of critically attending to the ideas of past thinkers, let us consider, in more detail, the foundational question (FQ) that anchors the study presented in this book:

FQ: Why engage with the study, and critical evaluation, of the history of Western political philosophy?

No doubt many distinct answers could be given to this question, and this foundational question raises a number of more specific questions that it is prudent to address before trying to answer FQ. Three more specific questions are:

1. What constitutes the *classics* in the history of Western political philosophy?
2. Why study the *history* of Western political philosophy (versus more contemporary theories and arguments)?
3. Why study the history of *Western* political philosophy (versus non-Western traditions, such as Eastern philosophy (e.g., Confucius)?

With respect to the first question, "What constitutes the *classics* in the history of Western political philosophy?" we should acknowledge the elephant in the room—that the traditional canon of Western political philosophy typically taught at universities was composed, at least predominately if not exclusively, of dead, white, male thinkers. This has led to (I believe well-founded) criticisms that the discipline must be substantively revised. Some have called for decolonizing the teaching curriculum, and adopting a more inclusive range of thinkers (e.g., more female thinkers) within the canon.[9] This book aspires to takes such criticisms

---

9. Charles Mills, "Decolonising Western Political Philosophy," *New Political Science* 37, no. 1 (2015): 1–25; Penny Weiss, *Canon Fodder: Historical Women Political Thinkers* (University Park: Pennsylvania State University Press, 2009).

seriously, and while it covers many thinkers traditionally considered part of the canon (e.g., Plato, Aristotle, Hobbes, Locke, Mill, and Marx) it also substantively addresses the contributions of female political thinkers (e.g., Goldman, Pizan, Wollstonecraft, and Cooper) and Black political thinkers (Washington, Douglass, Du Bois, Fanon, and Martin Luther King Jr.) who have tended to be neglected or marginalized in the field.

The second, more specific, question noted above asks: "Why study the *history* of Western political philosophy versus more contemporary theories and arguments?" "The past is the past," a critic might argue when resisting engaging with thinkers long deceased. "The practical challenges of the twenty-first century are so unique and pressing," our skeptic might continue, "that there is little reason to believe that contemplating the arguments advanced by philosophers living in ancient Greece, or during the English Civil War, French Revolution, or Industrial Revolution, will really help us find sage insights into the problems of today."

Engaging with the arguments of philosophers long dead might appear as idle navel-gazing to some if attention is not given to the vast range of societal predicaments these thinkers theorized about, as well as the interdisciplinary scope and contemporary relevance of the modes of social inquiry they inspired. The innovative theorizing of past thinkers can serve as an important source of *learning* and *inspiration* to those of us living in the twenty-first century. When canvassing the concerns of these past thinkers I draw attention not just to the progressive and lasting positive contributions canonical thinkers have made to Western political culture but also to their "cognitive blind spots," problematic assumptions (e.g., prejudice) and glaring omissions in their theorizing about the problems of their time, which can still adversely impact how we view the political landscape today. For example, many of these political thinkers ignored the origins and persistence of sexual, racial, and cultural inequality. When Rousseau prescribed that our political lives should be governed by the "general will," which is supposed to "come from all" and "apply to all," he only considered men fit for exercising such civic responsibilities. And Marx assumed that technological progress could advance to "meet the needs of all" by exploiting the world's natural resources without concern for the long-term ecological impact on the planet and our future. By attending to the past we can reveal key insights that have been overlooked, even by insightful and progressive thinkers.

Furthermore, throughout this book the ideas of past thinkers are assessed in terms of more contemporary knowledge about topics like human nature, happiness, private property, gender, racism, and democracy. When relevant, I attempt to link the ideas of these past thinkers to contemporary concerns. Here are just five examples:

1. Plato's concerns about the rule of the ignorant parallels concerns about the recent rise of populism.
2. Locke's account of the right to private property connects to a range of divergent political interests and movements, ranging from Indigenous rights to libertarianism and taxation of income.
3. Conservatives emphasize, in the words of Michael Oakeshott, "the familiar to the unknown," "the tried to the untried." Does this mean that society should adopt a position of "bioconservatism" and resist adopting new genetic technologies like genome editing, a technology that might permit us to improve our biology?
4. The consequentialist outlook of Jeremy Bentham helps frame the strengths and weaknesses of cost-benefit analysis in public policy decision-making *and* provides the normative theoretical basis for arguments about animal rights.
5. Anna Cooper's attention to the overlapping problems of racism and sexism has direct relevance to the intersectional lens often deployed today to bring attention to the different ways oppression is manifest in contemporary societies.

The third and final specific question raised above is "Why study the history of *Western* political philosophy versus non-Western traditions (for example, Eastern philosophy, like Confucianism)?" Today's world is global and interconnected, and thus an exclusive focus on Western political philosophy might appear to some as a parochial interest or modern invention.[10] I think there is some validity to such concerns, though the arguments

---

10. Fred Dallmayr, "Toward a Comparative Political Theory," *Review of Politics* 59, no. 3 (1997): 421–27; Andrew March, "What Is Comparative Political Theory?," *Review of Politics* 71, no. 4 (2009): 531–65; Kwame Anthony Appiah, "There Is No Such Thing as Western Civilization," *Guardian*, July 9, 2016, https://www.theguardian.com/world/2016/nov/09/western-civilisation-appiah-reith-lecture.

advanced in this book are perfectly compatible with the conjecture that there is also great value in attending to the arguments and insights of thinkers outside the Western tradition. This book is not intended to provide an *exhaustive* coverage of all the thinkers and traditions worthy of study that have ever lived (nor an exhaustive list of thinkers within just the tradition of Western political philosophy).

To dedicate a book to the study of the Western canon should not be taken to imply that *only* that canon is worthy of study. I decided to write a book on the canon of Western political philosophy because I believe doing so can offer important, *distinctive* educative lessons that are crucial for students to learn in today's globalized world, lessons concerning the limits of state power, toleration, equality, freedom, happiness, property, racism, rebellion, technological progress, equality, democracy, and patriarchy. These lessons are really the focus of this book, though the lessons are taught via an engagement with thinkers in the history of Western political philosophy. Other important lessons could no doubt be taught by engaging with Islamic political thought or Confucianism, for example. But those topics would have to be covered in a different book than this one.

The issue of the value and centrality of, as well as the approach to teaching, the history of Western civilization is among one of the most contentious and divisive issues debated on university campuses today. The three specific questions addressed above have all weighed heavily on my own mind in my teaching, as well as in the design and writing of this book. When I started university as an undergraduate student back in the early 1990s in Canada, these questions were not live questions like they are today. What was considered the canon back then was much pretty much fixed, and this rigidity meant the list of thinkers deemed essential to learn about and engage with was often accepted uncritically. The value of studying that rigid canon was also taken as a given, as was the value of studying historical figures more generally and the value of focusing on Western political thinkers (versus non-Western thinkers). But a lot has changed over the past few decades, and in my view this change (on the whole) has been beneficial and long overdue.

What constitutes the canon to be taught to our undergraduate students in political science and philosophy courses, and how we teach that canon, are now regarded as moral, evaluative, and highly contested issues.

What we include and what we leave out (e.g., the voices of women, the experience of those who suffered the injustices of racial and cultural inequality) can help either combat or perpetuate different types of societal problems. This means such questions warrant a great deal of care, attention, and critical reflection rather than being treated as simply a descriptive and settled matter (e.g., "teach what we have tended to teach in the past!").

One might be tempted to take the limitations of Western political thought—like the fact that traditional canonical thinkers ignored issues like patriarchy, colonialism, and racial inequality—as a basis for neglecting, if not rejecting, the continued importance of seriously engaging with central historical thinkers in Western political thought. I think such a dismissive attitude is problematic and should be resisted. There is a valuable pedagogical lesson to be learned by acknowledging that insightful, even progressive, thinkers of the past had their own cognitive blind spots, biases, and prejudices. Rather than treat such thinkers as infallible "intellectual heroes" of Western civilization, we should engage with them in a nuanced and humble fashion. All these thinkers (like us today) were fallible, working with assumptions about human nature, culture, religion, race, and gender that can and should be challenged today. We study these thinkers not for the purpose of ridiculing them for all their faulty assumptions or glaring omissions, but to draw attention to the strengths, as well as acknowledge and redress the weaknesses, of the theories, assumptions, insights, and prescriptions they offered regarding how we should collectively live together.

The most timeless contributions of these thinkers continue to provide important insights we should consider and engage with in the twenty-first century. Our engagement with the canon should be one of critical inquiry, the middle ground between adoration/deference and the impulse to "cancel" and dismiss. Recall Dewey's apt insight that "the trained mind profits the most, in future thinking, by mistakes made in the past."[11] In the chapters to come I try my best to canvass both the strengths *and* weaknesses/limitations of the thinkers we will cover. By doing so I hope the book is a catalyst to the project of renewing and revising the classics in political philosophy.

---

11. John Dewey, *How We Think* (Boston: D. C. Health, 1910), 78.

Humanistic Education and Epistemic Virtue

Let us now return to answer the foundational question (FQ) raised earlier: *Why engage with the study, and critical evaluation, of the history of Western political philosophy?* I have a short answer to this question, and a longer one. The short answer will strike the reader as a generic type of answer often provided by instructors teaching in the humanities and social sciences: namely, that doing so helps encourage and refine *critical thinking*.

The critical thinking inherent in political philosophy concerns a specific domain of social inquiry: *how should we, both as individuals and collectively as societies, live our lives?* For example, when thinking about the legitimate scope, limits, and function of government, what we assume about human nature, gender, property, happiness, racial inequality, the experience and wisdom of the past, and so on will have a profound impact on what kind of future we aspire to bring into existence in the "here and now." The thinkers of the past theorized about their own "present and future collective lives," and thus we can learn a great deal by attending to the virtues and vices of the concepts, theories, assumptions, and aspirations they invoked when addressing the practical predicaments of their own time.

But if the reader will indulge me, I would like to elaborate further on this short answer with my longer answer to the FQ, as this will help explain the content and approach of this book. This book has been designed to be a contribution to *humanistic education*. The literature on humanistic education is vast and could be the focus of a book in itself. My own personal "philosophy of education" draws on a variety of humanistic thinkers, ranging from Socrates and Rabindranath Tagore to John Dewey, Carl Rogers, and Martha Nussbaum. I will just briefly summarize the vision of humanistic education that informs this book and has been the foundation of my teaching for over twenty years.

First and foremost, a humanistic education is *student-centered*; it treats students as *developing* human beings and reflective democratic citizens versus merely as students pursuing a degree who need to get a course credit, or future employees valued only for what they can contribute to the economy, or impressionable minds receptive to being swayed into adopting the specific political ideology an instructor advocates. Because humanistic education is conceived of as a reflexive, ongoing developmental process (versus a goal-oriented approach to education), it prioritizes the development and refinement of a number of specific *epistemic* or *intellectual virtues* that can help facilitate the self-realization of students. Three cornerstone epistemic virtues are integral to this work: (1) curiosity, (2) insight and nuanced understanding, and (3) optimism.

Epistemic Virtue #1: *Curiosity*

Curiosity can be defined as "a cognitive induced deprivation that arises from the perception of a gap in knowledge and understanding."[12] The curious intellect is motivated to try to make sense of what it currently does not know or understand. The intellectual activity of remedying this knowledge and understanding gap is an *enjoyable* activity for the genuinely curious mind. This book is written for the intellectually curious student. Such a student will often wonder about one or more of the following types of questions: "Why are our social and political lives the way that they are?" "Why is there government versus anarchism?" "Why is rule by democracy a desirable and defensible political aspiration?" "Why is there inequality in the world—socioeconomic inequality, gender inequality, and racial inequality?"

The motivation to engage with the political philosophy of the past is driven, at least in part, by the intrinsic reward of satisfying our intellectual curiosities of trying to understand, as well as critically assess, the political ideas and ideals of the past. Ideas and ideals concerning human nature, justice, equality, democracy, gender, race, happiness, and freedom have had, and continue to have, a real impact in politics. Engaging with the classics in political philosophy enables us to indulge our curiosity about the attraction and variation in, and limits of, political ideas and ideals. The study of political philosophy is serious business as it deals with important societal topics like political power, racial inequality, colonialism, patriarchy, democracy, and so on. But it can, and should, also be a fun topic to study if approached from a curious mindset.

---

12. George Loewenstein, "The Psychology of Curiosity: A Review and Reinterpretation," *Psychological Bulletin* 116, no. 1 (1994): 75–98.

A primary motivation for engaging with the canon of Western political thought should thus be a sense of *discovery*. What are the ideas, for better or worse, that have shaped the institutions and culture of Western liberal democracies? This sense of discovery was what motivated my interest in the field, first as a student and then (ever since) as a professor and scholar, so I have tried my best to write this book with a sense of discovery. By studying the classics in political philosophy, and by doing so in an inquisitive fashion, students will be exposed to intellectual giants that exemplify the epistemic virtue of curiosity. From Plato's classic examination of the question "What is justice?" and Hobbes's conjectures about what life is like in the "state of nature," to Goldman's defense of anarchism, Burke's reflections on the French Revolution, Wollestonecraft's criticism of sexual inequality, Du Bois's diagnosis of the ills of the Jim Crow era, and Marx's conjectures about class and class conflict, the thinkers covered in this book certainly thought outside the box for their times by critically reflecting on the societal predicaments they faced. By engaging with these inquisitive thinkers of the past, students in the twenty-first century can be inspired to exercise and celebrate their own curiosity about why things are the way they are, and how we might collectively act to bring about a more desirable future.

Epistemic Virtue #2: *Insight and Nuanced Understanding*

Everyday politics is often a rancorous business. Disagreement is omnipresent. Sometimes political arguments stem from disagreement over what constitutes the relevant facts concerning a particular policy or societal issue. Will policy A boost the economy more than policy B? Will strategy X help combat the harms of climate change in the future more effectively than strategy Y? But often political disagreements are disagreements about moral and political values. For example, is it more important to grow the economy or to ensure its benefits are more evenly distributed? What moral obligations do we have to future generations and who should take on most of the burdens of mitigating the harmful effects of climate change (e.g., the biggest carbon emitters today, or those who emitted the most historically, or those who can most afford to reduce their reliance on carbon, etc.)? When can government justifiably interfere in our liberty?

The ideas of past political thinkers have helped shape the evaluative judgments embedded in diverse political traditions, such as liberalism, feminism, conservativism, Marxism, and critical race theory. By critically engaging with the historical thinkers that inspired and shaped these political positions, we are exposed to a wide array of normative insights that can help us develop a better understanding of, and appreciation for, the diversity of insights and opinions in contemporary political life.

Epistemic Virtue #3: *Optimism*

As a general character trait, optimism is commonly described as a disposition that expects good (versus bad) things to happen. But the type of optimism I have in mind for cultivating in this book is a more narrow and specific type of optimism, conceived of as a distinctively *epistemic virtue*. When faced with adversity, an optimist adopts a creative (or open) mindset to *problem-solving* the collective predicaments that must be addressed. This can be contrasted with a pessimistic (or fixed) mindset, which fails to competently think or act because it is consumed with despair or a fatalism about the circumstances. Optimism is thus a *hopeful* disposition. Hope is something essential to the political theory of John Dewey,[13] a thinker who inspired this student-focused book. Hope is not deluded "wishful thinking" that somehow things will just work out for the better. Rather, the epistemic manifestation of hope and optimism is the belief that we can *learn* from the past, and that these lessons will help us better address the societal challenges of today and bring about a better tomorrow.

This optimism is based in the reality that ideas have had, and will continue to have, a substantive impact in the real world. Ideas of racial and gender supremacy helped create and sustain societal hierarchies, whereas ideals of equality and inclusion have helped challenge and dismantle such hierarchies. Ideas concerning nationalism have contributed to the rise of fascism and provided justifications for starting world wars, whereas ideas about the importance of individual freedom and toleration have helped

---

13. Stephen M. Fishman and Lucille McCarthy, *John Dewey and the Philosophy and Practice of Hope* (Urbana: University of Illinois Press, 2007).

limit state authoritarianism and xenophobic attitudes. Ideas concerning the right of the nobility to rule over others legitimated feudalism and reinforced the pretense for the humanitarian theology behind colonialism, whereas ideas about government accountability and political representation can inspire democratic reform and gender quotas for political parties. Ideas can have a profound, tangible impact on the life prospects of the world's populations. They are a subject worthy of study and careful critical examination.

CHAPTER 2

Plato, Justice, and Epistocracy

Our engagement with the classics in political philosophy begins by going back over two thousand years, to the fourth century BC in ancient Greece. Plato is one of the most significant figures in the history of philosophy, and Plato's *Republic* is certainly one of the foundational works (if not the most important one) in political philosophy. The *Republic*, like Plato's other writings, takes the form of a dialogue with interlocutors debating philosophical questions. The question that is the focus of the *Republic* is "What is justice?" In this chapter we will primarily focus on the *Republic* but also address the *Apology* and *Crito*. The *Apology* deals with the trial of Socrates, where Socrates is condemned to death for impiety and corrupting the minds of young Athenians. Plato's *Crito* takes place in Socrates's prison cell shortly before his death, and it addresses the issue of political obligation.

The central character in Plato's dialogues is the character of Socrates. Socrates was a real person and (an older) contemporary of Plato's. What we know about Socrates comes from the writings of Plato and others (e.g., Aristophanes and Xenophon). There is debate among Platonic scholars concerning the extent to which the character of Socrates in Plato's writings is Plato simply reporting the insights and arguments of his mentor Socrates versus the extent to which Plato simply utilized Socrates as a character in his dialogues to champion Plato's own views on the topics of discussion. For our purposes, which are to engage in the critical thinking pedagogy Plato's *Republic* offers (versus an in-depth historical and textual analysis of Plato's writings), when we refer to the character of Socrates we shall simply take that to represent Plato's position. We will treat the character of Socrates in Plato's dialogues as a character who represents the actual positions and arguments of Plato, while recognizing that the issue of interpreting Plato's actual position versus that of Socrates is much more complex.

Ancient Athens

At the time that Plato lived, Greece was not the country that it is today. Ancient Greece was composed of a number of distinct city-states (*polis*, pl. *poleis*). Athens, where Plato lived, had a population of approximately 250,000 people. What makes ancient Athens of particular interest to political philosophers is that it was the first experiment with *democratic* governance. During its prime, Athens stood out as the most successful of the Greek city-states, by nearly all important criteria of comparison: wealth, power, stability, cultural influence, and so on.[1]

The main rival to ancient Athens during the lifetime of Plato was Sparta, an oligarchy ("rule by the few") and military state. Sparta invested heavily in the military training of its citizenry, and discipline was highly prized. As such, Sparta was less innovative and experimental compared to the Athenian democratic form of governance, an approach that could tap into the wisdom of "many and diverse minds." Diverse knowledge, rather than just military specialization, proved more successful in achieving the prosperity and security for a polity. Trade, the cultural benefits of art and philosophy, and the system of democratic governance meant the Athenians could adapt efficiently to the changes and challenges of their environment.

Athenian democracy was very different from the conception of democratic government that exists today. First, today's democracies are more expansive about citizenship and the enfranchisement of adult citizens. In ancient Athens the vast majority of the population—slaves, women, and noncitizens who moved to Athens from other city-states—were excluded from citizenship. Furthermore, Athenian democracy was a form of direct versus representative democracy. There were no elected politicians who made the decisions typically made by the US Congress. In ancient Athens the "ruling council" had five hundred members, all men, who were chosen by lot for a year at a time and had the responsibility of preparing the agenda for meetings of the Assembly—when citizens would have the opportunity to participate in a form of direct democracy to determine the collective decisions of the polis.

---

1. Josiah Ober, *Democracy and Knowledge* (Princeton, NJ: Princeton University Press, 2008).

In *Democracy and Its Critics*, Robert Dahl characterizes the following six features that were considered necessary ingredients of the Greek view of the democratic order during the time of Plato:

1. Citizens have to be sufficiently harmonious in their interests so that they can share, and act on, a strong sense of a general good that is not in marked contradiction to their personal aims or interests.
2. Citizens must also be highly homogeneous in other respects to avoid conflict and disagreement over the common good (e.g., economic prosperity, language, education, religion, ethnicity).
3. The citizen body must be small in size.
4. Citizens must be able to assemble and directly decide on laws and policies.
5. Participation also meant participating in the administration of the city.
6. The city-state must remain autonomous (it should be self-sufficient—politically, economically, and militarily).[2]

These features of a viable democratic city-state can be contrasted with the values, aspirations, and realities of today's large (consisting of millions, even hundreds of millions, of citizens), multicultural, representative democracies that exist in a globalized world. For example, while the democracies of today also need a vision of the common good to flourish and be sustained over time, such societies are often characterized as "pluralistic" (along religious, linguistic, and ethnic lines), "individualistic" (with constitutions protecting individual rights like free speech and freedom of religion, and the consumerism of a capitalist economy), with significant socioeconomic inequalities that would contravene the highly homogenous conception of a well-functioning, small-scale society that the ancient Athenians envisioned. A citizen body consisting of tens, let alone hundreds, of millions of people living in the economically interdependent state of a globalized economy would also have been beyond

---

2. Robert Dahl, *Democracy and Its Critics* (New Haven, CT: Yale University Press, 1989), 18–19.

the realm of what was conceivable (let alone feasible) for the small-scale experiment of democracy in ancient Athens.

Plato's *Republic* takes place during ancient Athens's experiment with direct democracy. The main character of the dialogue, Socrates, had a prominent reputation for asking profound questions and engaging in prolonged debates about the answers to these questions. This does not always go down well, and as we shall see in our examination of Plato's *Apology*, it leads to criminal accusations against Socrates that he corrupted the minds of the young and committed impiety. And this trial ultimately leads to his being found guilty and sentenced to death by drinking hemlock.

Socrates had an (in)famous reputation for engaging in the "Socratic method," a mode of critical thinking that is embodied in a process of *social inquiry*. The Socratic method involves the positing of questions (e.g., "what is justice?"; "what is beauty?"), the provision of potential answers to those questions, and (most importantly) the critical scrutiny of the viability of those answers. The method presumes an authentic commitment to specific *epistemic* virtues by its practitioners, such as intellectual humility, curiosity, attention to details, and an adaptive intellect. By exercising these distinct "virtues of the mind,"[3] the practitioners of the Socratic method can display a fidelity to the genuine expression, probing, revision, rejection, modification, and vindication of their assumptions, beliefs, values, and aspirations.

The character of Socrates, who is presented as having a humble, curious, and sharp intellect, can be contrasted with his main foil in the *Republic*, Thrasymachus. Thrasymachus was a famous *sophist*, or public speaker who would charge money to teach the skills of rhetoric to Athenians. In Plato's *Republic* Thrasymachus comes across as an arrogant character who is impatient with Socrates's methodical thinking and thus aspires to best Socrates in the game of intellectual jousting. For Plato, the influence the sophists enjoyed in ancient Athens reveals the folly of democratic governance. Skilled in deception and manipulation, the sophists would teach, for a fee, how to win any argument by simply pandering to the masses. Unlike the philosopher Socrates, who pursued the truth, Plato believed the sophists engaged in superficial argumentation that amounted to little more than simply telling people what they wanted to hear. This meant that the

---

3. Linda Trinkaus Zagzebski, *Virtues of the Mind: An Inquiry into the Nature of Virtue and the Ethical Foundations of Knowledge* (Cambridge: Cambridge University Press, 1996).

exercise of political power was in grave danger as it would be wielded not from the hands of knowledge, but instead from the hands of those skilled and effective with the intellectual vices of fallacious reasoning, begging the question, and pandering to the masses, none of which could lead to the discovery of the true knowledge needed to ensure the polis would flourish. To understand Plato's critique of democracy we must first consider the foundational normative question of the *Republic*: "What is justice?"

What Is Justice? Some Preliminary Answers

The *Republic* begins with Socrates returning from a festival with Glaucon, Plato's brother. They are met by Polemarchus, who invites them to the home of his father Cephalus. Cephalus is an elder and wealthy metic, a person who was neither a citizen nor a slave. Metics were foreigners who were born outside of Athens. Cephalus is welcoming of Socrates, and tells him he wishes he could see Socrates more frequently as he enjoys engaging in the intellectual discussions and debates for which Socrates was famous.

The question Socrates poses, which is the focus of Plato's *Republic*, is "What is justice?" The discussion and debate that ensues involves a number of different characters and interlocutors, some of whom are major contributors to the *Republic* and others who are minor characters. What follows will be an abbreviated account of the dialogue concerning the potential answers to the question "What is justice?" In addition to Socrates, the other five main characters in the dialogue are Cephalus (the dialogue takes place in his home), his son Polemarchus, the sophist Thrasymachus, and Plato's brothers Glaucon and Adeimantus.

The first answer to the question "What is justice?" is put forth by Cephalus. Cephalus dedicated his life to amassing his wealth and his family's prosperity, and he views justice through the lens of a businessperson. Thus his answer represents a common Athenian conception of justice at the time:

Answer #1: JUSTICE IS TELLING THE TRUTH AND RETURNING ANYTHING WE BORROWED. (331c)

Socrates then critically scrutinizes this hypothesis. There are of course many clear cases where this hypothesis would appear to be a sage account of the virtue of justice. For example, if a friend asked if you wanted to travel together with them on a weekend trip up to their cottage, you should answer the question truthfully. Or if you borrowed some money from a family member to help you pay for a new car, you should repay that debt when you are able to do so.

But just because there are some instances where the maxim "tell the truth and return anything we borrowed" appears just, that does not establish its validity as an account of justice. So Socrates considers a case where justice would appear to *contradict* answer #1. Suppose you have borrowed a weapon from your neighbor. You are going hunting in the morning and ask to borrow your neighbor's spear for the day. After a successful day of hunting, you return back home and are in your back garden unpacking your gear when you overhear a heated argument coming from your neighbor's house. It is the same neighbor that lent you the spear that morning, and he is arguing with a family member. The shouting is somewhat inaudible, but you make out the last words very clearly. It was your neighbor yelling, "I am going to get my spear and kill you with it!"

Alarmed at hearing this declaration, you then hear the door to your neighbor's home slam shut, and a few moments later you notice your neighbor coming to your front door. He bangs on your door very loudly. You go inside your house and open the front door to find your neighbor, face flushed and eyes glazed over, demanding you return the weapon he lent you that morning. What do you do?

If you simply apply Cephalus's maxim "Justice is telling the truth and returning anything you borrowed," then you should return the spear to your neighbor, even when he is in this highly emotive, volatile state of mind. However, doing so will most likely lead to murder. Whatever justice is, it certainly cannot be a virtue that prescribes aiding in the murder of another person. On this particular occasion it seems clear that justice, whatever it may be, would prescribe that we lie rather than tell the truth and return the weapon. The just person might tell their neighbor that they accidentally broke the spear and thus left it in the forest but intend to replace it at a future time (when the neighbor is not in an unstable state of mind!). The just person would not simply hand the weapon over to the neighbor in these circumstances.

By bringing up counterexamples to a tentative answer to the question of "What is justice?" Socrates's friend-and-weapon example reveals the deficiency in the first answer. It must either be revised, to account for such hard cases, or rejected as an account of justice.

The son of Cephalus, Polemarchus, attempts to reformulate his father's position by reformulating the answer as the following:

Answer #2: JUSTICE IS GIVING A MAN HIS DUE. (332a)

But this revision is also inadequate, argues Socrates, as the example of the weapon and neighbor is one where we would say that the neighbor does *deserve* to have the weapon returned (after all, it is *his* spear), but on this particular occasion, when giving a man his due will help aid in the killing of another (presumably innocent) person, we should not honor that maxim. And thus Socrates concludes that this second definition of justice is also inadequate.

Polemarchus then attempts to reformulate his answer further, providing the following answer:

Answer #3: JUSTICE IS TO BENEFIT ONE'S FRIENDS AND HARM ONE'S ENEMIES. (332b)

To our contemporary ears, this answer might sound rather vengeful. But it would have been a widely affirmed conviction of the ancient Athenians, as the precarious circumstances of life meant that there were always enemies (e.g., combatants from a warring city-state) ready to attack and take advantage when the opportunity arose.

This new formulation of the answer does resolve the dilemma posed by the weapon example. If our neighbor is a friend, then we would not want to return the weapon to him when he is in an enraged, unstable state of mind, which would harm him because he will commit serious wrongdoing to a loved one. Thus this third formulation has successfully fended off the original challenge that Socrates raised against Cephalus's first answer. However, that does not mean this new answer is not itself subject to other compelling objections or counterarguments.

To dismantle the viability of answer #3, Socrates considers the reality that we are fallible, and thus can make mistakes in our judgments concerning who our true friends are (and the same is true about those we might think are our enemies). There may have been someone in your history you once considered a good friend, when in reality they did not treat you as a friend ought to. Perhaps you found out that they were spreading gossip about you to others, maybe even spreading lies and rumors, which diminished your social capital. Such cases reveal the kind of human fallibility that Socrates has in mind.

Conversely, there might be people we believe are our enemies who are not in fact our enemies. Perhaps we formed the impression they were our enemies because of gossip and lies that have been spread by others about them. Or we misinterpreted their actions, constructing faulty intentions (e.g., "They brought up an issue at an important work meeting simply to embarrass me and make me look bad in front of my boss!" but in reality they brought up the issue because it was important to address). We might mistakenly believe that a coworker is trying to sabotage our potential job promotion, or steal a romantic partner away from us, when in fact they are simply perfectionists at work or genuinely overly friendly with everyone they meet.

Because we are fallible, if we follow Polemarchus's maxim of "Benefit one's friends and harm one's enemies," then we may actually be benefiting people that do not deserve to be benefited, and harming people that do not deserve to be harmed. Polemarchus concedes that such an outcome would not be just, and thus his formulation of justice is also rejected.

After Socrates's dismantling of the first three accounts of justice, the arrogant sophist Thrasymachus, who has been agitated by the attention given to Socrates, is keen to upstage him. So Thrasymachus abruptly inserts himself into the exchange, offering the following formulation of the answer to the question "What is justice?"

Answer #4: JUSTICE IS THE INTEREST OF THE STRONGER PARTY. (338c)

Thrasymachus's argument contains two somewhat inconsistent strains. The Platonic scholar Julia Annas contends that "Thrasymachus is presented as a hasty and confused thinker."[4] To help bring some clarity to the two strains of his argument, Annas refers to them as (a) *conventionalism* and (b) *immoralism*. Conventionalism is the idea that justice is nothing

---

4. Julia Annas, *An Introduction to Plato's Republic* (Oxford: Oxford University Press, 1981), 38.

but obeying the laws. This tenet is captured in Thrasymachus's claim that "justice is obedience to laws" (339b). Immoralism is the conjecture that justice is nothing but the advantage of another (343c) and thus there is nothing noble or praiseworthy about the virtue of justice understood in this way. It is this second strain of Thrasymachus's argument that Socrates gets Thrasymachus to commit to as a refinement of his initial general answer that justice is the interest of the stronger party.

Socrates begins to challenge answer #4 by questioning the idea that the "stronger party" is infallible, and thus always likely to govern in their own interest. It is possible that rulers might wage wars, impose taxes, or implement other policies that actually end up harming their own interests. But Thrasymachus abruptly shuts down this kind of rebuttal, claiming that a skilled ruler does not make mistakes.

Rather than challenge the validity of Thrasymachus's highly suspect premise (history is replete with examples of skilled rulers who still managed to make grave errors of judgment that proved to be disadvantageous to their own interests), Socrates instead decides to unravel Thrasymachus's argument by critically scrutinizing the idea of "skill" that Thrasymachus employs. If ruling is a skill, and the perfect ruler never makes a mistake, then perhaps we should consider other skill domains to better understand who actually benefits from a skill. Socrates argues that all skills aim at the good of their subjects. A physician, for example, "is a healer of the sick rather than a maker of money." The captain of the ship aims to safely bring the crew and merchandise to its destination. All skills aim at *the good of their subjects*, contends Socrates. And if this is so, then the skilled ruler must rule in the interest of their subjects. However, this conflicts with the original maxim that "justice is the interest of the stronger party."

Answer #5: JUSTICE IS MERELY A MATTER OF CONVENIENCE. (359a)

We might have expected Thrasymachus, the influential sophist with a reputation for training others in intellectual skills, to be the foil to Socrates in the *Republic*. But it is evident, from both the tone and the inconsistency of Thrasymachus's argument in the *Republic*, that Plato does not present him in a favorable light. After being bested by Socrates, it is Glaucon, aided by Adeimantus, who takes up Thrasymachus's challenge. They present the most formidable challenge to Socrates, compelling Socrates to formulate his own positive account of what justice is versus simply dismantling the hypotheses put forth by the others.

The immoralism sentiment first expressed by Thrasymachus—that injustice pays more than justice—raises the question of what type of good justice is. Socrates distinguishes between three possible answers to this question (357–58):

> Is justice something that we value:
> 1. as an end in itself (meaning it has *intrinsic* value)?
>   or
> 2. as a good that has only *instrumental* value (meaning we value it only as a means to some other end)?
>   or
> 3. as a good that has *both* intrinsic and instrumental value?

The most significant challenge raised against Socrates is now mounted by Glaucon, who argues that Thrasymachus's argument is a commitment to the second option, the position that "justice is merely a matter of convenience." Glaucon advances two lines of argumentation to reinforce the validity of answer #5: the example of the ring of Gyges, and a comparison between the life of the person who has all the accolades of being just but is actually unjust versus the person who is perceived and treated as unjust by others but is actually just.

The ring of Gyges is a mythical story about a shepherd, named Gyges, who discovered a magic ring that made him invisible. When wearing the ring he could commit any immoral action he wanted, free from the fear of being detected. With the invisible ring Gyges seduced the queen, murdered the king, and seized the power to rule for himself.

Glaucon postulates that if two invisible rings existed, and one ring was given to a just person and the second to an unjust person, they would behave in the same manner. The just person, when shielded against the disadvantages of being detected for committing unjust acts, would have no reason to behave justly. If justice is merely a matter of convenience, then in the fictional scenario Glaucon describes with the ring of Gyges, the person who was initially a just person would now commit theft and murder without fear of the negative repercussions. This shows that justice only has instrumental, and not intrinsic, value. There would be no reason to behave justly when you can reap the rewards of being unjust without incurring the risks of detection and the punishments that come with detection.

A second example Glaucon raises, which illustrates the same point, is to consider the choice between two lives—the perfectly just person and the perfectly unjust person. The former is stripped of everything but their justness. That is, they have the reputation of being a wrong doer even though they have never committed a crime. In their heart they know they have been a virtuous person, yet they suffer all the social condemnation befitting of someone who lived a life of vice versus virtue. They are imprisoned, and tortured for crimes they never committed. By contrast, the perfectly wicked person is in their heart an unjust person. They commit serious wrongdoings—lying, manipulating, cheating, and so on—to advance their own personal interests, but they are a master at concealing their wrongdoing and successfully cultivate the reputation for being virtuous. So they receive the external accolades befitting of a good person—they can become a partner in any business, have wealth, and ally themself to any family they choose through marriage. They do not deserve these accolades, but they enjoy them nonetheless.

Given the choice between these two lives, Glaucon believes we would choose the life of the perfectly unjust person over the perfectly just person. This is because there is no intrinsic value to being just. The perfectly wicked person reaps all the instrumental benefits we could expect from actually being just. And thus that life is preferable to the life that has none of those instrumental benefits.

Glaucon's challenge proves to be the most formidable one raised by Socrates's interlocutors. In Book VI we see a shift in the style and substance of the dialogue take place. Rather than the rapid rebuttal of accounts of justice offered by his contemporaries, now Socrates begins to detail his own answer to the question "What is justice?"

The Just Society

To meet the challenge posed by Glaucon—the hypothesis that justice only has instrumental (and not intrinsic) value—Socrates must now advance a positive account of what justice is as a virtue. He does so both at the level of the individual person and at the level of the city-state. He begins with the latter as he reasons it is easier to determine justice on the larger scale than it is on the smaller scale.

Socrates conjectures about the creation of society. We are not, as individuals, self-sufficient at meeting our needs. Unlike the fictional character Robinson Crusoe (from Daniel Defoe's famous novel) who sustains all his material needs by himself on an isolated island, in the real world we meet our needs by cooperating with others. People we cooperate with have different talents and abilities, such as fishing, carpentry, weaving, and music. Socrates reasons that it is by tapping into the productive efficiency of a "division of labor" among the diversity of specialization of skills that this society would grow in population and sustain itself over time.

As this polis grew in size, conflict with those living outside the polity was inevitable. Thus Socrates claims this city-state would need soldiers, an army of "Guardians." And this Guardian class is composed of two categories: Rulers and Auxiliaries (soldiers). A third class, the most populous class, is composed of workers (e.g., agricultural and other manual workers).

The education of the Rulers, a class of philosophers (both male and female) committed to the truth and governing for the best interest of the polity, is of central importance to Plato's vision of the just society. Their education involves a total training of character and thus requires strict regulation, especially of art and literature. Private interests and affections (e.g., having children) threaten to distract the Rulers from their duties to their community. Thus in the just society Socrates contends that the abolishment of private property for the Rulers would be implemented, to eliminate the profit motive from politics. The family is also abolished for this class. State nurseries would permit female members of the Ruling class to be free from these parental responsibilities.

Plato has conflicting views concerning the extent to which the ideal society he advocates is meritocratic. Sometimes he suggests it is a meritocracy, where children are raised according to their aptitude regardless of their class origin. But at other times in the *Republic* it appears class membership is inherited. He proposes that sexual intercourse be strictly regulated so that suitable partners mate and produce the best Rulers. Critics of Plato point out the authoritarian (indeed, some claim totalitarian[5]) aspirations and eugenic implications of his utopian society as providing sufficient grounds for rejecting it as a political ideal to strive for.

The hierarchal vision of Plato's just society is explicitly affirmed by Socrates's invocation of the Noble Lie (the "myth of the metals," *Republic* 414b–415d). This is the myth that those suited to be the philosopher rulers are made of gold, the auxiliaries silver, and the workers iron and bronze. Plato, like the ancient Greeks more generally, conceptualized ethics and the ideal society in terms of virtue or character traits. His ideal society thus consists of a polity that exercises the following four virtues:

Wisdom: this virtue is the "good council" of society's affairs provided by rulers who possess knowledge.

Courage: this virtue is exercised by the soldiers, who possess the steadfast character needed to protect the interests of the polis from hostile threats.

Self-discipline (or harmony): this virtue is a harmony between the distinct classes.

Justice: justice is doing what you are suited to do ("do their own thing and not meddle with that of another" [433a]).

It is not clear how the virtues of self-discipline (harmony) and justice are distinct virtues, as they seem to express the same or similar sentiments. The first answer Socrates provides to the "What is justice?" question is thus "do what you are suited to do," at least when applied at the level of a society. This implies people are best suited to specific tasks—some to fish and farm, others to protect and fight, some to govern, and so on—and that the best thing for the city-state is for people to do the thing they are best suited to do over something that they lack the competence and skill needed to do. Having detailed what justice writ large entails, at the societal level, Socrates then turns to justice at the level of the individual person.

---

5. Karl Popper, *The Open Society and Its Enemies*, vol. 1: *The Spell of Plato*, 5th ed. (Princeton, NJ: Princeton University Press, 1971).

Was Plato a Feminist?

Before considering what justice is at the level of the individual person, one interesting feature of Plato's ideal society that warrants some further attention and reflection is the fact that his description of the Guardian class, as elitist and exclusionary as it was, is progressive and inclusive at least to the extent that Plato believed women could be competent members of the Ruler class. Recall that women were not citizens in ancient Athens, and thus were not granted the right to vote. Does the fact that Plato was open to women becoming members of the Ruler class mean that his political philosophy is feminist, or based on a vision of equality between the sexes?[6] Platonic scholar Julia Annas[7] takes up that question and posits three reasons for answering "No, Plato shouldn't be considered a feminist."

The first concern that Annas emphasizes is that Plato's stance on women being members of the Guardian class is open to the antifeminist objection that men are better suited to be Guardians because (1) Plato claims that, in general, "Men are better equipped both mentally and physically" (455b4–c6) and (2) his account of the ideal society is predicated on the premise "that each person is to do his own work, according to his nature" (453b5). This leaves Plato open to the objection that the best among men are those naturally suited to be Guardians. This would have been the standard objection Plato's contemporaries would have raised against his inclusion of women in the Guardian class. What Plato really needed to establish, claims Annas, is the point that there are no occupations that *only* men are suited to do—being a doctor, taking part in politics, or owning property. But Plato does not establish that, and as such, he leaves his argument open to the antifeminist objection.

Second, Annas argues that feminists should not accept Plato's theory because it is neither predicated on nor makes any reference to women's interests or desires. Plato's suggestion that women be included in the

---

6. Abigail L. Rosenthal, "Feminism without Contradictions," *Monist* 57, no. 1 (1973): 28–42.

7. Julia Annas, "Plato's *Republic* and Feminism," *Philosophy* 51, no. 197 (July 1976): 307–21.

Guardian class is not motivated, for example, by a genuine concern to improve the life of these women.

Third, and this relates to the second point, Annas contends that Plato's account of justice is irrelevant to the injustice of sexual inequality. Plato is not concerned with women as a group, to emancipate them from patriarchal practices and institutions. The inclusive aspects of Plato's position on women being members of the Guardian class are purely instrumental to his concern with the ideal city-state being realized. The ultimate goal of including women as Guardians is not equality for women, but rather the fulfillment of Plato's demand that the just society is one where we do what we are suited to do. The sole rationale Plato provides for the inclusion of some women in the Guardian class is that this is beneficial for creating and sustaining the ideal society. It has nothing to do with the emancipation of women per se. Annas remarks:

> The Guardians will not be tied to houses and families; all their emotional energy will be released for service to the state, and will not be wasted in quarrels over individual concerns. . . . Plato is uninterested in the question of whether the life of an individual is stunted by the nuclear family. His obsession with unity and stability in a state points in the opposite direction from increasing free self-realization and self-direction on the part of the individual.[8]

Just Person

Having canvassed his account of the ideal society, Socrates then turns to the issue of what constitutes a just *person*. It is in the details of Plato's account of the just individual that we find his response to the challenges Glaucon had raised for Socrates in his conjecture that justice is merely a matter of convenience. If justice is, as Plato maintains, *intrinsically* valuable (as an "end in itself") as well instrumentally valuable, then Socrates must be able to give a convincing response to the ring of Gyges example.

---

8. Annas, "Plato's *Republic* and Feminism," 318–19.

Socrates must also explain why we would have reason to choose the life of the just person who has nothing but their justness over the life of the perfectly wicked person who has all the reputational benefits and accolades of being just (but actually lacks that virtue).

In his discussion of the just person, in Books IV, VIII, and IX of the *Republic*, Plato distinguishes between three distinct parts of our soul, which correspond to the three classes within the ideal state—there is reason (which corresponds to the philosopher Rulers), courage (or Spirit, which corresponds to the Auxiliary class), and our appetites (which correspond to the Worker class).

According to Plato, reason is the part of our soul that yearns for knowledge and truth. Reason ensures that our practical reasoning is guided by a concern for our complete well-being versus what might simply bring us short-term hedonic pleasure at any given moment. Courage, or spirit, refers to that part of our nature that, when it is harnessed by the right sort of training (44 1 e–44n), can be brave (versus angry). And appetites include our desires for wealth, food, drink, and sex.

Having detailed the central thrust of Socrates's account of the just person, we can conclude by returning to Glaucon's challenge: *why should we be just?* The answer Plato provides is predicated on theological assumptions about the soul—that by acting justly we achieve the proper psychic ordering of the soul needed to achieve the immortality of the soul. A ring that makes us invisible would not lead us to alter our behavior, because reason would not authorize committing the immoral acts that depraved persons, blinded by their perverse desires, might seek to realize. Similarly, the perfectly wicked person who enjoys the societal benefits of having the reputation for being a just person does not achieve this internal harmony between reason, courage, and appetites.

The unjust person perverts the internal harmony between reason, courage, and appetites. And in doing so, the unjust person makes decisions that are detrimental, versus beneficial, to that person's well-being. For example, a person who desires to make more wealth through gambling, and thus impulsively puts all their wages for the week on the roll of a die, is not guided by reason. They risk the health and well-being of their family for the short-term gain of some potential additional wealth. The wise decision regarding improving one's financial resources would be to consider working longer hours, or changing jobs, not risking what few resources one has on the roll of the dice. A person who is addicted to gambling is driven to act by the dopamine rush they experience from gambling instead of their reason.

What are we to make of Socrates's response to Glaucon's challenge? Unless one is persuaded by Plato's moral psychology, and the theological commitments it has to the soul (and immortality of the soul), we will find it questionable. The ring of Gyges is a challenging example to consider because it presents an ethical dilemma where pursuing our own self-interest conflicts with respecting the interests of others. Plato's strategy is to claim that we actually have self-regarding reasons for not committing injustices, even when we cannot be detected by others because of the stealth the ring affords us. Acting unjustly threatens the harmony (and thus the immortality) of our soul, which Plato took to be integral to our well-being. For Plato the just person would not jeopardize the proper psychic ordering of their soul for the ill-perceived benefits of immorality. A contemporary defender of Plato may be able to refine his position to advance a coherent and persuasive secular account (e.g., one not predicated on the assumption of the immortality of the soul) of human flourishing that highlights the self-regarding reasons for not committing injustice. But Glaucon's challenge—that justice has only instrumental value—remains a live and debated topic in political philosophy over two thousand years after Plato's *Republic*.

The Fate of Socrates

Socrates was infamous in ancient Athens for asking challenging questions of his contemporaries. When the critic challenges the central beliefs and assumptions of his contemporaries, this can create societal disapproval and even hostility toward the critic. Socrates's inquisitive nature, sharp wit, and skilled intellect were not appreciated by many of his contemporaries. Some prominent Athenians (like Thrasymachus) saw Socrates as a nuisance and a societal problem rather than a beacon of enlightenment and critical thinking. Eventually the societal disapproval of Socrates had grown to a level where critics claimed he was guilty of impiety and corrupting the minds of young Athenians. At age seventy, Socrates was judged in a trial by 501 jurors.

The trial of Socrates is portrayed in Plato's dialogue titled the *Apology*. Plato actually witnessed the trial firsthand. In the first part of the trial, the jurors had to decide if Socrates is guilty or innocent of the charges. If he is found guilty, the jury then must decide what the appropriate punishment should be. Socrates is given an allotted amount of time to make his defense.

If Socrates had taken the strategy of apologizing to his peers and asked for mercy from them, then the outcome of the trial would perhaps have been different. But that is not Socrates's character. He approaches the trial as a (somewhat provocative!) philosopher would—he critically examines the legitimacy of the charges against him, subjecting them to critical scrutiny. He starts with common allegations that Socrates is a "busybody who makes the weaker argument the stronger." He recounts the story of the Oracle at Delphi. Delphi was considered to be the center of the world, and the religious site was built around a sacred spring. At this religious site a friend of Socrates asked a priestess if anyone was wiser than Socrates. Her reply was "No."

In his defense speech Socrates ponders what the priestess could have meant by such a proclamation. Socrates admits he is not wise about anything. He purposely seeks out people who have the reputations for being wise, to ask their opinions about questions pertaining to beauty, the good life, and justice. But in doing so Socrates may have angered them. He conjectures that he is only wiser than these alleged "experts" because he knows how ignorant he is, while they proclaim to have knowledge but remain ignorant about their own ignorance. This further provokes his jurors.

Foreshadowing the outcome of the trial, Socrates ponders if receiving the death penalty would actually be a bad outcome for him. To fear death one must believe death is something to be feared. But Socrates claims he does not know this. Perhaps death is like a good night's sleep (except you never wake up from it!), or if there is an afterlife, Socrates wonders if there would be the opportunity to converse with the great minds of the past. In either case, death is not an outcome he believes he should fear.

Rather than using his allotted time to try to save his own life, Socrates uses the platform of the trial to make his case for the kind of life he has led—the life of the critically reflective mind. He comments:

All I do is to go about and try to persuade you, both young and old, not to care for your bodies or your monies first, and to care more exceedingly for the soul, to make it as good as possible; and I tell you that virtue comes not from money, but from virtue comes both money and all other good things for mankind, both in private and in public. If, then, by saying these things I corrupt the young, these things must be mischievous; but if anyone says I say anything else, he talks nonsense. . . . I will never do anything else, even if I am to die many deaths.[9]

The jurors vote, and they conclude that Socrates is guilty of the charges brought against him. Now they must decide what the appropriate punishment should be. Should Socrates be exiled from Athens or sentenced to death? Socrates is again given the chance to make a speech before the vote, and he again adopts a combative approach. He ponders the question of what the appropriate punishment should be for not having an idle life, for trying to persuade his fellow citizens that they should be good and wise. Socrates declares his most famous slogan "The unexamined life is not worth living," and concludes that free board in the town hall would be the appropriate response to his actions. Needless to say this does not go down well with the jury either. On the final vote the outcome is decisive: Socrates is to be put to death by drinking hemlock.

While awaiting his execution, Socrates spends the last few weeks of his life in a prison cell. His friend Crito, who had also attended his trial, has bribed the prison guard to let him enter Socrates's cell and help Socrates escape. The Platonic dialogue *Crito* takes place a few days before Socrates's day of execution. Crito enters Socrates's cell and appeals to him, as his friend, to escape. Crito doesn't want to lose him as a friend, and if Socrates doesn't escape he will be put to death. Crito also notes that Crito's own reputation will be tainted if Socrates does not escape, as people will think Crito was too cheap to bribe the guard for Socrates's escape. Further, Crito brings up Socrates's children and asks who will support and educate them if Socrates is killed. Finally, Crito notes that Socrates will

---

9. Plato, *Crito*, in *Great Dialogues of Plato*, trans. W. H. D. Rouse (New York: Penguin Random House, 1999), 518.

not be able to teach philosophy anymore if he is dead, and thus his critics will have succeeded in silencing him.

Socrates then engages in his typical Socratic method to analyze and evaluate the premises of Crito's arguments. In the *Apology* Socrates argued that no evil can happen to a good man, either living or dead. To be harmed means one must become less virtuous, less excellent. So the important question that Socrates must ponder now is whether escaping or accepting his punishment would harm his friends. And that question can only be answered by considering the question: is escaping just or unjust? If it is an unjust act, then Socrates would not be a good teacher, father, or example of virtue, and this would harm his friends, family, and philosophy.

At this stage Socrates imagines that *The Laws* appear before him in the cell. Socrates contemplates what kind of justification could be provided to explain to *The Laws* why he would not accept the punishment that has been given to him. He argues that there is no adequate justification. Socrates has spent his life living in the city-state of Athens; if he did not agree with *The Laws* he could have left at any previous time, but he did not. He reaped the benefits of staying in Athens and now, at the time its laws demand his death, Crito is encouraging him to defect from this legal decision. This would constitute a violation of the social contract that Socrates endorsed by choosing to remain throughout his life in Athens, the city-state that has nurtured and educated him and his children. Should he, only now, decide to challenge and jeopardize the legal order? Socrates argues that this would be unjust. By remaining in Athens and enjoying the benefits of its legal system he is morally obligated to accept the burdens it also imposes upon him.

So in the end Socrates refuses to escape with Crito. He accepts the punishment the Athenians have assigned to him; he is put to death by drinking hemlock a few days later. Socrates's drinking of the hemlock is represented in the famous painting by the French painter Jacques-Louis David, *The Death of Socrates* (1787).

Plato's Critique of Democracy

Plato's ideal society governed by philosopher Rulers may not sound either attractive or feasible to citizens living in democracies in the twenty-first century. Nonetheless, Plato's critique of democracy is still very relevant today. In Book VI of the *Republic* Socrates likens democracy to a ship with an incompetent captain. Imagine the captain in charge of navigating a ship was the captain only because they were physically stronger than anyone else, or the most liked among the crew members, or the richest person who paid for the privilege to captain the ship. But such a captain actually lacked the knowledge and skills needed to safely navigate the ship to its destination. Placing such a person at the helm of the ship would be a disaster for everyone.

Plato believes the same fate awaits democracy. We can perhaps sympathize with Plato on this point when we bear in mind that it was Athenian democracy that sentenced his mentor, Socrates, to death for engaging in critical inquiry. Today's democracies are representative rather than direct democracies, but Plato's critique remains relevant. Politicians and political leaders are often elected because they know how to pander to the masses, coining effective "sound bites" or social media posts that exploit the fears and anxieties of the masses versus genuinely endorsing sound principles and public policies that will actually be best for all living in a country.

Unlike the direct democracy of ancient Athens, the constitutional democracies of the twenty-first century have a number of institutional features that were intentionally designed to guard against the "tyranny of the majority." For example, constitutions are the supreme law of the land, and they limit the power of legislative majorities by taking off the political agenda (or making it more difficult to contravene) basic rights and freedoms, such as freedom of expression, freedom of political association, and the right to vote.

The social scientist Jon Elster describes constitutions as a "pre-commitment" device.[10] Pre-commitment devices involve binding ourselves to avoid the weaknesses of human nature. The classic example of self-binding is represented in Homer's *Odyssey*, which depicts the journey of the Greek king of Ithaca, Odysseus, also known by the Latin name Ulysses, returning home from the Trojan War. At one stage in the story Ulysses must sail past the island of the sirens, whose enchanted singing lures sailors toward the island and certain death. The goddess

---

10. Jon Elster, *Ulysses and the Sirens: Studies in Rationality and Irrationality* (Cambridge: Cambridge University Press, 1979).

Circe provides Ulysses with advice for surviving the perils of the sirens' fatal enchanting song: Ulysses's men are to fill their ears with beeswax so they will not be able to hear the sirens' song. Ulysses must also have his men bind him to the mast of the ship, so that Ulysses (who does not use the beeswax) will not succumb to the sirens' song and steer the ship into the rocks. By binding himself to the mast of the ship, Ulysses employs a pre-commitment device to protect himself from passion and weakness of will. Modern-day democracies pre-commit themselves to a constitution as a similar type of guard against the tyranny of the majority that might wish to promote the greater good by inflicting injustices (e.g., violating individual rights) on the minority. This helps guard against some of the concerns Plato raises against direct democracy. But of course constitutions can be amended or ignored, and thus there is no guarantee that if the majority wish to violate or limit their own constitution, they may not do so.

Society could also redress the concerns Plato has about democratic rule by trying to ensure that moral and epistemic virtues are more widely dispersed in society via *public education*. In ancient Greece the type of education Plato offered in his Academy was very selective, available to only an elite few in Athens. But in modern societies today children receive many years of formal education, and this education extends into early adulthood if they attend an institution of higher learning. In her book *Not for Profit* the philosopher Martha Nussbaum outlines two rival models of education: *education for economic growth* and *education for democratic citizenship*.[11] The former emphasizes literacy, numeracy, computer skills, and technology, along with some understanding of history and facts. Its central focus is on standardized tests, but critical thinking is not considered important and can actually be seen as a threat to the goal of creating an obedient workforce. Nussbaum disagrees with the model of education for economic growth, which does not equip citizens with the intellectual skills necessary to ensure they can self-govern responsibly.

Instead of adopting a model of economic growth, Nussbaum argues that today's democracies should strive to realize the aspirations of the second model of education, the model of democratic citizenship. This model prioritizes the importance of human dignity. It aspires to cultivate and

---

11. Martha Nussbaum, *Not for Profit* (Princeton, NJ: Princeton University Press, 2010).

refine a diverse array of moral and intellectual virtues in the citizenry, such as thinking clearly about political issues, recognizing others as people with equal rights, empathizing with others, critically judging political leaders, and so on.

Nussbaum believes that Socratic pedagogy is a critical social practice that can inspire students to think and argue for themselves rather than simply appeal to tradition. The arts and literature, argues Nussbaum, can help students bridge the gulfs of geography, language, and nationality. Fiction can help one develop the narrative imagination necessary for understanding the emotions of another person. It can also help students transcend their own place and time, so they can grasp the predicaments of humanity as a whole. Education for democratic citizenship aspires to create curious citizens who are capable of critical thinking, and this can serve as a check on the potential vices of democratic rule.

In chapter 10 on utilitarianism we will return to some of these issues when we consider John Stuart Mill's suggestion of giving plural votes to the more educated, and Jason Brennan's suggestion that the right to vote should entail a competency test.[12] Regardless of what one thinks about Plato's arguments for the just society and person, his epistemic critique of democracy remains as apt and significant for the world's democracies today as it did for the embryonic stages of democratic governance in ancient Athens.

---

12. Jason Brennan, *Against Democracy* (Princeton, NJ: Princeton University Press, 2016); Jason Brennan, "The Right to a Competent Electorate," *Philosophical Quarterly* 61, no. 245 (2011): 700–724.

CHAPTER 3

Aristotle, Virtue Ethics, and Happiness

Aristotle was born in Macedon, which is now part of Greece, in 384 BC. He spent the majority of his life living in Athens and was a student in Plato's Academy for nearly twenty years, until Plato died in 347 BC. Aristotle was a polymath, interested in topics as varied as biology, physics, logic, ethics, and politics. He tutored Alexander the Great and eventually founded his own academy of philosophy called the Lyceum.

The surviving writings of Aristotle, which only represent a small portion of his philosophical corpus, were based on his lectures (and it is worth noting his lectures were aimed at young, affluent men). We shall focus on one of Aristotle's most important and influential works, the *Nicomachean Ethics*, and how Aristotle's ideas continue to influence and inform research in the twenty-first century on topics in epistemology, legal theory, and the psychology of human happiness. Aristotle is considered one of the, if not the most, influential philosophers in the history of Western civilization. He was influenced by his mentor, Plato, but Aristotle developed and refined his own account of the good life and politics.

Like many other historical figures we cover in this book, it is worth noting from the outset that Aristotle did not endorse many of the foundational normative premises (e.g., the equality of all persons) that we, living in the twenty-first century, would take to be nonnegotiables for any defensible political philosophy. "Aristotle believed that the majority of human beings may be enslaved without injustice, because they are slaves by nature."[1] Non-Greeks, for example, were considered natural slaves by Aristotle, and women were also considered to be inferior. So while, in principle, it is admirable that a polymath may aspire to apply insights from biology to ethics and politics, the value and defensibility of doing so is only as sound as the biological and ethical premises one begins with.

---

1. Malcolm Heath, "Aristotle on Natural Slavery," *Phronesis* 53 (2008): 243–70, 243.

And in Aristotle's case there are inherently problematic premises in many aspects of his writings. This has led some to contemplate whether or not Aristotle should be "canceled."[2] Including Aristotle here makes it clear that I believe Aristotle is an important thinker worth taking seriously today, flaws and all.

In what follows I focus on those aspects of Aristotle's writings that I think remain important and insightful for us in the twenty-first century. Nonetheless, it is important to recognize that even profound and revolutionary thinkers (like Aristotle) can be swayed and biased by the limited understanding, cognitive blind spots, and prejudice of their own time. And it is important to acknowledge this before addressing the other aspects of Aristotle's work, for we need to be careful not to permit these problematic hierarchal premises to inform any substantive conclusions that we may be inclined to seriously entertain today. The task of disentangling "the good, the bad, and the ugly" in Western political philosophy can be a laborious task, but it is a crucial task that can serve an important pedagogical function. At a minimum it should make us humble and introspective about our own biases and limited understanding. Like Aristotle, we may also be functioning with problematic moral premises in our normative theorizing.

We begin our introduction to Aristotle by considering the "virtue ethics" tradition, of which Aristotle is (rightly) considered the foremost proponent. What makes an action or public policy morally right or wrong? This is a foundational question in moral and political philosophy, and there are many distinct theoretical traditions that attempt to answer this question. One position, which is the central rival to the virtue ethics tradition (and which we will cover in chapter 10 on utilitarianism) is called "consequentialism." According to consequentialists, what makes one decision or course of action morally right or wrong is determined by its consequences. Suppose, for example, you promised to pick up your friend from work at 5:00 p.m. today so the two of you could enjoy dinner together and catch up on things before your friend starts their second, evening, job at 7:00 p.m. On the way to get your friend you witness a

---

2. See, for example, Agnes Callard, "Should We Cancel Aristotle?," *New York Times*, July 21, 2020, https://www.nytimes.com/2020/07/21/opinion/should-we-cancel-aristotle.html.

single-car accident—a driver lost control and veered off a quiet rural road and crashed into a tree—and you observe that the driver, the sole occupant in the car, is seriously injured and in need of medical care. If you stop to attend to the injured driver, taking the time to call an ambulance and then waiting to make sure the injured person gets the medical treatment they need, you will be delayed by at least an hour. You now face an ethical dilemma. Should you stop and aid the person in need? Or, alternatively, should you fulfill the promise you made to pick up your friend from work at the time you agreed on, so you can both enjoy dinner together?

For a consequentialist, the answer to such predicaments is determined by the consequences of one's actions. If you stop to help the injured driver, you increase the odds of their survival by ensuring that the paramedics are called and that the injured person is cared for and reassured until the medical team arrives. But this will also mean your friend will not be picked up at 5:00 p.m., and thus you will not have time to enjoy dinner together. Alternatively, if you continue on driving to pick up your friend, you can meet to have dinner together, but in doing so you risk the increased suffering, and potential death, of the injured driver (if no other passerby happens to see them and stops to help on the quiet rural road).

In this simplistic example the consequences being compared are between "possibly saving a life" versus "the inconvenience of missing a planned dinner with a friend." Unless one subscribes to an egotistical conceptional of morality, most would agree that the best consequences in this scenario are to help the injured person and accept that doing so will impose some minimal burden of inconvenience on you personally.

In more complex ethical predicaments the consequences might not be as straightforward as with the choice between saving a life and postponing dinner plans. For example, mitigating the harms of climate change might impose financial hardships, which might be severe if the countries involved are lower- or even middle-income countries that are heavily reliant on fossil fuels for most of their energy and economic growth.

Furthermore, consequentialists have offered different ways of construing what constitutes the "best consequences." Should those consequences simply be, as Jeremy Bentham (1748–1832) proposed, the maximization of pleasure and the minimization of pain? Or perhaps the relevant consequences are those that satisfy people's preferences (whatever those preferences are), or that cohere with some "objective list" of human goods (e.g., health, bodily integrity, play, etc.)? There is no consensus on this issue among consequentialists. But what consequentialists do agree on is that, of the options available, the morally defensible course of action to take is determined by the expected benefits and harms of those actions to all affected.

By contrast, Aristotle and other virtue ethicists believe that the focus of ethics and politics ought to be primarily concerned with *character traits* versus the consequences of our individual or collective actions. For the Aristotelian, it is a mistake to think that the foundational moral question "How ought I to act?" is best answered by appeals to some cost-benefit analysis of the likely consequences of our actions. Instead, the focus of moral inquiry ought to be directed toward the question "How would a virtuous person, in these same circumstances, act?" Admittedly this is a more nuanced, and critics might say too ambiguous and indeterminate, account of moral life.

Aristotle makes a distinction between the intellectual virtues (*phronesis*, or practical wisdom) and the moral virtues. The moral virtues involve the nonrational desires, which cooperate with reason to enable virtuous agents to attain complete virtue and flourish. The following section canvasses the moral virtues and Aristotle's doctrine of "the mean"—that a virtuous agent occupies the middle ground between possessing an excess or deficiency of emotion. For Aristotle's account of the moral virtues we will limit most of our attention to two important virtues: courage and justice. But Aristotle covers a wide array of other moral virtues, such as temperance, magnanimity, truthfulness, friendliness, and so on. For each of the moral virtues, Aristotle contends that the virtuous agent's character is a state that occupies the mean between the extremes of possessing too much of the feeling/emotion and too little of it. We then address virtue epistemology and the intellectual virtues, which relate to what Aristotle refers to as the "rational" desires of the soul.

Courage and Justice

For the moral virtue of courage or bravery, the virtuous agent is in a state that is the mean between the feelings of excessive fear (cowardice) and overconfidence (or rashness). Aristotle notes it is natural and good for us to fear things that are bad for us, such as damage to our reputation, sickness, and death. But a person who is too fearful, a coward with an excess of fear, cannot stand firm against something frightening when doing so is the right thing to do. For example, in battle a brave soldier must risk their own life to protect family, friends, and compatriots from hostile invaders. The soldier who runs away in the face of any danger is in a state of moral vice rather than moral virtue.

For Aristotle, the coward is a person who is afraid of everything and possesses a despairing temperament. By contrast the courageous person possesses hope. They are not immobilized by fear, but neither are they so foolhardy as to recklessly seek out risks of harm for trivial reasons. The overconfident or rash person possesses an excess of feeling because they are impetuous. The soldier who cavalierly seeks out violent confrontation with others, and relishes such conflict for its own sake, possesses (like the coward) moral vice rather than virtue. Aristotle contends that the courageous or brave person "has the intermediate or right state" (1116a, SS12).[3]

For virtue ethicists, moral virtues involve being in the state of having the correct amount of feeling—neither too much nor too little. The other moral virtues Aristotle identifies, like truthfulness, also involve occupying the mean between extremes. With respect to truthfulness Aristotle argues it is the mean between the self-deprecator (who belittles their own accomplishments or skills) and the boaster (who embellishes their accomplishments). For example, consider a timid teacher who, on learning from the school principal that they have been nominated for a prestigious teaching award, responds by saying, "But I am a terrible teacher!" Or, for the opposite extreme, the boastful colleague who, on hearing the news of the nomination of their colleague for the teaching award, blurts out, "But I am by far the best teacher in this school. The reason I did not get nominated for the award is because I do not play nice with 'school politics.'" The timid teacher lacks truthfulness, distorting the truth about their own accomplishments because they feel uncomfortable receiving praise. By contrast, the boastful person possesses an excess of the feeling of truthfulness, embellishing/exaggerating the truth. The virtuous person occupies the mean between these two extremes. "The intermediate person is straightforward, and therefore truthful in what he says and does, acknowledging the qualities he has without exaggerating or belittling" (*NE* 1127a).

---

3. Aristotle, *Nicomachean Ethics*, trans. Terence Irwin (Indianapolis: Hackett, 1999). All references to *NE* are to this translation.

Aristotle's account of the moral virtue of justice is a more complex view, as he introduces a couple of distinct kinds and accounts of justice. Book V of *Nicomachean Ethics* is devoted to the topic of justice. Aristotle distinguishes between two kinds of justice: the broad sense of justice as lawfulness, and the narrow sense of justice as equality or proportionality.[4] With respect to the broad sense of justice, Aristotle remarks:

> Now the law instructs us to do the actions of a brave person—for instance, not to leave the battle-line, or to flee, or to throw away our weapons; of a temperate person—not to commit adultery or wanton aggression; of a mild person—not to strike or revile another; and similarly requires actions in accord with the other virtues, and prohibits actions in accord with the vices. The correctly established law does this correctly, and the less carefully framed one does this worse. (*NE* 1129b20–26)

On a first reading of this passage one might infer that Aristotle's broad conception of justice as lawfulness simply equates being just with following the law. If this were the case, then Aristotle's conception of justice would be very conservative. Whatever laws happen to exist in a community determines what justice demands, even if those laws clearly jeopardize the common good. But this is not Aristotle's position. When articulating the broad conception of justice, Aristotle is explicit that his account is a perfectionist ideal theory, for he claims that "In every manner that they deal with, the laws aim either at the common benefit of all, or at the benefit of those in control, whose control rests on virtue or on some other such basis" (*NE* 1129b15–17). Thus justice as lawfulness means that justice is the production and maintenance of the ultimate end: happiness. Justice is not to be equated with the proclamations of a tyrannical ruler who governs for their own self-interest, inflicting misery and suffering on the citizenry. Furthermore, as Kraut notes, the Greek term *nomos* (translated as "law") means more than just the enactments of the lawmaker; it also encompasses the customs, norms, and unwritten rules of a community.[5]

---

4. Richard Kraut, *Aristotle: Political Philosophy* (Oxford: Oxford University Press, 2002), 98.

5. Kraut, *Aristotle*, 195.

Charles Young contends that Aristotle's equation of universal justice with lawfulness runs into at least two kinds of problems.[6] First, the lawmakers may be functioning with a mistaken conception of happiness, but they are successful in designing laws that promote this (ill-conceived) conception of happiness. Suppose the lawmakers subscribe to the view that happiness is equated with experiencing hedonic pleasures. So the laws of this society are designed to maximize these types of base pleasures. They mandate citizens pursue ends that make them feel good in the short term but discourage showing any regard for long-term pursuits and activities that would add meaning and purpose to their lives. Such a society aspires to promote and maintain "happiness," but what is understood to constitute happiness is impoverished. Such laws create a society where few experience any meaning or purpose, but instead pursue the fleeting sensations of a hedonic maximizer.

Second, Young argues that even if the lawmakers do function with an adequate understanding of happiness, they might do a poor job of successfully promoting happiness. It is not difficult to conceive of a situation where the government might justify a certain law or policy by reasoning that its expected benefits would be increasing morally laudable aims such as more meaning and purpose. But if such laws are ill crafted, they may not only fail to realize those ends, but they could actually undermine them.

To illustrate this point with another example, suppose a government decides that friendship (a topic that is the focus of Book IX of *Nicomachean Ethics*) is important for the good life. In order to promote the good of friendship, it enacts a number of laws that compel persons to make new friends and to spend a certain amount of substantive time with their already existing friends. Such a law would be ill conceived because it overlooks important aspects of the good of friendship, such as the fact that true friendship must be free and voluntary. Making a new friend with someone, simply because the law requires citizens to invest in such social relationships, will sabotage the realization of genuine friendships. The latter must arise from free and voluntary decisions and from organic mutual investment in new relationships. Serendipity, versus state compulsion, is often the catalyst for most genuine new friendships.

---

6. Charles Young, "Aristotle's Justice," in *The Blackwell Guide to Aristotle's Nicomachean Ethics*, ed. Richard Kraut (Oxford: Blackwell, 2006), 179–97, 182.

Having put forth his broad sense of justice, Aristotle contends that justice is lawfulness and injustice is lawlessness. But there is another type of justice and injustice, which concerns fairness. Justice is being fair, and injustice is unfair. This refers to Aristotle's narrow sense of justice, which he categorizes into three different types:

1. Justice in distribution;
2. Justice in rectification;
3. Justice in exchange.

Distributive justice, for Aristotle, concerns itself with the distribution of honors and wealth. Distributive justice is the intermediate between the extremes of too much and too little. Young describes Aristotle's understanding of distributive justice as follows:

> Suppose that Socrates and Plato invest money in some enterprise, and the time comes when the profits earned are distributed. Distributive justice requires that equal persons receive equal shares. Here the measure of equality of persons is the size of the investment each has made. Suppose that Socrates has invested 20 minae, that Plato has invested 10 minae, and that there are now 60 minae in profits to divide between them. Plainly it is just to give Socrates, who has invested twice as much as Plato has, twice as much of the profits as Plato: 40 minae for Socrates vs 20 minae for Plato. An unjust distribution would be one that violates this proportion.[7]

Distributive justice thus involves having a sense of proportionality, and treating "like cases alike." Another example can illustrate this point. Suppose a student in my class receives a C grade on their essay. On the previous assignments in the course this student had received all A grades, so they come to see me and ask if they can receive a higher grade on the latest assignment. They inform me that the C is much lower than what they have received in the past. I look over the essay again, reading the comments and feedback I had provided on my assessment. After doing so I determine that the C was in fact a fair grade. I inform the student that

---

7. Young, "Aristotle's Justice," 185.

this latest essay is not similar in its quality to the other A-level material they have submitted in the past. The most recent essay did not have a clear thesis, the argumentation for their position was somewhat weak, the paper could have been structured more effectively, and there were some (as an example) careless spelling mistakes. "But . . ." the student pleads, "I need an A to boost my average and get on the dean's list." I tell them that grades in the course are assigned on the basis of "desert," not "need." It would be a violation of Aristotle's doctrine of distributive justice if I gave higher marks to students simply because they complained about their marks, or desired to be on the dean's list. Students must be treated equally when their grades are awarded, and this means their work should be assessed based on its merits (or demerits) versus considerations that have nothing to do with the quality of the work submitted. Proportional equality in the distribution of honors captures the first kind of justice Aristotle identifies with the narrow sense of justice.

The second species of narrow justice that Aristotle identifies is justice in rectification. Consider the case of a robbery and physical assault. Person X physically injures an innocent victim, stealing their money after beating them up. X's transgression creates an inequality that did not exist before—diminishing the well-being (the physical and mental well-being, as well as their financial situation) of the victim, and improving the financial situation of X. The "equal" in this situation is the intermediate position between the "profit" and "loss" of X and the victim. The judge acts as a mediator, determining the intermediate position between doing nothing (which would result in an inequality in favor of X over the victim) and an overly severe punishment for X (which would result in a new inequality arising in favor of the victim over X). This example summarizes the basic idea of justice in rectification.

Aristotle's third type of justice, in the narrow sense, is justice in exchange, or reciprocity. He considers the case of an exchange between a shoemaker and a builder. The shoemaker makes shoes, and the builder builds houses. For an exchange between them to be fair, proportionate equality and reciprocity require the exchange be such that the quality of workmanship be comparable (one cannot be significantly superior in quality), and some measure, between the number of shoes per house, satisfied. Otherwise the exchange will be unjust. Aristotle contends it is this need that holds a community together (*NE* 1133b7–10).

The Intellectual Virtues

In addition to the moral virtues, which apply to the nonrational parts of the soul, in Book VI of the *Nicomachean Ethics* Aristotle addresses the "intellectual virtues" or "virtues of thought," which apply to the rational part of the soul. Instead of detailing (as we did in the previous section on the moral virtues) Aristotle's own account of the intellectual virtues, in this section we shall consider a contemporary Aristotelian account of "virtue epistemology." "Epistemology" refers to the branch of philosophy concerned with knowledge, and there is a burgeoning field of study referred to as "virtue epistemology" that has been influenced by Aristotle's account of virtue ethics. In her book *Virtues of the Mind: An Inquiry into the Nature of Virtue and the Ethical Foundations of Knowledge*, Linda Zagzebski advances a contemporary Aristotelian account of intellectual virtue. We will consider some of the tenets of her account.

Virtue epistemology is often characterized as an extension of virtue ethics. For the latter, the focus of moral inquiry and evaluation is our actions. So virtue ethics concerns itself with questions like "Should we always tell the truth?" (e.g., even when doing so will harm people we care about) or "How should we distribute different types of societal benefits (e.g., wealth) and burdens (e.g., punishment)?" But virtue epistemology shifts the focus from human actions to the kind of person we should be, and more specifically the cognitive processing that precedes our actions.

Zagzebski contends that, when it comes to determining the rightness or wrongness of actions, virtue ethicists maintain that "a *right act, all things considered*, is what a person with *phronesis* might do in like circumstances. A *wrong act, all things considered*, is what a person with *phronesis* would not do in like circumstances." Virtue epistemology maintains a structural similarity with virtue ethics, but it shifts the focus of moral evaluation from actions to beliefs. Thus "a justified belief, *all things considered*, is what a person with *phronesis* might believe in like circumstances. An *unjustified belief, all things considered*, is what a person with *phronesis* would not believe in like circumstances."[8] In Book VI Aristotle describes *phronesis*

---

8. Linda Trinkaus Zagzebski, *Virtues of the Mind: An Inquiry into the Nature of Virtue and the Ethical Foundations of Knowledge* (Cambridge: Cambridge University Press, 1996), 239–40, 246 (emphasis in original).

as a "reasoned and true state of capacity to act with regard to human goods" (VI.5.1140b20–21). As such it is a higher-order virtue that governs the moral and intellectual virtues. And knowledge, which is critical to enabling us to flourish (and helping prevent misfortune) is defined by Zagzebski as "a state of cognitive contact with reality arising out of acts of intellectual virtue."[9] Another virtue epistemologist characterizes knowledge as "success from ability."[10]

So what kinds of "intellectual virtues" could help enable us to succeed in today's uncertain and often precarious environment? Human populations face threats from infectious diseases, climate change, war, economic recessions, and so on. Zagzebski identifies the following lengthy list of "virtues of the mind":

1. The ability to recognize the salient facts; sensitivity to details;
2. Open-mindedness in collecting and appraising evidence;
3. Fairness in evaluating the arguments of others;
4. Intellectual humility;
5. Intellectual perseverance, diligence, care, and thoroughness;
6. Adaptability of intellect;
7. The detective's virtues: thinking of coherent explanations of the facts;
8. Being able to recognize reliable authority;
9. Insight into persons, problems, theories;
10. The teaching virtues: the social virtues of being communicative, including intellectual candor and knowing your audience and how they respond.[11]

We shall limit our examination of the intellectual virtues to just the first five of these virtues, and see how they may play out in different societal predicaments for government policy and individual decision-making.

---

9. Zagzebski, *Virtues of the Mind*, 270.

10. John Greco, *Achieving Knowledge: A Virtue-Theoretic Account of Epistemic Normativity* (Cambridge: Cambridge University Press, 2010), 3.

11. Zagzebski, *Virtues of the Mind*, 114.

The ability to recognize the salient facts, and having a sensitivity to details, is critical for sagely combating the threats of an infectious disease, for example. Suppose, as occurred in late 2019, a new infectious disease emerges that threatens the health of the global population. A number of "relevant facts" are important to pay attention to when public health officials are figuring out how to respond to a novel infectious disease. For example, how does the disease spread? Some infectious diseases are transmitted sexually (e.g., like HIV/AIDS); others are transmitted via food and contaminated water (e.g., typhoid); yet others (e.g., like SARS-CoV-2) can be transmitted via droplets or particles from an infected person's cough or sneeze. In order to know which public health measures are more effective in reducing the transmission of an infectious disease, we must first pay attention to details like the evidence of how it is transmitted. That information will help us determine whether the appropriate response is to clean contaminated water versus advise the wearing of condoms versus advise the wearing of face masks, and so forth. The details of how a disease is transmitted are important for determining how serious a public health threat it is (e.g., how quickly a new virus may spread), as well as the precautions that can be taken to help contain or reduce its transmission.

Other salient facts to consider in responding to the public health threats of a novel infectious disease would be to determine the lethality of the disease. Is it fatal to only a very small percentage of people who are exposed to the pathogen, or is the probability of death after exposure very high (e.g., as in the case of rabies)? Also, are there asymptomatic as well as symptomatic infections? This might be relevant in terms of determining both the severity of a novel disease and the feasibility of containing or reducing transmission once the disease is already widespread. In the early months of 2020 there was uncertainty on all of these points with respect to the COVID-19 pandemic, which made it particularly challenging to determine the best way to respond to the public health crisis. Should schools for children be closed? Crowded environments mean an increased risk of virus transmission. But what about the educational deficits and social isolation that occur with prolonged school closures? The COVID-19 pandemic is a vivid example of the importance of the "intellectual virtues" for global health. We return to this issue in more detail in the concluding chapter.

Openness to collecting and appraising the evidence is an intellectual virtue that is critical for forensic science and law enforcement. Suppose Peter is the prime suspect in the murder of his boss. Peter has a clear motive: his boss had fired him the day before the murder. And Peter has no good alibi. He says he took a long nap at home that day, but no one could confirm that is where he was. The lead detective in the case does not jump to the conclusion that Peter should be arrested for the crime. Instead, she has the victim's house examined for fingerprints and DNA evidence. A murder weapon is found in the park outside the boss's house, and the fingerprints of the boss's neighbor are found on the weapon. It turns out that the boss and neighbor had a long and heated argument over the backyard fence the boss had constructed. Because of the detective's "openness to collecting evidence and appraising that evidence," the injustice of charging an innocent person (Peter) with murder was avoided.

A third intellectual virtue is fairness in evaluating the arguments of others. Consider how this virtue could improve the health of democratic government. Two political opponents are debating their respective policy agendas at a town hall event. They both disagree passionately about how the city should deal with the growing problem of the scarcity of affordable housing. One candidate believes the best solution is to increase the minimum wage so that more citizens can afford housing. The other candidate believes the better option is for the government to approve new zoning bylaws that would permit more construction of low-cost housing. If both sides remain polarized on this issue, with both candidates belittling their opponent's proposals, it is unlikely that a workable solution will be implemented. But if both candidates possess the virtue of fairness in evaluating their opponent's arguments, perhaps they can find a feasible middle ground that helps rectify the economic vulnerability of the poor while also stimulating the building of new affordable housing in the city.

Intellectual humility is an important virtue for persons, organizations, and societies. Consider how this virtue could apply to the success of running a business. The owner of a business has had success selling their product on the market for the past ten years. This has enabled the business to expand, resulting in hiring dozens more employees. However, the business owner knows that commercial success in the past does not necessarily mean commercial success in the future. They hire an outside firm to observe and critically assess the business model they have been using for the last decade. These external advisors find that there are some practices the company adopted that made sense ten years ago but now actually cause some inefficiencies for the company. The business owner takes the advice of this consulting firm and makes changes to eliminate those inefficiencies. After doing so, the company continues to grow and expand for the foreseeable future.

Finally, consider the intellectual virtues of *perseverance, diligence, care,* and *thoroughness*. These are intellectual virtues that are critical to innovation in all areas of technology and industry. For example, the three 1903 Nobel Prize winners for physics were Henri Becquerel, Marie Curie, and Pierre Curie. Becquerel accidentally discovered spontaneous radioactivity while studying how uranium salts were affected by light. His discovery was then studied further by the Curies (husband and wife) who undertook painstaking methodical research on polonium and radium. Marie Curie was awarded a second Nobel Prize in 1911, this time in chemistry, for the separation of polonium and radium. Undertaking scientific research worthy of a Nobel Prize requires great care, thoroughness, and a desire to persevere with research that can take years, even decades, to complete. Moreover, the eventual success of such research is never a given. Scientific research would be stifled if researchers did not aspire to exercise the intellectual virtues of perseverance, diligence, care, and thoroughness.

Virtue Jurisprudence

Aristotle's emphasis on virtue ethics has also been applied by philosophers to contemporary topics in law and judicial decision-making. Lawrence Solum characterizes virtue jurisprudence as a normative and explanatory theory of law that utilizes the resources of virtue ethics to answer the central questions of legal theory.[12] This approach to legal theory can be distinguished from legal realism and legal formalism. Both of these terms have a long history in legal thought, and both have multiple meanings.[13] Legal

---

12. Lawrence Solum, "Virtue Jurisprudence: A Virtue-Centred Theory of Judging," *Metaphilosophy* 34, nos. 1–2 (2003): 178–213; Colin Farrelly and Lawrence Solum, eds., *Virtue Jurisprudence* (Basingstoke, UK: Palgrave Macmillan, 2008).

13. Richard A. Posner, "Legal Formalism, Legal Realism, and the Interpretation of Statutes and the Constitution," *Case Western Reserve Law Review* 37, no. 2 (1986): 179–217.

realism maintains that laws reflect political power and societal interests. In this respect legal realism echoes Thrasymachus's contention, articulated in Plato's *Republic*, that political right makes legal right.[14] This account of judicial decision-making thus rejects the idea that judges are "independent" and "impartial," at least with respect to making legal decisions that are not biased by their own political ideologies and policy preferences. Legal realists thus challenge the position known as legal formalism.

In contrast to legal realism, legal formalism characterizes judicial decision-making as judges apply the facts to the rules created by lawmakers, but judges themselves are not swayed by social interests and politics. In this account of law, judges apply, versus make up, the law. The term "originalism," for example, refers to a type of formalism that espouses the judicial philosophy that judges ought to interpret the law in accordance with the original intention of the lawmakers. Former US Supreme Court justice Antonin Scalia (1936–2016), for example, was a prominent proponent of originalism. When deciding on contentious constitutional cases dealing with issues like gun control or abortion, Justice Scalia maintained that a judge should consider what the original meaning of the US Constitution was.

Virtue jurisprudence involves utilizing insights from the virtue ethics tradition to help legal theory progress beyond the traditional dichotomy of legal realism and formalism. The selection of judges, especially in the United States and particularly for the US Supreme Court, is a very contentious social issue, as political parties often make their own policy and political preferences (e.g., for or against affirmative action, the right to abortion, gun control, etc.) major elements of the judicial selection process. In "Virtue Jurisprudence: A Virtue-Centred Theory of Judging" Solum begins by first asking what constitutes judicial "vices." Suppose the judge is presiding over the criminal proceedings of a well-known gangster who has a long history of being involved in organized crime. The evidence regarding the criminal wrongdoing of the defendant is very strong. There is video evidence of someone of similar size and clothing to the suspect fleeing the crime scene shortly after the victim was killed. A gun was found on the suspect's property, and the bullet found in the

---

14. Richard A. Posner, *The Problems of Jurisprudence* (Cambridge, MA: Harvard University Press, 1990), 9.

deceased person's body (a known rival of the suspect) was matched to the gun found on the suspect's property. A few eyewitnesses have also testified that they saw the suspect arguing with the victim shortly before the victim was killed. But the defendant also has witnesses who testify that he was nowhere near the victim at the time of the killing. The defendant's close friends and family all testify that he was enjoying dinner with them on the other side of town.

One obvious judicial vice is *corruption*. If the judge finds the notorious gangster not guilty because the judge has been paid a handsome bribe to make sure the suspect is released from custody, this would clearly violate judicial virtue. And yet judicial corruption is a real and persistent threat in legal jurisdictions throughout the world.

A second judicial vice Solum identifies is *judicial cowardice*. Suppose that, instead of making their decision based on receiving a bribe, the judge decided to give the verdict "not guilty" because the suspect was well liked by the general population. Despite having a reputation as a person involved in organized crime, the suspect was also well liked on social media, with millions of followers. Additionally, they also had political ambitions and are (despite the ongoing criminal investigation) the front-runner to easily win the next election for governor of their state. The judge, not wishing to risk the ire of public opinion, renders the decision "not guilty" because they lack the courage to stand by justice when such decisions might be unpopular with the masses.

Other judicial vices include *temper* (e.g., a judge who lets their emotions influence their decision about a case), *incompetence* (e.g., a judge who fails to understand the law), and *foolishness* (e.g., a judge who fails to distinguish between those aspects of a dispute that are important and those that are trivial).[15] After canvassing the judicial vices, Solum identifies the following five aspects of judicial virtue: (1) judicial temperance, (2) judicial courage, (3) judicial temperament, (4) judicial intelligence, and (5) judicial wisdom.

Temperance is having control of one's own desires and emotions. This means a virtuous judge will not let their own desires influence or sway their decisions. Offers of bribes from defendants, for example, would not pervert the decision-making of the temperate judge because they place

---

15. Solum, "Virtue Jurisprudence," 188.

justice above their own hedonic pleasures (and thus are not tempted to take such bribes). *Judicial courage* means a judge will be willing to risk their career and reputation for the sake of justice. *Judicial temperament* entails that the judge has good control of their anger. A long day of court decisions may make a judge tired and hungry, but such matters do not influence the decisions of a virtuous judge. They do not increase the severity of punishment for a crime simply because they are "hangry."

Judicial intelligence involves the exercise of intellectual virtues related to legal decision-making. This means the virtuous judge will understand the laws governing the jurisdiction they are deciding on, and the facts and specifics of the dispute in question. Finally there is the virtue of *judicial wisdom*. "Judicial wisdom is simply the virtue of practical wisdom as applied to the choices that must be made by judges. The practically wise judge has developed excellence in knowing what goals to pursue in the particular case and excellence in choosing the means to accomplish those goals."[16]

Eudaimonia and the "Science of Happiness"

Our focus thus far has been on Aristotle's account of virtue ethics, and how moral and intellectual virtues can be, and have been, applied to topics in ethics, epistemology, and law. Now we turn our attention to what is arguably the most important theme throughout Aristotle's moral and political philosophy—his account of happiness (the Greek word is *eudaimonia*). Aristotle begins the *Nicomachean Ethics* by asserting that "every craft and every inquiry, and likewise every action and decision, seems to seek some good" (*NE* I, 1. 1094a). The end of medicine, Aristotle contends, is health. The end of shipbuilding is a vessel, and the end of household management is wealth. But, he continues, what is the highest end? Aristotle conjectures that there must be some higher end, an end that all other ends seek to promote.

This highest of ends is the proper subject of politics, the master science that prescribes which other sciences must be studied. For Aristotle, politics is a science that examines what preserves and destroys cities. Which laws

---

16. Solum, "Virtue Jurisprudence," 192.

and customs would create the best kind of political system? And what is the standard by which we would assess how good such a political system is? The highest end, which the science of politics is ultimately concerned with, is happiness or *eudaimonia*. The good society is one that enables persons to flourish.

In Book I, chapter 5, Aristotle distinguishes between different understandings of happiness. The most vulgar and popular understanding of happiness reduces happiness to gratification or pleasure. We shall see the utilitarian Jeremy Bentham espouse this account of happiness in his defense of utilitarianism and hedonism in chapter 10. For Aristotle, the pursuit of hedonic satisfaction is a slavish, animal-like existence. It does not constitute the good life for humans.

Another understanding of happiness is honor, the type of happiness Aristotle believes people active in politics pursue. But this cannot be the highest of goods, argues Aristotle. The honor pursued in politics is something that is fleeting and contingent on the approval of others. When such approval disappears, so too does the good of honor. And the highest good is something that others cannot take away from us. The highest of ends, *eudaimonia*, is the "activity of the soul in accordance with complete virtue" (*NE* 1102a5–10).

While contemporary psychologists who study the science of happiness (known as the field of "positive psychology") do not invoke Aristotle's vague reference to the "activity of the soul," many have found inspiration in Aristotle's eudaimonic account of well-being, an account that has helped the empirical study of well-being transcend the limitations of the hedonic account of happiness. In *Flourish*, for example, Martin Seligman—one of the pioneers in the field of positive psychology—argues that the science of happiness must move away from equating life satisfaction with cheerful mood and instead focus on well-being. The latter, Seligman contends, is composed of the following five elements: positive emotion, engagement, relationships, meaning, and accomplishment (referred to as PERMA). This multifaceted understanding of human flourishing has significant political implications for things like the importance to be placed on economic growth and affluence. Unlike the hedonic account of happiness, which would equate greater wealth with greater happiness if it satiates our consumer preferences, Seligman argues (as Aristotle does) that material prosperity only matters insofar as it increases well-being.[17] Accumulating wealth should not be considered an end in itself. While it is certainly true that lifting a country out of poverty improves the life satisfaction of a population—reducing the hardships and stressors of poverty, famine, war, and so on—Seligman contends that making more money rapidly reaches a point of diminishing returns and does not have a significant impact on well-being (e.g., positive emotion, engagement, and meaning).

Despite the significant improvements in our health and economic prospects since the time of the ancient Greeks, the problems of anxiety and boredom remain significant challenges for even the world's wealthiest nations. Another contemporary psychologist who draws on insights from Aristotle to inform empirical research on how we can improve happiness today is Mihaly Csikszentmihalyi. A key insight in his book *FLOW: The Psychology of Optimal Experience* is that happiness does not depend on external events (e.g., good fortune), but rather on how we *interpret* these events. Csikszentmihalyi argues that the most important trait in life is the ability to persevere through adversity, "to transform hopeless situations into challenges to overcome."[18] Our self-growth is facilitated by engaging in *flow activities* that possess the following eight major components of enjoyment:

1. The experience usually occurs when we confront tasks we have a chance of completing.
2. We must be able to concentrate on what we are doing.
3. The concentration is possible because the task undertaken has clear goals.
4. The task provides immediate feedback.
5. One acts with deep but effortless involvement that removes from awareness the worries and frustrations of everyday life.
6. They allow us to exercise a sense of control over our actions.
7. Concern for the self disappears, yet paradoxically the sense of self emerges stronger after the flow experience is over.

---

17. Martin Seligman, *Flourish* (New York: Free Press, 2011), 221.
18. Mihaly Csikszentmihalyi, *FLOW: The Psychology of Optimal Experience* (New York: Harper Collins, 2008), 24.

8. The sense of duration of time is altered; hours pass by in minutes, and minutes can stretch out to seem like hours.[19]

Like Aristotle's strong emphasis on our social nature, Csikszentmihalyi's analysis of flow begins with the foundational premise that we are "biologically programmed to find other human beings the most important objects in the world." People can make our lives very interesting and fulfilling, yet they can also make our lives miserable. How we manage human relationships thus has a significant impact on our happiness and well-being. "If we learn to make our relationships with others more like flow experiences, our quality of life as a whole is going to be much improved."[20] In democracies the health, or lack thereof, of our democratic practices, institutions, and culture can impact our well-being as they represent the quality of our relationship with our compatriots (e.g., civility, intolerance, misunderstanding, empathy, indifference, etc.). "Who should we vote for?" "Which principles and policy priorities ought to govern collective decision-making?" "How should the interests of future generations factor into the current generation's deliberations concerning the determinates of good governance in the twenty-first century?" These normative questions often permeate our individual and collective deliberations about democratic politics. If we are, as Aristotle contends, social animals who enjoy the exercise of our practice reason, then it is worthwhile considering the relationship between democracy and happiness.

Voting, Democracy, and Happiness

Scholars who substantively engage with the contemporary implications of Aristotle's moral and political philosophy face a dilemma. Many aspects of Aristotle's views are flawed and morally objectionable, such as his stances on inequality, women, and slavery. Josiah Ober notes these problems and remarks:

---

19. Csikszentmihalyi, *FLOW*, 49.
20. Csikszentmihalyi, *FLOW*, 164.

It goes almost without saying that there are aspects of Aristotle's political thought that are *not* relevant, at least in any positive, theory-building sense: Aristotle's defense of the claim that some persons are, by dint of an inborn psychological flaw, "slaves by nature," along with his military doctrine that asserts that it is just to employ organized violence to enslave a foreign population of putative natural slaves, is an obvious case in point. Aristotle also asserted that all women suffer a psychological disability that prevents them from reliably deliberating about public goods and that this disability debarred women from active citizenship. Aristotle further contended that the civic virtue essential for the effective performance of active citizenship is necessarily corrupted when an individual acts as an instrument of another's private advantage (whether that meant laboring under another's direction, or expert musical performance enjoyed by another). It follows that everyone who works for a living is rendered, *ipso facto*, slavish by habit and thereby unsuited for political action. I will call these three claims "Aristotle's useless arguments."[21]

An example of how Aristotle's flawed and morally objectionable presuppositions inform his political theory is his constitutional theorizing about the organizational arrangements ("constitution" or "government"), which Aristotle takes to constitute the supreme authority in states (*Politics*, Books III, VI) of a political community in the *Politics*. Aristotle posits a six-fold classification of "deviant" and "correct" constitutions for the three potential forms of government of *rule by one*, *rule by the few*, and *rule by the multitude*. The correct constitutions for these three forms are kingship, aristocracy and polity, respectively; the deviant forms are tyranny, oligarchy, and democracy. Aristotle defines democracy as rule of the poor, in contrast to the correct version of rule by the multitude—a polity—which is rule by the middle class (the middle ground between rule by the poor and rule by the most affluent).

To our twenty-first-century moral sensibilities, with the empirical knowledge we now have about the pros and cons of democratic rule versus

---

21. Josiah Ober, "Political Animals Revisited," *Good Society* 22, no. 2 (2013): 201–14, 201.

dictatorships, there could be no "correct" form of rule by one person, or even rule by the few, that we would entertain seriously as a form of desirable or legitimate government. But rather than amplify the elements of Aristotle's arguments that are, as Ober notes, "useless" to theorists today, we can instead attempt to draw some inspiration from Aristotle's emphasis on our political nature and the human search for meaning and explore how these might apply to democratic theory and voting behavior.

Political science has long concerned itself with the question "Why vote?" In electoral systems with millions of voters, the probability that any person's single vote will determine the outcome in an election is close to zero. However, the act of voting incurs some cost or burden on the voter. Economists call this an "opportunity cost." At a minimum, a voter must take the time to travel to the voting station, wait in line to verify they are eligible to vote, and then cast their ballot. Another way to describe this is to say voting incurs *burdens* (even if they are minimal) but not any likely *benefits*.

This form of reasoning, called *rational choice theory*, was employed by the economist Anthony Downs in his seminal book *An Economic Theory of Democracy*. Downs called this the "paradox of not voting."[22] At least when viewed through the lens of rational choice theory, voting thus appears to be irrational activity.[23] And if the act of voting is irrational, one could contend that investing the time and energy to become an informed voter (e.g., learning about the party platforms and candidates, etc.) is itself irrational. Thus it might appear that the coherence of the system of democratic governance itself may be in jeopardy.

Critics of rational choice theory often criticize the simplistic characterization of human motivation it presumes. When acting as consumers in market decisions, people may act (though many obviously do not!) as *rational consumers*. Such consumers will seek out the cheapest price for products of similar quality. But the critic will contend that it is a category mistake to think this does (or should) apply to voting behavior. Voting is a *political* act, an expression of how the collective political power of a society should be wielded. By contrast, purchasing a new electric toothbrush or a meal is a private act of consumption. Aristotle's account of our "political

---

22. Anthony Downs, *An Economic Theory of Democracy* (New York: Harper, 1957).
23. Gordon Tullock, *Toward a Mathematics of Politics* (Ann Arbor: University of Michigan Press, 1967).

nature" captures a much richer account of human motivation and behavior than that offered by rational choice theory.

Ober, for example, contends that the self-interest–centered account of the person employed by rational choice theory is a fiction, "an over-simplification of human psychology that gains analytic power by reduction—by stripping away, as analytically irrelevant, many complexities of real-world human motivation."[24] Rather than employing economic theory to explain political behavior, Ober believes that the Aristotelian account of human nature provides a more plausible account of the appeal of democratic governance and voting:

> Political participation has non-instrumental, as well as instrumental, value for humans because of the kind of beings we are. It is because we are, as Aristotle saw, a political-animal kind of being that the opportunity for exercising a natural capacity for practicing democracy, defined in a minimal sense as "association in public decision," is for us a good-in-itself that is both inherently happiness-producing and necessary to our full happiness. It is necessary to our complete happiness because, along with (for example) our capacities to reason and to love, the capacity to associate ourselves in decisions through the medium of speech is constitutive of our distinctive kind of being.[25]

Is there empirical evidence to support the conjecture that humans are the kind of animal that Aristotle claimed we are, and that voting and democracy are conducive to our well-being? Definitively answering such questions would exceed what we could examine in this book, and any evidence provided to support such conjectures is vulnerable to the charge that it is being selective. The critic might point to empirical studies that suggest (at least some) people are indifferent to political participation. But there is certainly some research that suggests Aristotle was on to something with his account of both human nature and happiness, and

---

24. Josiah Ober, *Democracy and Knowledge* (Princeton, NJ: Princeton University Press, 2008), 10.

25. Josiah Ober, "Natural Capacities and Democracy as a Good-In-Itself," *Philosophical Studies* 132 (2007): 59–73, 60.

these insights have significance for our understanding of the relationship between democracy (and voting) and happiness.

For example, one study examined the daily social behavior of happy people by using an electronically activated recorder to record the conversations of the participants and group them into "small talk" (e.g., banal conversations, such as about the weather) and "substantive talk" (e.g., discussions about meaningful things, such as relationships).[26] The researchers found that higher well-being was associated with having less small talk and more substantive conversations. Such a finding would make sense if people are, as Aristotle conjectured, political animals who derive intrinsic pleasure from conversations that express our capacity to reason and love. Like meaningful conversations, the act of voting can represent an expression of our deliberation and reflection on questions about the common good and future direction of a polity.

Voter turnout is of course influenced by many factors. Some of these factors are external factors, such as the (real or perceived) quality of democratic institutions and practices, the economy, the type of election (e.g., federal versus local), and how close the competition is. But there are also important (internal) factors related to the *identity* of voters, such as their age, income, education level, race, gender, rural versus urban location, and so on. This means that any attempt to present a concise and persuasive account of human nature and voting faces significant challenges. There are many nuances related to the history of the societal and political problems facing a polity, the quality of the dialogue and debate among political parties, the influence of media, circumstances people face at different stages of their lives (e.g., young voters versus parents of young children versus retirees living on a pension), and so forth. Nonetheless, Aristotle's contention that we are political animals is one that continues to have traction in debates about democracy and politics. Further empirical research into human happiness and well-being might help shed light on novel ways to improve the health of democracies in the twenty-first century.

---

26. M. R. Mehl, S. Vazire, S. E. Holleran, and C. S. Clark, "Eavesdropping on Happiness: Well-being Is Related to Having Less Small Talk and More Substantive Conversations," *Psychological Science* 21 (2010): 539–41.

Chapter 4

Hobbes, Human Nature, and Anarchism

The social contract tradition has a long, influential, and somewhat tumultuous history in Western political thought. Philosophically, the idea of construing society and government as constituting a kind of "social contract" often has a great deal of intuitive appeal and attraction. The problem of political authority would seem to be resolved if the scope and limits of political authority were derived from a social contract. If it were factually true that "everyone agreed to this societal arrangement," then it would appear there can be no reasonable basis on which to complain that we are not morally bound to obey the laws of such a society. But the philosophical appeal of the social contract becomes strained when we recognize reality, where consent, equality, and inclusion have not been the norm in any society. Social hierarchies along lines of social class, gender, race, and so on have a long history in human societies. If the argument from the social contract tradition glosses over, or implicitly legitimates, such inequalities, the outcome of such theorizing will be antithetical to, rather than exemplary of, generating emancipatory knowledge to help us think sagely about the functions of government and what constitutes fair terms of cooperation in the complex situation of real-world societies. This concern is one we shall address with the three main social contract theorists considered in this book: Thomas Hobbes's argument for an absolute sovereign in *Leviathan*, John Locke's argument for limited government in the *Two Treatises of Government*, and Jean-Jacques Rousseau's argument for democratic governance in *The Social Contract*.

The social contract tradition can be divided into two different types of contract theories: the "interest-based" and "right-based" contract traditions.[1] For the former, of which Thomas Hobbes is the paradigmatic

---

1. Samuel Freeman, "Reason and Agreement in Social Contract Views," *Philosophy and Public Affairs* 19, no. 2 (1990): 122–57.

proponent, the account of the social contract is not predicated on any moral premises. Social cooperation is understood as a system of *mutual advantage*. In other words, agreeing to the social contract improves the bargaining position of everyone compared to the baseline of comparison of noncooperation. This account of the social contract has appeal, its proponents claim, because it is rational for contractors to accept the social contract. From the perspective of their own self-interest, each participant moves from a position of nonagreement (i.e., life in the state of nature) to agreement to the social contract, and this improves the life prospects of everyone bound by the contract. The agreement is not predicated on some suspect theological or moral premises concerning the dictates of a religious authority or the natural rights of persons.

In contrast to the *interest-based* contract theory of Hobbes, *right-based* contract theories explicitly rely on *moral premises*. "The common feature of these accounts is not that they base the agreement on an assumption of prior individual rights . . . rather, that principles of right and justice cannot be accounted for without appeal to certain irreducible moral notions."[2] In John Locke's account of government, people possess the natural rights to life, liberty, and property in the state of nature, before any government or laws have been created. For Jean-Jacques Rousseau, the argument for binding ourselves to the democratic form of government guided by the "general will" is predicated on the moral premise that people (or at least men) are *political equals*.

These two different contract traditions—interest-based versus right-based—have their own strengths and weaknesses. Defenders of the interest-based approach see it as a strength of the approach that it does not assume the moral premises that it is trying to justify in the first place. As such, if successful, it should be a normative theory that can provide even the moral skeptic with a compelling reason for agreeing with the social contract—namely, that it is in their own self-interest to do so.

Right-based critics of the interest-based approach typically highlight the problematic *conclusions* of the interest-based approach. In the case of Hobbes, he comes to the conclusion that an absolute sovereign is justified. To those of us living in democracies in the twenty-first century, this is not going to be a morally palatable conclusion. The conception of

---

2. Freeman, "Reason and Agreement," 124.

morality entailed in Hobbes's political theory—that morality simply is what is mutually advantageous—also raises the problem of what should be done in circumstances where it may not be rational to cooperate, such as with future generations, nonhuman animals, weaker countries, and so on. A vision of morality that permits the exploitation of future generations, nonhuman animals, and weaker countries (when cooperation is not mutually beneficial) is inherently defective, claim the critics of the interest-based approach to the social contract.

Hobbes and the English Civil War

Thomas Hobbes was born in 1588 in England. In his autobiography Hobbes claims that he was born prematurely, when his mother became distressed at the news that the Spanish Armada was approaching England. Fear was something Hobbes believed had brought him into this world early, and fear looms large in his political philosophy and justification of the absolute sovereign. How to interpret Hobbes's contributions to political philosophy and ethics is the subject of much debate, as is the case with most of the thinkers canvassed in this book. Historians, political scientists, and philosophers apply different intellectual tools—textual insights, historical factors, and pedagogical agendas—to the study of the thinkers they address. Throughout this book my primary goal is to bring to the fore the philosophical engagement with important thinkers, with an orientation toward revealing and critically assessing the contemporary relevance of these thinkers.

Hobbes is an important thinker for many reasons, but in this chapter we will focus on what Jean Hampton has called the "systematic camp of Hobbes interpreters."[3] This camp treats Hobbes's arguments as the expression of a single argument for absolute sovereignty based on premises concerning human nature and our psychology. And it is these components of Hobbes's contribution to political philosophy we shall focus on, and critically evaluate, in this chapter. But it is worth noting that there is

---

3. Jean Hampton, *Hobbes and the Social Contract Tradition* (Cambridge: Cambridge University Press, 2012), 2.

another camp of Hobbes interpreters, the "anti-systematic camp,"[4] that maintains that Hobbes's argument for an absolute sovereign is predicated on the foundation of natural law developed in medieval Christian philosophy.

To make sense of the Hobbesian project of an interest-based social contract theory, we must understand the historical context in which Hobbes was writing in the seventeenth century. The time Hobbes was writing *Leviathan* was very turbulent in England for many distinct reasons. First, it was a time of great religious and political instability, with ongoing conflict between royalists and parliamentarians. The former defended the king's right to rule over the subjects as part of the doctrine of divine right. By contrast, the parliamentarians maintained that there were constraints and limits on the rule of the monarchy. Furthermore, there were also religious tensions after decades of the Reformation in Europe had fractured Christianity, challenging established traditions and power arrangements. Finally, there was an emerging scientific revolution. Significant scientific progress was made during the seventeenth century by scientists such as Galileo Galilei (1564–1642) and Isaac Newton (1643–1727). Observations of astronomical and other natural phenomenon led to the discovery of scientific laws that helped us make predictions about the orbits of the planets and the motion of objects on earth.

Hobbes was a proactive participant in this growing scientific revolution. He hoped to study the "science of man" with the same rigor that science had applied to the study of natural phenomena such as the movement of the planets. After his education at Oxford, he spent most of his adult life working as a tutor for the aristocratic family of the Earl of Devonshire. Hobbes had access to the latest books of his day and met prominent scientists such as Galileo Galilei and other philosophers such as René Descartes. Hobbes also traveled extensively in continental Europe and lived in France during the English Civil War.

---

4. Hampton includes A. E. Taylor, "The Ethical Doctrine of Hobbes," *Philosophy* 13 (1938): 407–8; and Howard Warrender, *The Political Philosophy of Hobbes* (New York: Oxford University Press, 1957) as the leading advocates of this interpretation of Hobbes. More recent and more intricate interpretations of Hobbes include Arash Abizadeh, *Hobbes and the Two Faces of Ethics* (Cambridge: Cambridge University Press, 2018), and Jeffrey Collins, *The Allegiance of Thomas Hobbes* (Oxford: Oxford University Press, 2007).

The publication of *Leviathan* in 1651 came at a time of significant turmoil and stress in British politics. For decades tension between King Charles I and Parliament had been mounting. The king needed the approval of Parliament to impose taxes. But wars in France and Spain, and rebellions in Ireland and Scotland, strained the relationship between Parliament and the monarchy, with King Charles I dissolving Parliament three times between 1625 and 1629, after which Charles I started his "eleven years of personal rule." Tax revenue could be raised without the approval of Parliament through "ship money," a levy that could be imposed on coastal communities to defend the realm. Rather than amassing ships for protection when there was no eminent threat, the Crown instead used the levy to raise revenue via taxation. This was not well received by the critics of Charles I.

The growing unrest in England motivated Hobbes to flee to France, where he lived for eleven years and wrote *Leviathan*. During that time, in 1642, civil war broke out in England between royalists and parliamentarians. Charles I was defeated, then tried and convicted of high treason. He was beheaded in 1649.

Hobbes's argument in *Leviathan* was controversial at the time, rejecting the popular justification for the rule of the monarchy—the divine right of kings—but at the same time arguing for the legitimacy of an absolute monarch. The potential appeal of Hobbes's project, from a philosophical perspective, is that *if* he could provide a justification for the state that does not presuppose the acceptance of any particular religious or moral assumptions, it would provide a strong argument that all rational persons could accept. Our focus will be on the central assumptions Hobbes puts forth in *Leviathan* for the necessity and legitimacy of the state.

The State of Nature

The interest-based Hobbesian argument for the social contract represented an innovative way of arguing for the state and about politics and ethics. Hobbes challenged both dominant justifications for monarchal rule: the divine right of kings and also the dominance of Aristotelianism. "Almost all of the best-known philosophers and scientists of the seventeenth century saw Aristotle's philosophy as a significant impediment to the progress of knowledge, and believed that progress could only begin once the edifice of Aristotle's system had been razed and philosophy could rebuild on new foundations."[5] Hobbes was very proactively engaged in debunking the grip of Aristotelianism.

Predicating a political theory on nonmoral premises, Hobbes believed he could advance a *science of politics* that was capable of demonstrating why the social contract legitimated the rule by an absolute monarch. Acceptance of the social contract did not require the commitment to particular religious or moral doctrines, such as Catholicism, Protestantism, or Aristotle's "teleology." Such foundations would erode the security of any society where there is disagreement and pluralism in what people believe.

Hobbes aspired instead to advance a political theory predicated on what he believed to be "universal truths" for us as humans. These included truths about our nature and psychology, such as our rough equality in terms of physical and mental powers, the emotion of fear and our concern for self-preservation, our ability to simulate future states of affair in our mind, and truths about the external world we inhabit, such as the scarcity of goods.

Gary Herbert describes Hobbes's significance to the discipline as follows:

> Thomas Hobbes laid the philosophical groundwork for political modernity by purging natural right of the residues of stoic and medieval morality. He rejected altogether the idea of natural right based on the reliability of moral motivations or moral exhortation, on man's elusive natural sociability, or on the exogenous authority of God's admittedly ambiguous commands. He appealed to one natural motive—the inexorable concern each human being has for his or her own interests.[6]

There are three foundational assumptions to Hobbes's interest-based account of the social contract:

1. *Felicity*: we want to satisfy our desires and get power.
2. *Our rough equality* of physical and mental powers.
3. Our *asocial* nature.

---

5. Donald Rutherford, "In Pursuit of Happiness: Hobbes's New Science of Ethics," *Philosophical Topics* 31, nos. 1–2 (2003): 369–93, 369.

6. Gary Herbert, "Fear of Death and the Foundations of Natural Right in the Philosophy of Thomas Hobbes," *Hobbes Studies* 7, no. 1 (1994): 56–68, 56.

Referring to Aristotle's arguments as "absurd," "repugnant," and "ignorant," Hobbes instead advances a political philosophy he believed was predicated on science. His account attempts to explain behavior in the same way that science explained the movement of the planets. What drives humans to behave the way we do, contends Hobbes, is "felicity": our desire for power, to get what we need in order to achieve self-preservation. In chapter 6 of *Leviathan*, Hobbes remarks:

> *Continual Success* in obtaining those things which a man from time to time desireth, that is to say, continual prospering, is that men call FELICITY; I mean the felicity of this life. For there is no such thing as perpetual tranquility of mind while we live here; because life itself is but motion, and can never be without desire, nor without fear, no more than without sense.[7]

The key strategy for elaborating on the content of his version of the social contract is Hobbes's employment of a device other social contract theorists will also employ: imagining what life was like in "the state of nature" before human cooperation and the institutions of government existed. The state of nature, Hobbes contends, is a state of perpetual war of all against all. The most famous passage from *Leviathan* is the following, where Hobbes describes what he believed life would be like for humans without the artifice of government:

> In such condition, there is no place for Industry; because the fruit thereof is uncertain: and consequently no Culture on the Earth; no Navigation, nor use of the commodities that may be imported by the Sea; no commodious Building; no Instruments of moving, and removing such things as require much force; no Knowledge of the face of the Earth; no account of Time; no Arts; no Letters; no Society; and which is worst of all, continual fear, and danger of violent death; And the life of man, solitary, nasty, brutish and short.[8]

---

7. Thomas Hobbes, *Leviathan* [1651], in David Wootton, *Modern Political Thought: Readings from Machiavelli to Nietzsche* (Indianapolis: Hackett, 2008), 116–277, 136.

8. Hobbes, *Leviathan*, 159.

Why is life in the state of nature "nasty, brutish and short"? There are competing interpretations of Hobbes on this point. The dominant interpretation, which we will focus on, is often referred to as the "rationality account" of conflict.[9] This account maintains that there is conflict in the Hobbesian state of nature because of

1. Competition for resources
2. Diffidence
3. Glory seeking

Let us expound on each of these points briefly.

First, humans are driven by felicity, which means we seek to get the things we need to ensure our self-preservation. However, resources in the state of nature are scarce, and we have to compete for these finite resources. We are bound to run into others also searching for resources to meet their needs, and if they take resources, that means there is less for us. There is thus what is called a *zero-sum game* situation, which means the needs of some can only be met by the needs of others going unmet. This is one reason why conflict is omnipresent in the Hobbesian state of nature.

Hobbes also maintains that humans are naturally suspicious of others, an anxiety he calls "diffidence." Diffidence is the reason we lock our front doors when we go to sleep every night. We think there are some individuals who would be out to violate our life and property if given the opportunity. Hobbes states:

> And from this diffidence of one another, there is no way for any man to secure himself, so reasonable, as anticipation; that is, by force, or wiles, to master the persons of all men he can, so long, till he see no other power great enough to endanger him: And this is no more than his own conservation requireth, and is generally allowed.[10]

In the state of nature, with no government authorities to enforce the law and protect our security, we must remain constantly vigilant. This can

---

9. Hampton, *Hobbes and the Social Contract Tradition*, 58.
10. Hobbes, *Leviathan*, 158.

motivate us to engage in preemptive strikes against others (what Hobbes refers to as a "principle of anticipation"). For example, imagine you are struggling for survival in the Hobbesian state of nature. You have made a campsite with a fire to stay warm for the evening, and you have with you enough provisions for another two days. Before falling asleep you notice in the distance the flame from someone else's campsite a mile away. Diffidence will make you wonder and worry, "If they see my campsite, will they attack me once I fall asleep, and steal my provisions?" Rather than falling asleep and risking being the victim of a surprise attack in the middle of the night, the rational thing to do, from the perspective of your self-interest, is to sneak over to the other campsite and be the attacker. You should eliminate the potential enemy and take their provisions before they have the opportunity to take yours!

A final cause of conflict in the Hobbesian state of nature concerns our preoccupation with our reputation. Hobbes describes humans in the state of nature as "glory seekers": we have "a desire for prestige and a desire to acquire power over others."[11] Hobbes's emphasis on our concern for reputation is at odds with the asocial description of humans, as it seems odd that atomistic individuals in the state of nature would care so much about how they are perceived by others. But as rational individuals concerned with self-preservation, it is not unreasonable to assume that we would want to cultivate a reputation of not being someone others should try to exploit or take advantage of.

Rational individuals in the Hobbesian state of nature seek their self-preservation and are in a constant state of war because of the competition for resources, diffidence, and the desire for glory. In the state of nature Hobbes claims there is no right or wrong; we have a "right to all things," to take any actions necessary to ensure our survival. The Hobbesian state of nature is often described by contemporary authors as a "prisoner's dilemma." This game theory representation is based on the mathematician A. W. Tucker's example from the early 1950s, and the literature on the dilemma can be very technical. The original example is called the prisoner's dilemma because it concerns two suspected criminals who committed a crime and are interrogated by the police separately. They

---

11. Gabriella Slomp, *Hobbes and the Political Philosophy of Glory* (New York: St. Martin's, 2000), 33.

can receive different lengths of prison sentences for their crime depending on whether they and/or their accomplice confess to the police. To make this example easier to understand, below I apply the prisoner's dilemma to a two-person example in the Hobbesian state of nature.

The Prisoner's Dilemma

The game theory device of the prisoner's dilemma was not available for Hobbes to use to help explain why Hobbesian individuals in the state of nature would agree to leave it and create a state. But I believe he would have utilized it if it were available as it nicely captures his concerns about life in the state of nature.

Imagine two individuals living in the Hobbesian state of nature. Both are rational (i.e., seeking their own self-preservation), suspicious, and glory seekers; the environment in which they coexist is characterized by scarcity. Our two individuals, A and B, have spent the morning searching for food. Both are hungry, and they both happen to come across a valuable find at the exact same time—bilberry shrubs that have produced bilberries, ripe for the picking! Wild bilberries are nutritional, edible berries with a sweet taste. The resource of bilberries A and B have stumbled upon approximates about four generous handfuls, if care is taken to delicately pull them off the shrubs, which takes some time and effort.

A and B thus face a predicament. Both want access to the bilberries to ease their hunger pains. If they work together, investing about fifteen minutes of time cooperatively and delicately picking the berries, they could pick a total of four generous handfuls of bilberries. Splitting the yield fifty-fifty, they each would consume two handfuls of bilberries, which would sustain them for the remainder of the day. This would be the outcome of **mutual cooperation.**

However, if they both decide to defect (e.g., attack versus work together), this strategy has the outcome that both would spend the fifteen minutes in combat, while also trying to consume whatever bilberries they can eat while fending off their opponent. In this scenario they each end up consuming only one handful of berries each; the rest of the berries were stepped on and destroyed during the physical combat between them. At the end of the interaction both A and B are exhausted and injured. This would be the outcome of **mutual defection.**

The first two outcomes describe the scenarios where both A and B choose *identical* strategies—either both cooperate or both defect. But there are two further possibilities, namely, they choose opposite strategies—A might choose to cooperate while B chooses defection, and vice versa. If, for example, A decides to work cooperatively, and B is intent on defection, both A and B spend a few minutes picking the bilberries together, but then, when an opportune moment presents itself, B hits A on the head with a rock, knocking A unconscious. B then reaps all the proceeds and nets a total of three handfuls of bilberries (one handful of berries was crushed when A collapsed on them). This is the outcome of **exploitation (if you are B)/being exploited (if you are A)**.

When A and B meet in the Hobbesian state of nature, what would be the rational course of action for A and B to choose, cooperation or defection? The rational thing to want is to get the most berries you can. The worst possible outcome is to be exploited (you get none). The best possible outcome is exploiting the other person (you get three handfuls of berries). You have no way of knowing if the other person will fulfill their promise to cooperate or exploit you when the opportune moment arises. This is the predicament of a prisoner's dilemma. In such a circumstance it is rational for both parties to choose defection. This of course results in the suboptimal payoff of only one handful of berries each, along with the exertion of valuable calories in combat and the risk of serious injury.

A better solution to mutual defection and being exploited, for both A and B, is the outcome of mutual cooperation. But the problem is there is no way of ensuring the other person will comply with the agreement. What is needed is some way of *enforcing* the agreement; for Hobbes this is the state. The state can ensure both A and B work cooperatively because it will punish those who violate the contract. Given the disadvantages associated with defection when the state is there to enforce compliance, the contracting parties have a compelling reason to work cooperatively.

Escaping the Prisoner's Dilemma: The Laws of Nature

The rational individuals in a prisoner's dilemma state of nature will reason that this "nasty, brutish, and short" life is suboptimal. They would prefer to move from the strategy of mutual defection to a situation of mutual cooperation. Reason thus helps them deduce what Hobbes calls the *Laws of Nature*. We will focus only on the first three of these laws.

The first Law of Nature is that we should seek peace. We seek peace because it is best for our own self-interest to live in a peaceful (versus conflictual) state. Hobbes remarks: *"that every man, ought to endeavour peace, as far as he has hope of obtaining it; and when he cannot obtain it, that he may seek, and use, all helps, and advantages of war."*[12] It is worth noting the second part of the Law, which makes our seeking peace contingent on the compliance of others. It is not rational to put yourself in a situation where you are exploited by someone else. To seek peace without the sincere commitment of others would be irrational.

The second Law of Nature is the law that we lay down our right to all things. In the state of nature there is no morality, and thus we have a right to steal, attack, and so forth to preserve our survival. To make peace feasible, I must lay down my right to all things, but only if you do as well. Hobbes claims: *"that a man be willing, when others are so too, as far-forth, as for peace, and defence of himself he shall think it necessary, to lay down this right to all things; and be contented with so much liberty against other men, as he would allow other men against himself."*[13]

In the Hobbesian state of nature we would realize that peace and laying down a right to all things are rational and mutually advantageous. In order to make that state of affairs a reality, we must transcend the prisoner's dilemma. Hence the derivation of the third Law of Nature: **That men perform their Covenants made.** This means we should live by the social contract of the sovereign ruling, an outcome that is rational to prefer over life in the state of nature with no government.

Critical Assessment

Hobbes advanced an interest-based account of the social contract, one that defends the rule of an absolute monarchy on the basis that the creation of the state would be mutually advantageous for everyone compared to the short, nasty, and brutish life circumstances we face in the absence of

---

12. Hobbes, *Leviathan*, 160.
13. Hobbes, *Leviathan*, 160.

government. There are a number of objections critics have raised against the Hobbesian argument for the state. We shall consider some of the most central objections.

First, there is the question about whether the individuals in the Hobbesian state of nature could actually escape the state of nature in the first place. If the original situation is a prisoner's dilemma and there is no trust or compliance initially, how do we create the government that will thus enforce compliance? By characterizing life in the state of nature in such a negative way, Hobbes's argument is open to the critique that such individuals could never escape it. They need government to enforce the social contract, but in the absence of that government, they would never institute it in the first place. Furthermore, if they could cooperate to create and comply with a social contract before the creation of government, then they do not need to create government as they are able to cooperate prior to the establishment of government.

Another obvious objection would be to take issue with the specific type of government Hobbes endorses. We may agree that creating government is mutually advantageous compared to life in the state of nature. Moreover, while the absolute sovereign might achieve peace and security for all, we might expect more from our government. We might also expect some liberty, and some political equality so that our government is accountable to all. Limited, democratic government, not an absolute monarchy, might be the conclusion one reasonably reaches from an interest-based approach to the social contract. Hobbes had a limited vision of what government could and should deliver.

Hobbes's characterization of life in the state of nature has serious implications for colonialism, as Indigenous peoples could be considered as living in nonpolitical and nonsovereign circumstances. In chapter 13 Hobbes notes in particular the circumstances of Native Americans:

> It may peradventure be thought, there was never such a time, nor condition of war as this; and I believe it was never generally so, over all the world: but there are many places where they live so now. For the savage people in many places of *America*, except the government of small families, the concord whereof depends on

natural lust, have no government at all; and live at this day in that brutish manner, as I said before.[14]

Nichols argues that from 1922 to 1924, the Iroquois Confederacy—a federal union of six aboriginal nations—sought resolution of a dispute between themselves and Canada at the League of Nations. However, the Confederacy was denied the right to participate at the international level on a par with other peoples because they were not considered political and sovereign.[15] As we shall also see in chapter 5 on John Locke, the critics of the social contract highlight many deficiencies and blind spots of the theory with respect to its implications for the territorial claims of Indigenous persons, as well as the treatment of women, slavery, and racism. This is captured by the threefold criticisms of the "settler contract," the "sexual contract," and the "racial contract."[16] The critics of the social contract tradition maintain that it is a theoretical framework ill equipped for dealing with the problems of colonialism, patriarchy, and racism. Indeed, its most vocal critics maintain that the social tradition has contributed to each of these problems, providing theoretical justifications for such injustices.

A final objection to Hobbes's argument, which we shall consider in greater detail in the following section, is that Hobbes was wrong to presume the state is a solution to violence and conflict. For anarchists, for example, it is the state that enacts large-scale violence, leading to war and genocide. According to anarchists, human nature is much more prosocial and cooperative than Hobbes presumes. We shall now consider a number of arguments from historical and more contemporary anarchist philosophers.

---

14. Hobbes, *Leviathan*, 159.

15. Robert Lee Nichols, "Realizing the Social Contract: The Case of Colonialism and Indigenous Peoples," *Contemporary Political Theory* 4 (2005): 42–62.

16. Robert Nichols, "Indigeneity and the Settler Contract Today," *Philosophy and Social Criticism* 39, no. 2 (2013): 165–86; Carole Pateman, *The Sexual Contract* (Palo Alto, CA: Stanford University Press, 1998); Charles Mills, *The Racial Contract* (Ithaca, NY: Cornell University Press, 1997).

Anarchism: Kropotkin, Goldman, Taylor, and Wolff

Hobbes is a significant political philosopher for many reasons. What he effectively demonstrates is that the starting premises of one's political theory—that humans are asocial, suspicious glory seekers driven by felicity—substantively impacts what theoretical conclusions one is likely to come to regarding the limits and functions of government. In the chapters to come we shall consider other social contract theorists who begin with premises very different from Hobbes. John Locke, for example, believes that morality does apply in the original state of nature. Locke also contends that we possess the rights to "life, liberty, and property," and that the creation of government arose from our consent to leave this original, rather idyllic state of affairs, to redress some inconveniences that can arise in interpreting the law of nature without government. Rousseau's social contract contests Hobbes's starting assumptions that we are, by nature, suspicious and glory seekers. For Rousseau, these negative qualities of character are the product of civilization, and would not arise in the original state of nature. In contrast to Hobbes's conclusion that rule by an absolute sovereign is legitimate, Rousseau's social contract entails substantive commitments to democratic government.

One of the most important and interesting challenges to Hobbes's general conclusion that a state is necessary (as a solution to the conflict of life in the state of nature) comes from *anarchism*. Anarchism is a rich and varied political tradition. We shall address a few historical and more contemporary arguments, contrasting them with Hobbes.

The most obvious anarchist foil to Hobbes was the Russian nobleman turned scientist/explorer/anarchist Peter Kropotkin. Born in Moscow in 1842 to Russian aristocrats, Kropotkin, like Hobbes, was interested in the science of his day. But in the mid-eighteenth century that science had become transformed by the most important biologist to have ever lived: Charles Darwin. Darwin's book *On the Origin of Species* was published in 1859 and detailed the principle of evolution by natural selection. In this process, organisms evolve over time, and the heritable traits that prove most beneficial to survival and reproduction in a given environment become more prevalent in a species.

In *Mutual Aid* (1902), Kropotkin argues that the war and misery Hobbes describes do not arise from human nature, nor would they be persistent and widespread in the state of nature. The worst forms of conflict and war are perpetuated by the state itself. Far from being the solution to war, Kropotkin believes government is the source of the problem. Kropotkin thus has a much more optimistic view of human nature. His argument invokes insights from comparative biology: we can observe *prosocial* behavior in other species that cooperate without any government. Very few species survive and thrive in the kind of isolation Hobbes believes existed before government. There is strength in numbers, and from an evolutionary perspective it is beneficial for a species to rely on others for defense, hunting, storing food, rearing offspring, and so on. While Kropotkin does not deny that conflict arises in the animal kingdom, he believes that "peace and mutual support are the rule within the tribe or the species, and that those species which best know how to combine, and to avoid competition, have the best chances of survival and of a further progressive development."[17]

Hobbes's Reply

Hobbes and Kropotkin were not contemporaries, and thus Hobbes did not have the opportunity to respond to the challenge from anarchists like Kropotkin. Yet in chapter 17 of *Leviathan* there is an interesting discussion of "bees and ants" that seems to anticipate the kind of objection Kropotkin makes. In that chapter Hobbes considers the issue that nonhuman animals can cooperate and coexist without coercive power, so why can't the same be true for humans? Hobbes contends that there are five important differences between humans and other animals that should preclude us from jumping to conclusions about human behavior based on our observations of the cooperative behavior of other species.

First, Hobbes contends that humans, unlike other species, are in competition for honor and dignity. Other species might come into sporadic conflict over competition for food or mates, for example, but they do not go to war because they are envious of others or hate them. Hobbes believes the latter is a unique trait of human beings.

---

17. Peter Alekseevich Kropotkin, *Mutual Aid: A Factor of Evolution* (Mineola, NY: Dover, 2006), 62.

Second, for animals the "common good" is synonymous with the "private good." The thriving of the beehive is what is good for any individual bee. Hobbes's point is comedically captured in 2007's animated *Bee Movie*. The lead character in the film, a bee named Barry B. Benson (voiced by comedian/actor Jerry Seinfeld), is discontented with his fate of being a regular worker bee. Instead of following the expected nature of a honeybee, he instead ventures out of the hive looking for adventure. To the bee Barry B. Benson, his own personal good is conceptually distinct from the good of the beehive as a whole. This is because Barry thinks, acts, and talks, like a human! But real bees do not critically reflect on and question if their own individual lives would go better if they diverted from the behaviors that are best for the hive.

Third, Hobbes claims that nonhuman animals cannot reason, and thus do not perceive any fault in the administration of their business. In *Bee Movie* the reason Barry sees a problem with the existence provided by the day-to-day operations of the beehive is because he possesses the human capacity to reason. It is common for humans, like Hobbes's contemporaries who agitated to overthrow King Charles I, to think they can do a better job of running things. We strive to reform, overthrow, and innovate, and this can bring about civil war. But bees do not experience anything comparable to a civil war being instigated because of the perceived flaws of a queen bee, which is why they are highly successful as a species.

Fourth, Hobbes contends that animals do not have language, and thus cannot deceive each other, which often leads to conflict. Humans can use "the art of words," such as metaphors (e.g., "the king is a tyrant"), to convey information to others in ways that alter their perception of reality for the sake of the manipulative ends of the communicator deploying such language. Alliances can be solidified, or undermined, by the language invoked to frame and convey selected information about the current state of affairs.

Finally, Hobbes notes that agreement among creatures is natural, but for humans it is artificial. We need a common power to ensure we "perform our Covenants made." Nonhuman animals do not need this.

But this last assumption is the real crux of the disagreement between Kropotkin and Hobbes. Hobbes believes conflict and war are the default "status quo" of human existence, and the state is the solution to this conflict. But Kropotkin contends that it is the state itself that is the cause of most conflict, and that humans (like other species) do have a strong instinct to aid each other. In *Mutual Aid* Kropotkin remarks:

> The mutual-aid tendency in man has so remote an origin, and is so deeply interwoven with all the past evolution of the human race, that it has been maintained by mankind up to the present time, notwithstanding all vicissitudes of history. It was chiefly evolved during periods of peace and prosperity; but when even the greatest calamities befell men—when whole countries were laid waste by wars, and whole populations were decimated by misery, or groaned under the yoke of tyranny—the same tendency continued to live in the villages and among the poorer classes in the towns; it still kept them together, and in the long run it reacted even upon those ruling, fighting, and devastating minorities which dismissed it as sentimental nonsense. And whenever mankind had to work out a new social organization, adapted to new phases of development, its constructive genius always drew the elements and the inspiration for the new departure from that same ever-living tendency.[18]

The worst types of human conflict, such as the two world wars in the twentieth century that led to the deaths of millions of humans, were state-led conflicts. But is life actually more or less violent today than it was in earlier times, before the development of sophisticated governmental institutions to codify and enforce laws? The psychologist Steven Pinker contends in his book *The Better Angels of Our Nature: Why Violence Has Declined* that life today is much less violent for humans. Pinker documents the historical record of violence over thousands of years and argues that the rate of violent deaths per capita has declined. Some critics of Pinker have responded that a more appropriate measure is the absolute number of violent deaths (not per capita). By that measure, violence is not declining.[19] So the debate between Hobbes and Kropotkin, concerning the cause of violence and conflict, continues to this day.

---

18. Kropotkin, *Mutual Aid*, 184.

19. Robert Epstein, "Book Review: *The Better Angels of Our Nature: Why Violence Has Declined*," *Scientific American*, October 7, 2011, https://www.scientificamerican.com/article/bookreview-steven-pinker-the-better-angels-of-our-nature-why-violence-has-declined/.

Anarchism and Freedom

In contrast to Hobbes's reduction of human interests to self-preservation and peace, many anarchist philosophers champion anarchism as the only mode of social life compatible with human freedom. For example, Emma Goldman (1869–1940) was an early twentieth-century anarchist who championed free speech and women's equality, and she criticized military conscription during World War I as well as the war itself. She published an anarchist monthly magazine that permitted her to challenge the legitimacy of state actions. Goldman was born in what is now Lithuania, and her family immigrated to the United States when she was a teenager. As a result of her social and political radicalism, Goldman was eventually deported from the United States in 1919.

In *Anarchism: What It Really Stands For* (1910), Goldman describes anarchism as follows: "The philosophy of a new social order based on liberty unrestricted by man-made law; the theory that all forms of government rest on violence, and are therefore wrong and harmful, as well as unnecessary."[20] For Goldman, a Hobbesian sovereign cannot be a solution to the problem of violence, since by definition the state is a form of violence. Goldman identifies a number of features of society that threaten liberty and social equality. Religion, for example, she describes as a fetter on the human mind; it makes god everything but humans nothing. Private property is also problematic, fostering our appetite for greater wealth and leading to the enslavement and domination of others. And the state itself enslaves the human spirit, contends Goldman. The aim of government is to subordinate the individual. The government's only function is to maintain property and a monopoly over the use of force. It does not secure the natural rights to "life and liberty" that we will find in John Locke's account of life in the state of nature (for example).

In a direct response to the Hobbesian contention that the state is needed to protect us from crime, Goldman argues:

> The most absurd apology for authority and law is that they serve to diminish crime. Aside from the fact that the State is itself the

---

20. Emma Goldman, *Anarchism and Other Essays* (New York: Mother Earth, 1911), 56.

greatest criminal, breaking every written and natural law, stealing in the form of taxes, killing in the form of war and capital punishment, it has come to an absolute standstill in coping with crime. It has failed utterly to destroy or even minimize the horrible scourge of its own creation.[21]

The horrific police killing of George Floyd in the summer of 2020 renewed such concerns and criticism of the brutality of the state, though now with the added dimension of the role of institutional racism. In the Black Lives Matter (BLM) protests following Floyd's killing, there arose a number of "autonomous zones" (e.g., in Seattle) that had anarchist aspirations. Critics will of course ask, if the authority of the state is not necessary, how would anarchism achieve and sustain human cooperation? The common answer, which both Kropotkin and Goldman give, is "community." Is it possible for humans to respect each other's rights, beyond simple security of the person, without the state?

In *Community, Anarchy, and Liberty*, Michael Taylor makes the case for answering "yes" to this question by highlighting the importance and viability of community to anarchist philosophy and aspirations. According to Taylor, anarchy does not mean chaos or lack of order; it simply means a state of *statelessness*, where "the state" is understood (following Max Weber's definition of a state) as existing, at a minimum, when "there is *some* concentration of the means of using of force, or equivalently some inequality in its distribution."[22] By contrast, in a pure anarchy there is no concentration of the use of force in the hands of the few; it is perfectly dispersed.

Rather than relying on a concentration of the means of using force, which is the hallmark strategy of maintaining stability for states, Taylor argues that small-scale societies relied on *community* to survive and persist over time. He identifies three features of community. First, people must have common beliefs and values. Second, the relations between members should be direct and many-sided. Finally, reciprocity is required, so that there is sharing and mutual aid among the community members.

---

21. Goldman, *Anarchism*, 65.

22. Michael Taylor, *Community, Anarchy, and Liberty* (Cambridge: Cambridge University Press, 1982), 5.

Taylor's claim for the possibility of anarchism draws on the evidence that, for most of the time our species has existed, we survived in stateless "hunter-gatherer" societies. In these types of societies there is "only the minimum concentration of force and scarcely any political specialization at all."[23] Indigenous societies thus provide a critical body of knowledge that challenges the Hobbesian argument for the state. As noted earlier, critics charge that Hobbes's argument for statism legitimates colonialism by perpetuating a narrative that life in the state of nature is so violent and lawless that expanding colonial rule should be a welcome development for the security and stability it brings over anarchy. The Hobbesian framing strategy of characterizing life in the state of nature as "nasty, brutish, and short," critics charge, enabled the expansion of colonial rule beyond the subjugation of those already living within European nation-states. Pat Moloney remarks:

> Hobbes linked European conceptions of individual freedom with the subordination of non-European societies in the colonial systems of European states. The entrapment of savage societies in his "hypothetical" state of nature had real and far-reaching consequences. If savages were free, sovereign individuals living in the state of nature (as Hobbes described them), then they could not also be bodies of men that constituted sovereign states.[24]

We shall pursue these anticolonial criticisms of the social contract in greater detail in the following chapter on John Locke. There, we will consider the criticism that Locke's arguments concerning private property helped support England's claim to American soil with little to no regard for the territorial claims of the Indigenous populations there.

Hobbes's argument for the state disputes the viability of (at least large-scale) reciprocity arising and persisting without an effective mechanism for enforcing compliance. Hobbes contends that people are prone to free ride when it is rational to do so, and if the state of nature is a prisoner's dilemma, then exploitation and domination will be the default

---

23. Taylor, *Community, Anarchy, and Liberty*, 33.
24. Pat Moloney, "Hobbes, Savagery, and International Anarchy," *American Political Science Review* 105, no. 1 (2011): 189–204, 189–90.

motivation of individuals versus reciprocity. What the dispute between statists and anarchists reveals is that our assumptions about human nature, as well as the potential pros and cons of the state versus community/anarchism, will profoundly influence which side of the debate one is likely to end up endorsing. Such a debate cannot be resolved via the philosopher's armchair.

Insights from the biological sciences suggest that perhaps a key factor for reciprocal cooperation might be the *size* of the group. In "The Evolution of Reciprocity in Sizable Groups," Boyd and Richerson note that in food foraging groups game is shared among the group members, even among those who did not participate in killing the game.[25] Moreover, in stateless societies warriors frequently risk their own lives to protect their group. None of these behaviors seems to align with the ever-defecting egoists of the Hobbesian state of nature. However, Boyd and Richerson contend that the reciprocal cooperation of stateless communities is feasible only when such communities are quite small. Invoking the anarchical practices of small communities of course may be of limited use when seeking to establish the potential viability of anarchism as a form of political organization for today's populations of billions of people.

Attending to our possibly anarchical past can serve many important pedagogical functions. First, it ensures we take a long view of human history when conjecturing about human nature. Insights from evolutionary biology, anthropology, and history can help the political philosopher develop more sound problem-solving skills for thinking about the potential pros and cons of the state versus anarchism. Second, attending to the actual history of prestate societies can help us identify and critically challenge the colonial assumptions within the statist argument championed by Hobbes. Third, a better understanding of the more distant past (e.g., the small size of communities where reciprocal cooperation took root) can help us better assess the attractions and limits of anarchical political aspirations invoked today for the world's much larger populations.

---

25. Robert Boyd and Peter J. Richerson, "The Evolution of Reciprocity in Sizable Groups," *Journal of Theoretical Biology* 132, no. 3 (1988): 337–56.

Wolff on "Philosophical Anarchism"

The final anarchist argument we will consider in this chapter is an account that arose out of the American countercultural period of the 1960s and early 1970s. In his book *In Defense of Anarchism*, Robert Wolff claims that the "state is a group of persons who have and exercise supreme authority within a territory," and "authority" means "the right to command, and correlatively, to be obeyed."[26] Wolff argues that the authority of the state is incompatible with the autonomy of the person. To be autonomous means we are not ruled by others. We ourselves must be the authors of the laws, if they are to be morally binding on us as autonomous agents. Wolff examines three possible political arrangements: (1) unanimous direct democracy; (2) representative democracy; and (3) majoritarian democracy. He finds that all three come up short in terms of adequately reconciling the values of authority and autonomy.

In principle, a unanimous direct democracy can reconcile these two conflicting values, but it would never work in practice. A direct democracy requires that we, as individuals, directly vote on the laws and policies that govern our society. The requirement of unanimity means that only those decisions that receive 100 percent support from the voters can be enacted. In principle, if the laws of our society were policies that every single person agreed on and directly supported with their vote, then the values of autonomy and authority would be compatible. This would be the case because the laws of this society would be identical to the laws you would personally endorse and adopt. But in practice this would not be viable.

A direct democracy would mean that all persons would become fulltime politicians. We would all have to be informed about the details of all public policy decisions and have the time to vote on them. This would be enormously time-consuming, leaving little time left over for citizens to do their real jobs, raise their families, and so forth. A true direct democracy would result in very low productivity outside the area of making laws.

A *unanimous* direct democracy would also have a low probability of ever passing any law or policy. All it takes is just one person who disagrees with everyone else, and the legislation in question would be voided. It

---

26. Robert Wolff, *In Defense of Anarchism* (Berkeley: University of California Press, 1970), 3, 4.

is not possible to get 100 percent agreement on decisions that involve complex empirical assumptions and estimates, as well as moral values. In practice Wolff believes a unanimous direct democracy would not be viable, even though on paper it appears to offer a solution to the resolution of authority and autonomy.

The second possible solution Wolff considers for reconciling the conflict between authority and autonomy is a representative democracy. This resolves some of the practical barriers of a direct democracy because now only the elected representatives have the job of refining and implementing the laws and policies of our society. However, should a responsible, autonomous person agree to give up their individual decision-making to a representative? We all know that what politicians promise when running for election does not always translate into what they do if they win. Thus even if their election platform looks as if it coheres with the priorities and policies we would choose if we were the lawmakers, real democratic politics seldom works out that way. This means we are sacrificing our true autonomy. Furthermore, argues Wolff, if none of the political party platforms conform to your own priorities and values, then there is no prospect of your autonomy being realized in a representative democracy.

The third and final solution Wolff considers is majoritarianism. In a democracy, the will of the majority rules the day. Perhaps this offers a way to resolve the tension between authority and autonomy. In chapter 6 we shall see Jean-Jacques Rousseau try precisely this type of argument. But Wolff notes the standard objection raised against majoritarianism: *what about the minority?* If the majority of the people living in my society believe growing the economy is more important than mitigating the potential harms of climate change, while I believe the opposite is true, I will not feel that the rules and priorities of my society are an expression of my autonomy. Thus Wolff concludes that majoritarianism also fails to reconcile authority with autonomy.

Given that none of the three main contenders for reconciling authority with autonomy is successful in Wolff's account, what does he conclude? His conclusion is provocative: we should embrace "philosophical anarchism," a position that treats all governments as illegitimate. This does not mean that a philosophical anarchist will seek to overthrow the government or disobey the law. For Wolff it just means they accept that authority which contravenes autonomy has no moral legitimacy. Nevertheless, there are other reasons for following the law (e.g., to avoid going to prison, etc.). Richard Dagger explains the difference in attitude between the philosophical anarchist and the average citizen this way:

> The philosophical anarchist, according to Wolff's account, is far different from the bomb-throwing anarchists of lore and the window-smashing, anti–World Trade Organization anarchists of recent days. Except, perhaps, for the "Question Authority" bumper stickers on their cars, there is nothing in the philosophical anarchists' appearance or actions to distinguish them from conventional, law-abiding citizens. The difference lies in their respective attitudes to authority and law. The philosophical anarchist and the conventional citizen both will obey the law in most circumstances, but they will obey it for different reasons. Conventional citizens believe that they have a moral duty or obligation to obey, but the philosophical anarchist rejects this belief and obeys simply because it is usually prudent or convenient.[27]

Thomas Hobbes's *Leviathan* remains a classic work in political philosophy, a book that is certainly worthy of critical engagement. Hobbes aspired to create a science of humanity and politics, though as we have highlighted throughout this chapter, one could contest a number of foundational premises in his argument for the state. From Hobbes's assumptions about what motivates humans to the colonial framing of "life in the state of nature" and the goods and opportunities we expect a (just) state to deliver, *Leviathan* continues to inspire discussion more than 350 years after its publication.

---

27. Richard Dagger, "Philosophical Anarchism and Its Fallacies: A Review Essay," *Law and Philosophy* 19, no. 3 (2000): 391–406, 391–92.

CHAPTER 5

Locke, Limited Government, and Toleration

In the last chapter we examined the interest-based social contract theory of Thomas Hobbes. It is now natural to address the next major social contract theorist, John Locke, who was born in 1632, just forty-four years after Hobbes was born. Locke is a central proponent of a right-based contract theory and a defender of limited government, and there are thus important contrasts between Hobbes and Locke, in terms of the practical concerns motivating their political theories, the starting assumptions of their accounts of human nature and the social contract, and the substantive conclusions they draw with respect to the purpose and function of government.

Locke is often characterized as the founder of modern liberal theory. Joshua Cohen succinctly summarizes the appeal and significance of Locke as a political thinker: "Locke held that human beings are by nature rational and equally free. On the basis of that rationality and equal freedom he argued against political absolutism and in defense of a constitutional state."[1] Liberalism is associated with the ideals of limited government, individual rights, and toleration, all of which we find addressed in the writings of John Locke in the seventeenth century. In this respect, Locke's writings are those of a progressive, even radical and revolutionary, political thinker.

"Liberalism emerged in opposition to slavery and absolutism."[2] Locke can be considered an innovative political thinker because he rejected the legitimacy of absolutism and its appeal to the divine right of kings, ideas

---

1. Joshua Cohen, "Structure, Choice, and Legitimacy: Locke's Theory of the State," *Philosophy & Public Affairs* 15, no. 4 (1986): 301–24, 301.

2. Holly Brewer, "Slavery, Sovereignty, and 'Inheritable Blood': Reconsidering John Locke and the Origins of American Slavery," *American Historical Review* 122, no. 4 (October 2017): 1038–78, 1043.

that cohered with the historical ideals of many of his contemporaries. Yet, as critics are quick to point out, liberalism and Locke in particular also have regressive and exclusive elements, often providing rationales that reinforced and justified colonialism. Colonialism "is typically understood as a practice that involves both the subjugation of one people to another and the political and economic control of a dependent territory (or parts of it)."[3]

In the following passage Bhikhu Parekh captures the tensions within liberalism when he remarks:

> Liberalism is full of strange paradoxes and reveals different faces depending on one's angle of vision. It offers one of the most inspiring statements of human equality, yet some of the greatest liberal philosophers justified colonialism with a clear conscience. Liberals condemned racist prejudices and misuse of political power in the colonies, but endorsed both the economic exploitation of the colonies and arrogant assertions of cultural superiority. They insisted on protection of the material interests of the colonial subjects, but thought little of destroying their ways of life.[4]

In this chapter we address Locke's arguments, explore some of the tensions that arise within his writings, and consider the ways some scholars have attempted to resolve these tensions.

The Historical Context of Locke

Recall from the previous chapter that a right-based contract theory, unlike an interest-based version, is predicated on moral premises. In contrast to Hobbes's contention that in the state of nature there is no right or wrong (and that we have a "right to all things"), John Locke's theory of government starts from a commitment to explicit moral and theological

---

3. Lea Ypi, "What's Wrong with Colonialism," *Philosophy & Public Affairs* 41, no. 2 (2013): 158–91, 162.

4. Bhikhu Parekh, "Liberalism and Colonialism: A Critique of Locke and Mill," in *The Decolonization of Imagination: Culture, Knowledge, and Power* (London: Zed, 1995), 81.

premises. Humans have a natural right to "self-ownership": rights to life, liberty, and property. In the initial state of nature, the world's resources are owned equally, argues Locke, for "God . . . hath given to men the world in common."[5]

After the turbulent period that culminated in the execution of Charles I, Oliver Cromwell, who led parliamentary forces in the English Civil War, eventually served a number of years as lord protector (head of state) until his death in 1658. The monarchy came back to prominence after Cromwell's death, with Charles II (son of Charles I) returning to the throne until his death in 1685. His brother, the Catholic James II, took over the throne but eventually fled to France during the "Glorious Revolution" of 1688, which replaced James II with his Protestant daughter Mary and her Dutch husband, William of Orange. In 1689, William III and Mary II signed into law the English Bill of Rights, which reaffirmed limited government. The Bill of Rights barred Roman Catholics from the throne, prohibited the arbitrary suspension of Parliament, established that the consent of Parliament was needed to raise taxes, protected freedom of speech for members of Parliament within parliamentary debates and proceedings, and made it illegal for the sovereign to keep military forces within the kingdom in times of peace without the consent of Parliament.

In this turbulent political environment, John Locke published the *Two Treatises of Government* in 1689. In contrast to Hobbes's argument for political absolutism, John Locke's political theory is considered foundational to modern liberalism, with its emphasis on the importance of natural rights, limited government, a right of rebellion, and defense of private property. The last point in particular is a source of criticism for Locke's detractors and critics.

Locke's *First Treatise of Government* takes critical aim at Robert Filmer's defense of the divine right of kings in *Natural Power of Kings* (*Patriarcha*) of 1680. Filmer argued that Adam and his heirs were the God-given rulers of the world. Locke refutes this, contending that no human has natural authority over the rest of humanity. Filmer assumed

---

5. John Locke, *Second Treatise of Government* [1689], in David Wootton, *Modern Political Thought: Readings from Machiavelli to Nietzsche* (Indianapolis: Hackett, 2008), 285–353, 293.

people were unequal, whereas Locke advances a political theory that takes seriously the contention that we are equals, and that the political obligation to obey government comes from consent.

Locke's *Second Treatise of Government*, in particular his account of life in the state of nature, consent, and private property, will be our focus in this chapter. Locke offers an account of life in the state of nature that is very different from that of Hobbes, and Locke also believes (contrary to anarchism) that a legitimate state can exist, one that is consistent with our natural rights. One of the distinctive contributions Locke makes to political philosophy is the notion of government by consent, predicated on the idea that all should be treated as political equals versus some people ruling over others in accordance with some divine proclamation. Finally, Locke defends the right to private property, an issue that remains an important source of political disagreement in the world today.

The Lockean State of Nature

Unlike the Hobbesian state of nature, where individuals have a "right to all things" and there is no right or wrong, the right-based social contract theory advanced by John Locke begins from the moral premise that "every man has a property in his own person: this no body has any right to but himself."[6] We can call this foundational moral right of Locke's liberalism the *right to self-ownership*. In the Lockean state of nature, persons have the right to life, liberty, and property. Persons also have the "executive power" of the law of nature, which means they can judge for themselves if the law of nature has been violated, prevent (by force if necessary) violations of the law of nature, and impose appropriate punishment when violations occur.

The right to self-ownership has strong intuitive appeal. A government should not enslave its people, tell us what to think or say, or stipulate which religion (if any) we must espouse. To do any of those things would constitute a violation of self-ownership. A society that takes the right of self-ownership seriously believes in the importance of individualism, that

---

6. Locke, *Second Treatise of Government*, 293.

each person should determine for themselves the kind of life they wish to lead.

If persons in the Lockean state of nature are at least minimally moral—meaning they respect the right to self-ownership of others—then why is government needed in the first place? There are different ways to interpret Locke on this point. One common interpretation is to claim that Locke believed that even among persons inclined to respect the right to self-ownership of others, disputes about interpreting the scope, limits, and application of this right are bound to occur. We tend to be biased toward our own interpretation of events, which can lead to conflict. For example, if I am driving my car in a parking lot and you pull out of your parking spot and we collide, we might both be biased as to who was responsible for the collision. I might claim that you didn't look behind you before backing up, for if you did, you would have waited until I drove past you before reversing. You retort that you did look behind and it was clear, but because I was speeding in the parking lot I appeared out of nowhere at the last second and a collision couldn't have been avoided by that stage. I demand compensation from you for the damage to my car, and you demand compensation from me for the damage to yours. We are at an impasse. If this impasse cannot be resolved, our disagreement is likely to escalate into a conflict much larger than the original fender bender.

Because of the ambiguities in applying the law of nature in specific cases, and our biased interpretation of the law, we must have a common, known interpretation of the law of nature. For Locke, this is what the function of political power is. In the *Second Treatise* he remarks:

> *Political power*, then, I take to be a *right* of making laws with penalties of death, and consequently all less penalties, for the regulating and preserving of property, and of employing the force of the community in the execution of such laws, and in the defence of the commonwealth from foreign injury, and all this only for the public good.[7]

Another way to interpret Locke's argument about why humans need to create political power in the state of nature where people mostly respect

---

7. Locke, *Second Treatise of Government*, 287.

the rights to life, liberty, and property is that his political theory is predicated on colonial premises about the primacy of Western ideas of political authority and civilization. Parekh claims that Locke's view of the Indigenous persons of North America (the so-called New World) as "savage" and "wild" were predicated on ideas of "English guardianship"[8] versus a plausible universal account of human nature and the possible ways in which to structure human civilizations. Parekh notes that Locke distinguished between two modes of colonization: "conquest by sword" (which Locke took to be represented by the Spanish) and "commerce" (represented by the English). Locke rejected the former, which would violate the natural rights of Indigenous persons. But improving the material prospects of all (colonialists and Indigenous alike) by expanding commerce (even without the communal consent of Indigenous communities) into the colonies was, for Locke, a justified mode of colonization. Thus Parekh contends that while Locke's liberalism could extend equal concern to Indigenous persons as individuals (thus entitled to individual rights), it could not extend such concern to them as collective actors deserving of political protection to govern themselves.

> Locke's principle of equality accepted them and other "savage" people as equal *objects* of concern, but not as self defining *subjects* entitled to full and equal self-determination. The manner in which Locke defined and defended equality thus had both egalitarian and inegalitarian implications, and *both* justified colonialism and regulated its excesses. It had an egalitarian form but its inegalitarian assumptions gave it an inegalitarian content, and it legitimized violence against the poor at home and the "savages" abroad provided, of course, that that violence did not exceed certain limits and served their long-term interests as defined by their masters.[9]

Like the challenge to Hobbes's argument that humans require a state/government to peacefully coexist, the anarchist will challenge the Lockean assumption that the state is necessary, let alone compatible with

---

8. Parekh, "Liberalism and Colonialism," 87.

9. Parekh, "Liberalism and Colonialism," 92.

the thesis of self-ownership. The core of Locke's social contract theory is his account of consent, and we shall now turn our attention to the role consent plays in his theory.

Consent

In the Lockean state of nature the "executive power" of the law of nature is in every person's hands. Due to the problems of making biased judgments, when interpreting the law of nature, an agreement was made to create government. To reach the conclusion that the existence of (limited) government is both justified and necessary, Locke invokes the idea of consent at two stages. First, there is the consent given to move from the state of nature to what Locke calls "the community." Second, consent is again given moving from "the community" to government.

In the first stage of the creation of the community, people in the state of nature agree (i.e., give their individual consent) to give up their right to exercise the executive power of nature for an equal share of political power. But the community is only halfway to a functional form of government. To fully achieve the latter Locke believes the community must choose a form of constitution via a majority decision. Locke remarks:

> Whosoever therefore out of a state of nature unite into a community, must be understood to give up all the power, necessary to the ends for which they unite into society, to the majority of the community, unless they expressly agreed in any number greater than the majority. And this is done by barely agreeing to *unite into one political society*, which is *all the compact* that is, or needs be, between the individuals, that enter into, or make up a commonwealth. And thus that, which begins and actually constitutes any political society, is nothing but the consent of any number of freemen capable of a majority to unite and incorporate into such a society. And this is that, and that only,

which did, or could give beginning to any lawful government in the world.[10]

D. A. Lloyd Thomas argues that it is best to understand Locke as invoking two different types of consent—*express* and *tacit* consent—both of which can be exercised as either *individual* or *collective* consent.[11] Express consent is the consent we provide when we agree verbally, in writing, or through some gesture (e.g., nodding our head "yes") to an agreement or promise. When the bride and groom both declare "I do" during the marriage ceremony, they are giving their individual express consent. When a bidder raises their hand in an auction, they give their individual express consent to pay the price the auctioneer has announced if their bid wins.

Express consent can also be exercised collectively by a group. For example, suppose I am a member of an organization—the local wine-tasting community—and each month this community votes on a particular type of wine that will be featured in the monthly wine-tasting social event. A "majority wins" decision-making procedure determines "the will of the wine group." For the upcoming September meeting I voted for merlot, one of my favorite wines, but the majority of the group voted for pinot grigio. While I might complain that this decision is not compatible with my individual consent, it was an expression of the collective express consent of the group. As a member of that community, rather than the dictator of my own wine-tasting group, I should be inclined to accept that majoritarian decision as legitimate because it was the expression of the express consent of the majority.

In contrast to express consent, Locke also invokes the notion of *tacit* consent. Tacit consent is a silent form of consent in which one accepts an agreement without actually having said "Yes, I agree to this!" Locke remarks: "The difficulty is, what ought to be looked upon as a *tacit consent*, and how far it binds, i.e., any one shall be looked on to have consented, and thereby submitted to any government, where he has made no expressions of it at all."[12]

---

10. Locke, *Second Treatise of Government*, 313.
11. D. A. Lloyd Thomas, *Locke on Government* (London: Routledge, 1997).
12. Locke, *Second Treatise of Government*, 318.

The idea of tacit consent is more problematic for Locke than express consent. In principle, if Locke's envisioned community was actually created via individuals giving their express consent to leave the state of nature (something Locke seems to believe was the case), and thus his account of legitimate (limited) government was actually something the majority of persons in the community chose, then his account might provide a compelling case for political obligation for those persons who were alive to make those choices. However, there is no basis for believing any persons actually did give their consent to leave the state of nature or to choose any particular form of government. Even if they did, a question remains: how does this bind future generations (such as those of us living now) to the social contract?

Locke's invocation of tacit consent is an attempt to bind those living today to the historical contract. To make the idea of tacit consent concrete, consider the example of a game of soccer (also known as football to most people in the world). Suppose I play left defense on my soccer team. The opposing team is approaching my team's goal, and their top striker kicks the ball high into the air toward the top of my team's goal. My goaltender is caught off guard and unable to stop the ball in time. However, I am near the net, and if I reach with my hands, I can deflect the ball over the net to prevent the opposing team from scoring. I use my hands to prevent the goal, and the referee immediately blows the whistle, awarding the other team a penalty shot and giving me a red card. I protest, claiming that I never gave my express consent to the rule that "only the goalie can use their hands to stop shots on the goal." The referee is unimpressed by my appeal, remarking, "This is soccer, and you tacitly agreed to the rules when you signed up to play in our soccer league. If you wanted to use your hands you should have joined the beach volleyball league instead." This is the idea behind Locke's appeal to tacit consent: we tacitly agree to the "rules of government" when we decide to live and participate in the society in which we live, just as I tacitly agree to the rules of soccer when I play soccer.

By invoking the idea of tacit consent, Locke's social contract faces a number of problems. What makes express consent appealing—that it is given both intentionally and voluntarily—does not necessarily apply with tacit consent. In my example of soccer these two conditions do hold; if I join a soccer league it is because I intend to play soccer (versus volleyball) and I voluntarily do so (I had other options, and did not have to choose soccer). But when it comes to living in a political society, these conditions often do not hold. I was born in Canada, but I had no control or intention over where I was born. I was simply born into the country my parents were living in when they had me. Simply being born into Canadian society doesn't seem like compelling grounds for claiming I have a political obligation to obey the laws of the country. Sometimes the critics of those who engage in civil disobedience (that is, peacefully breaking a law one believes is unjust) say, "If you don't like our laws, just leave!" But exiting a political community might not be a viable option for many people. Perhaps the laws of my political community are morally indefensible and problematic, but the laws in neighboring countries are even more unjust. Or perhaps there is no possibility of my entering another country, because I fail to meet the criteria they have imposed on people migrating there. In such a case I may choose to remain in the country where I was born, but it is not really a free and voluntary decision, just a prudent decision given the circumstances. Claiming that I have given my tacit consent by remaining, and that I am therefore politically obligated by the laws of the land, sounds unpersuasive to many. It certainly does not have the persuasion that cases involving express consent possess.

Carole Pateman has developed a feminist critique of the consent-based theory of Locke and social contract theory more generally. Pateman argues that when Locke and other liberals invoke the idea of consent and the social contract, they do so only within the context of theorizing about political obligation (e.g., whether the government's authority is justified). Yet this kind of liberalism ignores a very important power relationship in all societies that must also be theorized and addressed. That is power within the traditional family, the domination of husband over wife, and of men over women more generally.

The Lockean story of free and voluntary agents consenting to be governed overlooks the historical reality that women were not considered equal to men, and thus the family is an institution where immense power could be (and has been) exercised (by men over women) but in which genuine consent was not required or even on the radar of the social contract theorists. Pateman remarks:

> Consent as ideology cannot be distinguished from habitual acquiescence, assent, silent dissent, submission, or even enforced submission.

Unless refusal of consent or withdrawal of consent are real possibilities, we can no longer speak of "consent" in any genuine sense.[13]

Historically women were not even considered capable of consent. Women did not receive the right to vote at the same time that men did. Women were also excluded from education and work, leaving few options for them outside of marriage and motherhood, or prostitution. Thus, for Pateman, the idea of the social contract has actually helped facilitate the hierarchy of inequality between men and women, rather than being a tool to realize the political equality of all. She refers to this as the *sexual contract*.

Lockean liberalism focuses on the social ills of an absolute monarchy, making the case for limited government. But in doing so, the argument employed completely ignores the reality of the unequal power that exists within the family, between the husband and wife, and of the father over his children. This power is also extensive and unjustified, and yet Lockean liberalism does not consider what the demands of equality entail for addressing gender equality. These are themes we shall consider in greater detail in chapter 8 on feminist political thought.

Private Property

One of Locke's most influential impacts on contemporary political philosophy concerns his defense of a right to private property. As will become evident throughout this book, the right to private property is among the most contested issues in the history of political philosophy. Many thinkers, like Rousseau and Marx, condemn the right to private property, characterizing it as the catalyst of inequality and conflict (for Rousseau) and as a form of *ideology* and vehicle of exploitation and class conflict (for Marx). I will briefly canvass Locke's defense of the right to private property before considering some of the common critiques raised against it.

Unlike his defense of limited government, the argument for a right to private property is not predicated on consent. This would make the

---

13. Carole Pateman, *The Sexual Contract* (Palo Alto, CA: Stanford University Press, 1998), 150.

appropriation of external objects in the world simply unviable. If I had to get the consent of everyone before laying claim to an apple I picked from a tree, I would die from exhaustion traveling to get everyone's consent before enjoying any nutrients from the apple!

Locke's argument begins from a theological and moral premise: "God... has given the earth to the children of men, given it to mankind in common." The challenge Locke then sets for himself is to show "how men might come to have a *property* in several parts of that which God gave to mankind in common, and that without any express compact of all the commoners."[14]

The premise of equal ownership over the world's natural resources is combined with the thesis of self-ownership, which maintains that you own your body and the fruits of your own labor. If we own the world's resources in common, plus our individual labor, then the mixing of our own labor with that which is commonly owned can yield private property claims when certain conditions are met. The Lockean argument for private property is as follows:

> If you **mix your labour** with something in nature AND **leave enough and as good** for others AND **do not exceed as much as you could make use of** (before it spoils) THEN... you can claim it as your property.[15]

Each of the three underlined conditions must be elaborated in detail. The first is the idea that your claim to ownership of parts of the external world comes from mixing your labor with them. I have a potentially legitimate claim to the apple I picked from high above on an apple tree. I climbed the tree to pluck the apple from its high perch. I mixed my labor (admittedly it was not labor intensive, but still it took some effort and work) to appropriate the apple. If you walk by while I am climbing down the tree with the apple and object, "Hey, I want that apple!" I can say that I have a stronger claim to it because it was I who exerted the effort to pick the apple. My claim is stronger than yours.

---

14. Locke, *Second Treatise of Government*, 293.

15. John Christman, "Can Ownership Be Justified by Natural Rights?," *Philosophy and Public Affairs* 15, no. 2 (1986): 156–77, 160.

But for Locke, "mixing my labor" is only a necessary, but not sufficient, condition for my appropriating the apple. In addition to mixing my labor, I must also leave "enough and as good." If the apple I picked from the tree was the last apple and the only food supply for miles, then the person who contests my taking the apple would have a legitimate complaint against my claim. But if there are other comparable apples on that same tree or other trees nearby, then I passed the second test for legitimate ownership since my apple appropriation "leaves enough and as good for others."

Even if I have mixed my labor, and left enough and as good for others, there is one more requirement for Locke's account of private property: I must not exceed more than I could make use of. One apple easily satisfies this condition, but if I had spent the afternoon hoarding five large bags full of apples, even if there were more apples left for others, I would be violating Locke's third requirement. Hoarding of natural resources is not permitted. I should only take what I can use.

The argument presented thus far concerns the justified limitations on individual appropriation. However, the introduction of money alters these limitations. Once money is created, the limitation imposed by the spoilage proviso becomes moot as money does not perish. So my picking more apples than I can consume is permitted when I trade those apples to others who will consume them in exchange for money. In such a situation my appropriation of the apples does not lead to them being spoiled. But why would money be created? Many commentators, like C. B. MacPherson (1951), take Locke's argument concerning private property to be a justification for the unrestricted accumulation of capital. MacPherson claims:

> Locke saw money not merely as a medium of exchange but also as capital. Indeed, money's function as a medium of exchange was seen as subordinate to its function as capital, because the purpose of agriculture, industry, and commerce was in his view the accumulation of capital; and the purpose of capital was not to provide a consumable income for its owners, but to beget further capital by profitable investment. Mercantilist that he was, when Locke discussed the purpose of economic activity it was generally from

the point of view of the nation's rather than of the individual's wealth.[16]

Locke's defense of a natural right to private property has both its defenders and its critics. One influential defense of Locke's argumentced in 1974 by the libertarian philosopher Robert Nozick. In *Anarchy, State, and Utopia* Nozick defends a neo-Lockean account of free-market capitalism. But Nozick makes a number of modifications to Locke's argument to remedy what he considers its deficiencies.

First, Nozick points out that the labor mixing component of Locke's argument is inherently problematic and should be rejected. How can it be the case that something we own (our labor) can be mixed with something we do not own (objects in the external world) and then somehow the latter becomes part of the former? Nozick claims this is a metaphysical puzzle, and it is easy to conceive of cases where this is plausible, but equally so cases where it's not. For example, suppose that in the Lockean state of nature, I labor on the soil to produce some vegetables to sustain me. I clear the ground, plant some seeds, ensure they receive regular water, and protect them from weed growth. In this kind of scenario it might appear plausible to say I should have ownership over the land because the resulting value (the harvest from the vegetable garden) was created from my labor.

But Nozick points out there are cases where the opposite can appear intuitive. Suppose I create a bowl of vegetable soup from the harvest of my labor, then pour this soup into the Pacific Ocean. Does this mixing of something I own made from my labor (my bowl of soup) with something unowned (the Pacific Ocean) generate a moral entitlement to ownership of the Pacific Ocean? In other words, did I just make a much larger soup than a bowl of soup (a soup the size of the Pacific Ocean) by pouring the vegetables my labor has produced into that body of water, or have I simply lost my soup? Nozick contends it is the latter.

In addition to rejecting Locke's "labor mixing" requirement, Nozick also rejects, or rather modifies, Locke's "leaving enough and as good" proviso. This proviso is problematic, contends Nozick, because land is a finite resource and thus its acquisition is susceptible to what Nozick calls the

---

16. C. B. Macpherson, "Locke on Capitalist Appropriation," *Western Political Quarterly* 4, no. 1 (1951): 550–66, 558.

"regress argument." For example, in the twenty-first century there no longer exists any unowned land that one can appropriate in the country in which I live (Canada). This means that whoever appropriated the last bit of unowned land violated Locke's requirement that they leave "enough and as good" for others. In addition, the person who appropriated the second-to-last bit of unowned land also violated this proviso, because *they* did not leave "enough and as good" for the last person (because the last person cannot appropriate land without violating the proviso). This argument can be continuously applied going all the way back to the first person who appropriated land. The conclusion of the regress objection is that no land can be justifiably appropriated, given that land is a finite resource. This was something Locke did not seriously consider, as he believed (in the seventeenth century) one could simply extend such claims into the voluminous territory available in North America. But there no longer exists any unowned land in North America. If a theory is meant to justify a natural right to private property, this outcome is a problem.

What Nozick proposes to do instead, having dropped both the "labor mixing" requirement and the "enough and as good" proviso, is to advance a modified "enough and as good" proviso that encapsulates what he believes is the intuitive force of the original proviso. Rather than literally leaving "enough and as good" of external resources, Nozick's proviso requires that appropriation "not worsen (materially) the situation of others." When there is no unappropriated land left for me to claim, the question I need to ask is "Am I materially worse off compared to the situation when no one owned any of the land?" Nozick believes the answer will be no. In fact, we are likely to be better off because property rights increase the wealth and opportunities for everyone (albeit not equally). He remarks:

> Is the situation of persons who are unable to appropriate (there being no more accessible and useful unowned objects) worsened by a system allowing appropriation and permanent property? Here enter the various familiar social considerations favoring private property: it increases the social product by putting means of production in the hands of those who can use them most efficiently (profitably); experimentation is encouraged, because with separate persons controlling resources, there is no one person or small group whom someone with a new idea must convince to try

it out; private property enables people to decide on the pattern and types of risks they wish to bear, leading to specialized types of risk bearing; private property protects future persons by leading some of them to hold back resources from current consumption for future markets; it provides alternate sources of employment for unpopular persons who don't have to convince any one person or small group to hire them, and so on.[17]

Nozick's modified Lockean proviso of "not worsening the situation of others" presumes that the only morally relevant metric of well-being is economical, and that the only morally relevant baseline of comparison is a situation where there is no ownership of property at all. Critics reject both of these assumptions. Even if it is true that I can now be employed by the factory that owns a large area of land and paid a living wage for my labor, I might be worse off in other respects. For example, I might actually hate the job I do. As we will see in the chapter on Marx, for a lot of workers in modern capitalist societies the work is alienating, leaving workers feeling disconnected from what they produce and from their nature as human beings capable of creative, productive work.

Furthermore, rather than only comparing the situation of no ownership of land with how I fare when there is market capitalism, why not compare today with a situation of communal ownership?[18] Communal ownership might be more productive than a situation of private appropriation, and/or it might be more optimal for other aspects of human well-being.

Indigenous Rights

One aspect of Locke's work that has received significant attention in recent years concerns the colonial implications of his account of private property. Locke's *Second Treatise of Government* was published in 1690, and colonies in America had already been undertaken a century earlier. In the 1580s there were unsuccessful attempts to establish colonies in North Carolina, and in

---

17. Robert Nozick, *Anarchy, State, and Utopia* (New York: Basic Books, 1974), 177.

18. John Exdell, "Distributive Justice: Nozick on Property Rights," *Ethics* 87, no. 2 (1977): 142–49.

1606 King James I created the Virginia Company of London to establish colonies in America. Some commentators argue that Locke's philosophical defense of a natural right to private property helped advance a defense of England's right to American soil, despite the fact that Indigenous populations already inhabited those lands. Barbara Arneil, for example, argues:

> Locke's theory of property is consistent with two different but linked sets of arguments defending English colonialism. The first are those made by 17th century writers ... who defended the economic benefits of colonization by providing a clear blueprint of the successful plantation. ... The second set of arguments incorporated into Locke's theory of property are the ethical justifications of colonialists ... to appropriate aboriginal land.[19]

Like Arneil, James Tully contends that Locke's account of the initial acquisition of property in the state of nature was complicit with European imperialism and the dispossession of land previously used by Indigenous groups because they were considered savages or they used land wastefully and inefficiently. Tully claims:

> Locke's account covers over the real history of the interaction of European imperialism and Aboriginal resistance. The invasion of America, usurpation of Aboriginal nations, theft of the continent, imposition of European economic and political systems, and the steadfast resistance of the Aboriginal peoples are replaced with the captivating picture of the inevitable and benign progress of modern constitutionalism.[20]

In contrast to the colonial reading of Locke's political philosophy advanced by both Arneil and Tully, other scholars have argued that the connection between Locke's ideas and the dispossession of Indigenous persons is not so straightforward. Paul Corcoran (2018), for example, argues that interpretations of Locke that equate his account of the origins

---

19. Barbara Arneil, "The Wild Indian's Venison: Locke's Theory of Property and English Colonialism in America," *Political Studies* 44, no. 1 (1966): 60–74, 61.

20. James Tully, *Strange Multiplicity: Constitutionalism in an Age of Diversity* (Cambridge: Cambridge University Press, 1995), 78.

of private property with colonialism conflate the right to property with a theory of political sovereignty.[21] Such interpretations focus on the concept of *vacuum domicilium*, the idea that Native lands are uninhabited because they lack fixed inhabitants and fenced fields. Thus, according to this critique of Locke's account of property rights, Native Americans have no claim to the land they utilized in North America, nor any legitimate grievance to the English colonizing such land.

But such an interpretation, argues Corcoran, overlooks Locke's defense of the native right to property and possession. Corcoran claims that later chapters of Locke's *Second Treatise*—on conquest, usurpation, and tyranny—provide ample evidence that Locke does not advocate for a "might is simply right" position. Locke appears to explicitly reject the suggestion that imperial conquest of foreign lands is a legitimate way to appropriate property, which Corcoran claims is the basis for interpreting Locke as a defender of native rights to lands and possessions:

> The inhabitants of any country, who are descended, and derive a title to their estates from those who are subdued, and had a government forced upon them against their free consents, *retain a right to the possession of their ancestors* . . . for, the first conqueror *never having had a title to the land* of that country, the people who are the descendants of, or claim under those who were forced to submit to the yoke of a government by constraint, have always a right to shake it off, and free themselves from the usurpation or tyranny which the sword has brought in upon them. . . . Their persons *are free* by a native right, and their properties, be they more or less, *are their own, and at their own dispose*, and not at his or else it is no property.[22]

Did Locke have the Indigenous populations of North America in mind when writing this passage, or other European countries? This is a point of contention among Locke scholars.

---

21. Paul Corcoran, "John Locke on Native Right, Colonial Possession, and the Concept of *Vacuum domicilium*," *European Legacy* 23, no. 3 (2008): 225–50.
22. Locke, *Second Treatise of Government*, 338–39, 353.

Brian Smith contends that there is no convincing textual evidence for the claim that Locke advocated for the dispossession of the land of Indigenous peoples; he calls this *the punishment thesis*. First, Locke does not explicitly state that Native Americans violated the natural law or argue that they should be punished for violating the natural law. Without noting such violations there would be no principled Lockean grounds for the dispossession of the land of Indigenous peoples. Furthermore, when one considers Locke's involvement in the Carolina colony, Smith contends that "Locke appears to direct the brunt of his moral argument against European settlers, not the Native peoples."[23] Smith elaborates:

> Locke's work on toleration and his devotional writing suggest that, under the auspices of toleration and given the proper economic and social conditions, Native peoples might be convinced of the reasonableness of Christianity; their "paganism" should be tolerated, not punished. In some ideal sense, Locke believed that effective social and economic conditions could be fostered in the kind of political society which bore some, if only faint, resemblance to the Carolina colony described in the *Fundamental Constitutions*. . . . Part of these aspirations, I contend, were to model the kind of society that could empirically demonstrate the reasonableness of the natural law in such a way that even the Indigenous neighbors would ultimately be convinced of its truth. They might then become acquainted with the author of the natural law, and, in turn, come to hold some minimum set of Protestant dogmas. The agrarian form of the society was not merely a commitment to agricultural production; it also prefigured a set of political and spiritual relationships.

Given the conflicting threads of Locke's writings that have been utilized to both criticize and defend against the colonial reading of Locke, what are we to make of it all? Like all the thinkers we cover in the canon, it is a complicated and still unresolved issue. The historian

---

23. Brian Smith, "One Body of People: Locke on Punishment, Native Land Rights, and the Protestant Evangelism of North America," *Locke Studies* 18, no. 1 (2018): 1–40, 2.

David Armitage tries to resolve these tensions by claiming that Locke was certainly a "colonial thinker" *if* by that term we simply mean someone who devoted much thought and attention to the settlement and governance of colonies. But Armitage contends that Locke was not an "imperial" thinker. Imperial thinkers take the view that all non-European cultures are inferior, and thus can justifiably be subjugated to imperial rule. Armitage maintains that the label "imperial" cannot be applied to Locke because Locke "did not espouse or elaborate a hierarchical ordering of populations, least of all one that places Europeans above or even apart from other groups, because he saw rationality itself as evenly distributed among human populations."[24]

More tensions and debates arise when interpreting Locke's stance on slavery and racism. We now turn to these topics.

Slavery

Locke is considered to be the founder of modern liberal political theory. His defenses of limited government, political equality, and tolerance were radical positions to take in seventeenth-century England, when society was highly hierarchical, ruled by a monarchy its proponents believed was justified by the divine right of kings. To the defenders of liberalism, the ideas Locke espoused helped transform Western civilizations from their unequal, undemocratic traditions to political communities that take seriously the aspirations of limited government, political equality, and democracy. Yet to the critics of liberal political theory, liberalism is criticized as a racist, sexist, and colonial public ethic. Far from promoting equality and inclusion, its critics characterize liberalism as a political ideology that helps mask the true oppression that liberalism created and still helps perpetuate in the contemporary world.

In "Decolonizing Western Political Philosophy" Charles Mills argues that political philosophy must reject the abstract mode of reasoning employed by social contract theorists (both historical and contemporary)

---

24. David Armitage, "John Locke: Theorist of Empire?," in *Empire and Modern Political Thought*, ed. Sankar Muthu (Cambridge: Cambridge University Press, 2012), 84–111, 86.

and instead take seriously the empirical realities of history and the world today.

> The abstraction from the empirical which is its defining feature is generally taken to justify the ignoring of such real-world "deviations," because the important thing is the concepts employed. The aspiration to the timeless and universal then rationalizes an idealized form of abstraction which, through its obfuscation of the distinctive political experience of people of color in modernity, makes the representative political individual European. Whiteness as racelessness becomes abstractness becomes philosophical representativeness.[25]

For Mills, the roots of liberalism are racist. The ideology of individualism, equality, and consent are a *racialized* ideology, meaning they applied only to whites. Rather than condemning slavery and colonialism, Mills contends that liberalism has been complicit with them. With Locke's political philosophy, for example, does the thesis of self-ownership—that we own ourselves, our labor, and the fruits of our labor—apply to all human beings, or only to white people? Perhaps the obvious place to begin is with Locke's own words. In Locke's *First Treatise of Government* (SS 1) he claims that "slavery is so vile and miserable an Estate of Man, and so directly opposite to the generous Temper and Courage of our Nation; that 'tis hardly to be conceived, that an Englishman, much less a Gentleman, should plead for 't."[26] This statement clearly establishes Locke's opposition to slavery, which is a hierarchical relationship that violates consent and the natural rights to life, liberty, and property.

However, two decades before publishing these words condemning slavery, Locke drafted *The Fundamental Constitutions of Carolina* (1669), which explicitly supported heredity, nobility, and slavery. Furthermore, Locke owned stock in the Royal African Company, which ran the African slave trade in England. So how do we square these two different

---

25. Charles W. Mills, "Decolonizing Western Political Philosophy," *New Political Science* 37, no. 1 (2005): 1–24, 12.

26. John Locke, *Two Treatises of Government*, Peter Laslett, ed. (Cambridge: Cambridge University Press 1988), 141.

aspects of Locke's track record on slavery? If he was opposed to slavery, why would he author a constitution that supported the institution? Like many things in life and in history, it is a complicated story. Thinkers who published vast treatises and writings (not surprisingly) do not always maintain the same position on societal issues over their whole life, and historical context is important in understanding the predicaments of past times, as well as the way those predicaments were understood (or misunderstood) at the time.

When considering the existence of slavery in the seventeenth century, the historian Holly Brewer explains the tension we find in Locke's stance on slavery by pointing out that slavery predates Locke, and arose from the feudal principles of Locke's time (principles that he criticized). She argues:

> Slavery did not emerge within a liberal paradox. English kings of the Stuart dynasty—James I and his son Charles I and grandsons Charles II and James II and great-granddaughter Anne—justified their divine and hereditary status with the same principles they used to justify slavery. For the Stuarts, race was subsumed within a larger rationale celebrating hereditary status. One was born a slave, just as one was born a prince. Legally and ideologically, slavery was anchored in hierarchical and feudal principles that connected property in land to property in people, principles that were bent to new forms in England and its empire by Stuart kings.[27]

If hierarchical practices and feudal principles were the basis of colonial slavery, then Locke's ideas of individual rights, property, and political equality stand in opposition to slavery rather than being complicit with it. Mills could respond that even if the history of slavery predates Locke, Locke (and liberalism) were complicit with slavery because of its invocation of abstract theory,[28] such as the Lockean hypothetical state of nature where natural rights are respected versus the actual history of war, conflict,

---

27. Brewer, "Slavery, Sovereignty, and 'Inheritable Blood,'" 1043.
28. Charles W. Mills, "White Time: The Chronic Injustice of Ideal Theory," *Du Bois Review* 11, no. 1 (2014): 27–42.

and slavery. The marginalization of the empirical realities of the past and present impede the realization of racial equality. Such realities ought to be at the foreground of normative political theory today rather than ignored or marginalized. For example, rather than invoking the Lockean state of nature where all enjoy the rights of self-ownership and can acquire property rights by "mixing their labor" and "leaving enough and as good" for others, Locke should have focused on the actual violations of those rights (i.e., colonialism and slavery). But Locke did not, the critic will contend, because liberalism is a racial theory that only extended moral concern to the individual rights of whites.

Some commentators have tried to reconcile Locke's liberalism with the injustices of slavery and racial discrimination. The Black political philosopher Bernard Boxill, for example, argues that Locke's liberalism provides a defense for Black reparations for slavery in America. Boxill contends that "John Locke, if he were alive today, would support a case for reparation for African Americans based on the enslavement of their slave ancestors. At least he would do so if he reasoned consistently from his principles."[29]

Boxill's Lockean argument for Black reparations develops in two stages, integrating what he calls the "inheritance argument" and the "counterfactual argument." The inheritance argument utilizes Locke's comments on reparations in the *Second Treatise of Government*, where Locke claims that reparations are owed to the injured party when violations of natural rights have occurred. Locke argues:

> Besides the crime which consists in violating the law, and varying from the right rule of reason, ... there is commonly injury done to some Person or other, and some other Man receives damage by his transgression, in which case he who hath received any damage, has besides the right of punishment common to him with other men, a particular right to seek reparation from him that has done it.[30]

---

29. Bernard R. Boxill, "A Lockean Argument for Black Reparations," *Journal of Ethics* 7, no. 1 (2003): 63–91, 63.

30. Locke, *Second Treatise of Government*, 288.

It is clear that enslavers, by violating the liberty of enslaved persons, harmed them. Thus the enslaved were entitled to reparation for some portion of the property and wealth the enslavers acquired through forced labor. Furthermore, those who aided and abetted these harmful transgressions, such as the US government, also owe reparations for being complicit in slavery. Moreover, the living descendants of slavery are still harmed from slavery, even though it was formally abolished a long time ago. The legacy of racism, especially institutional racism, has disadvantaged Black Americans in many domains of life, from segregation in education to unequal treatment in housing, employment, health care, and the criminal justice system (e.g., higher rates of incarceration and police brutality, etc.).

Boxill concludes that the harm caused by slavery, and the subsequent failure to make reparations from the time of slavery to the present, justify Lockean moral demands for reparations. Slavery in the United States was abolished more than a century and a half ago, which means that both the transgressors (i.e., enslavers) and those who were transgressed (i.e., enslaved persons) are no longer living. Does this mean that the reparation claims are nullified? Boxill argues no. The descendants of the enslaved ought to inherit those reparations. Such a payment was never made, and that is why compensation is now owed to the descendants of enslaved persons.

How much compensation ought to be paid? This is a very complex question and is difficult to answer with much specificity. To make some headway on answering that question, Boxill invokes the "counterfactual argument." The standard counterfactual test for reparations is to claim that the appropriate compensation owed is to return the harmed person's or group's level of well-being to what it would have been had the injustice never occurred in the first place. For example, suppose you burglarize my house when I am not home, breaking my back window and stealing my new television. Had you not transgressed my rights to private property, I would still own a new television and my back window would not be broken. The counterfactual test stipulates that the appropriate reparations in such a case are the value of a new television and a repaired window. That would restore me to the level of well-being I had before your unjust actions.

However, this type of counterfactual test, when applied to rectification in the case of the historical injustices of slavery in America, often runs into a problem philosophers call the "nonidentity" problem. If we ask how well off existing descendants of American slaves would be had slavery never been permitted in the first place, then we must acknowledge that they would not have existed. They exist because their ancestors were brought (as slaves) to the United States and then propagated and gave birth to the specific line of descendants who now exist. However, if their ancestors had never been enslaved, they would have had a different line of descendants (coupling with potentially different partners, or at least at different times with different sperm and eggs than those for the currently existing people). An implication of this "nonidentity problem" is that the only potential world in which the current descendants could have lived is the actual world, with its history of slavery.

To avoid this counterintuitive conclusion of the counterfactual test, Boxill's counterfactual argument is integrated with the inheritance argument. The inheritance argument does not invoke the causal chain connection of the counterfactual test (e.g., how would the descendants of slaves have fared if the circumstances that led to their being born had never happened?). Instead, the inheritance argument maintains that the current generation has a claim to collect the compensation that was owed to their ancestors but was never paid. Boxill maintains that this inheritance argument is "a more elegant and streamlined argument" for reparations.[31]

The call for reparations for the injustices of slavery is not just an academic debate among scholars interested in, or critical of, John Locke's arguments about liberalism. Real proposals have been invoked in recent years to address the legacy of slavery, segregation, and institutional racism in the United States. For example, in 2021 the city council of Evanston, Illinois, a suburb of Chicago, voted to utilize funds from a new tax on legalized marijuana to compensate Black Americans currently living in the area for discrimination in housing in the city between 1919 and 1969. The funds would be given to be put toward down payments on property or home repairs. Furthermore, in 2020 the state of California enacted bill AB 3121, which established a task force to study and develop reparation proposals for African Americans. The bill states:

---

31. Boxill, "A Lockean Argument for Black Reparations," 69.

The institution of slavery is inextricably woven into the establishment, history, and prosperity of the United States. Constitutionally and statutorily sanctioned from 1619 to 1865, slavery deprived more than four million Africans and their descendants of life, liberty, citizenship, cultural heritage, and economic opportunity. Following the abolition of slavery, government entities at the federal, state, and local levels continued to perpetuate, condone, and often profit from practices that brutalized African Americans and excluded them from meaningful participation in society. This legacy of slavery and racial discrimination has resulted in debilitating economic, educational, and health hardships that are uniquely experienced by African Americans.[32]

Returning to Locke himself, should we view Locke as a defender of liberty and individual rights, or was his liberalism complicit with colonialism and slavery? There is textual evidence and support for both readings of Locke, depending on which parts of his political writings and professional life one wishes to emphasize as encapsulating Locke's "political philosophy."

Brewer argues that the way to understand Locke's position on slavery is to see him as a thinker whose views changed over time. Yes, earlier in his career Locke was involved in the Stuart slave program, a program that arose from laws and court decisions predicated on the principles of the divine right of kings. Yet it was through acquiring a working knowledge of the abuses of the royal state that Locke eventually became, argues Brewer, the critic of inherited status (the root of slavery).

The debates surrounding Locke's legacy in political philosophy reflect both the significance and the difficulty of understanding historical thinkers in their complex historical circumstances, as well as the legacy of their ideas and ideals. Regardless of the stance one takes on Locke and his legacy, all would agree that he has had an important impact (either positive or negative) on the history of Western political philosophy and civilization, and as such is a thinker worth seriously engaging with today. Engaging with Locke exposes us to not only the

---

32. Bill AB 3121: "Task Force to Study and Develop Reparation Proposals for African Americans," State of California, Department of Justice, Office of the Attorney General, November 19, 2022, https://oag.ca.gov/ab3121.

ideas that helped limit absolute monarchial rule but also the themes of patriarchy, colonialism, and racism.

Religious Toleration

In contrast to the interpretation of liberalism developed by critical race theorists such as Charles Mills, who argues that liberalism ignores the nonideal realities of human history and society, Locke's liberalism is predicated on some of the nonideal empirical observations of his day, in particular that religious sectarian warfare is the fundamental problem of politics and can be controlled by either absolutism or toleration.[33] I will conclude this chapter on Locke by considering some of the ideas developed in his 1689 essay "A Letter Concerning Toleration." One of the defining features of a liberal society is that it is pluralistic or tolerant. What does toleration mean, and why is it a political virtue?

In the everyday use of the word "tolerant" we often mean a person or society that is accepting of others. But in philosophical discussions of the concept, the definition is more specific. Toleration is distinct from "respecting" the viewpoints of others. In fact, the real test of toleration concerns the beliefs, customs, and traditions you find objectionable but still would not suppress.

The "core of the concept of toleration is the refusal, where one has the power to do so, to prohibit or seriously interfere with conduct one finds objectionable."[34] There are thus three important elements of the tolerant mindset:

1. The judgment that some belief or practice is objectionable (e.g., wrong)
2. The capacity to suppress the objectionable belief or practice
3. The decision not to suppress the belief or practice in question, despite its being objectionable

---

33. Robert P. Kraynak, "John Locke: From Absolutism to Toleration," *American Political Science Review* 74, no. 1 (1980): 53–69, 53.

34. John Horton, "Toleration as a Virtue," in *Toleration: An Elusive Virtue*, ed. David Heyd (Princeton, NJ: Princeton University Press, 1996), 28–43, 28.

The tension between (1) and (3) reveals what is often called the "paradox of toleration." It is paradoxical that you object to a belief or practice, yet at the same time, you would not seek to suppress the thing that you object to. Why tolerate something you object to?

During the seventeenth century the intolerance of religious persecution had taken a heavy toll on European life, with persistent conflict, the burning of heretics, and so on. Locke's essay on toleration is an attempt to dissuade authority from engaging in religious intolerance. In "Locke, Sincerity, and the Rationality of Persecution" Paul Bou-Habib distinguishes between two distinct lines of argumentation against religious persecution that Locke advances, which Bou-Habib calls the "belief-based argument" and the "sincerity argument."[35] Let us consider and assess both lines of argumentation.

The belief-based argument is an instrumental argument that religious intolerance is an ineffective governmental aspiration to pursue. While governments can use coercion to enforce compliance with performing certain actions (e.g., paying taxes, respecting the property rights of others, serving in the military, etc.), it cannot effectively control the beliefs of a person. A person's cognition cannot be controlled by a third party, at least not to the same extent that the latter can control a person's actions. We might draw an analogy with a so-called helicopter parent who wishes to micromanage the preferences and aspirations of their child. Such a parent might be able to control their teen's actions, for example, by threatening to ground them or by taking away their phone if the teen skips school or stays out late at a party. But the parent cannot actually control the beliefs of their children. They cannot use threats to alter their teen's belief that "spending time with my friends is more important than doing well in school or pleasing my parents."

"Belief is not subject to the will, and, since coercion influences only the will, people cannot accept one belief over another as a result of having their will subjected to coercion."[36] The premise of this Lockean argument for toleration is that belief is not voluntary, and thus you cannot genuinely

---

35. Paul Bou-Habib, "Locke, Sincerity, and the Rationality of Persecution," *Political Studies* 51, no. 4 (2003): 611–26.

36. Bou-Habib, "Locke," 615.

hand over control of your cognition to another person and say "Tell me what I should believe."

This account of Lockean toleration has been criticized by Jeremy Waldron, who argues that religious authorities could still influence the population's beliefs by banning certain texts they consider heretical so that people are not exposed to ideas that challenge the religious orthodoxy.[37] Since the seventeenth century, governments around the world have introduced mandatory public schooling. The twentieth century witnessed the propaganda campaigns of the Nazi regime, which demonstrated that governments can wield significant influence over people's beliefs. Additionally, new technologies like social media create new opportunities to permit governments to manipulate and control the information a population is exposed to. So rather than being an argument against religious intolerance, the belief-based argument is only compelling against direct, coercive attempts to persecute those whose beliefs contravene the religious orthodoxy. But governments can utilize indirect tools, from education to censorship, which may prove a more effective way of cultivating the religious identity of a population.

Locke's "sincerity argument" is expressed in the following passage:

> How great, soever, in fine, may be the pretence of good-will and charity, and concern for the salvation of men's souls, men cannot be forced to be saved whether they will or no; and therefore, when all is done, they must be left to their own consciences.[38]

The thrust of the sincerity argument for religious toleration is that people would not rationally consent to a government that aims to coerce them into its favored religion because salvation depends on sincere religion.

This argument is predicated on a contentious theological premise. If one denies the existence of god, as an atheist would, this argument would not have any plausibility (though atheists could have other reasons for opposing religious coercion). Within Locke's historical context, the idea

---

37. Jeremy Waldron, "Locke: Toleration and the Rationality of Persecution," in *John Locke: A Letter Concerning Toleration in Focus*, ed. John Horton and Susan Mendus (London: Routledge, 1991), 98–124, 116.

38. John Locke, *Letter Concerning Toleration* (1689), in *Political Writings of John Locke*, ed. David Wootton (London: Penguin, 1993), 390–436, 410.

of extending universal toleration to include atheists that do not believe in god was too radical even for a revolutionary thinker like Locke. Locke took belief in Christianity, god, and an afterlife as a critical link between the individual and society. Locke did not even advocate tolerating Catholics, who, because they were seen as loyal only to the pope, were considered outside the natural moral community.[39]

Contemporary liberal arguments for toleration typically invoke the values of autonomy and pluralism[40] rather than the theistic premises of Locke's arguments for toleration. The defense of civil and political liberties—like freedom of religion, freedom of political association, and freedom of expression—is now made by claiming that political equality requires that we respect the autonomy of others to decide for themselves what to believe, and accept that there will be disagreement around some issues (e.g., "What is the good life?"). Some contemporary liberals espouse the idea of "state neutrality,"[41] the principle that the government should not justify the coercive use of power by reference to a particular conception of the good life, like a specific religion. For example, the government cannot restrict people from practicing a particular religious faith on the grounds that the religion is heresy. But contemporary debates about state neutrality and toleration extend into more contentious policies, such as the regulation of pornography and hate speech. We shall consider these issues in greater detail in chapter 10 when we examine John Stuart Mill's arguments for free speech.

---

39. Richard Ashcraft, "Religion and Lockean Natural Rights," in *Religious Diversity and Human Rights*, ed. I. Bloom, J. P. Martin, and W. L. Proudfoot (New York: Columbia University Press, 1996), 195–212; Richard Ashcraft, *Revolutionary Politics and Locke's Two Treatises on Government* (Princeton, NJ: Princeton University Press, 1986).

40. Joseph Raz, *The Morality of Freedom* (Oxford: Clarendon, 1986); John Rawls, *A Theory of Justice* (Cambridge, MA: Belknap Press of Harvard University Press, 1971).

41. Peter de Marneffe, "Liberalism, Liberty, and Neutrality," *Philosophy & Public Affairs* 19, no. 3 (1990): 253–74.

CHAPTER 6

Rousseau, Inequality, and the General Will

The third and final historical social contract theorist we examine in this book is the Swiss philosopher Jean-Jacques Rousseau. Like Locke, Rousseau can be considered a proponent of right-based contractualism as his theory is predicated on moral premises about the equality of persons. While Hobbes's interest-based social contract theory yielded an argument for an absolute monarchy, and Locke's right-based social contract an argument for limited government and the rights of self-ownership, within Rousseau's writings we find the first spirited defense of *democratic governance*.

Rousseau (1712–78) was born in Geneva, which at that time was an independent city-state (and now is part of Switzerland). Rousseau's mother died a few days after he was born, an event that biographers of Rousseau believe had a deep and lasting impact on his political philosophy, which emphasized the importance of direct and immediate human relationships. Raised by his father, an educated watchmaker, as a teenager Rousseau was training to become an apprentice engraver. But at age sixteen Rousseau returned from a trip outside Geneva and found the gates to the city locked at nightfall. Instead of waiting for the gates to re-open the next day, and face a certain beating from his master, Rousseau decided to leave. He ventured off into the outside world and worked as a servant, gave music lessons, and ended up living in Paris as an adult.

In addition to his contributions to political philosophy, Rousseau also contributed to the philosophy of education with *Emile*, a treatise about the education of a young boy who is removed from the negative societal influences that accentuate the desires which would have brought him into conflict with others (e.g., relations of domination and suppression). Devoid of a preoccupation with fear and what others think, Emile is able to develop autonomously and live a content and happy life "in the present."

Rousseau was also an active composer and music theorist. In 1752 he composed *The Village Soothsayer*, which was performed for the French royalty. The king is reported to have enjoyed the opera and summoned for Rousseau, which meant Rousseau would probably have received a pension. However, Rousseau feigned an illness and did not respond to the summons because accepting such a pension from the king would have meant accepting obligations that violated the integrity of his independence.[1] Rousseau was also the principal contributor of the articles on music published in the first volume of *Encyclopédie*, edited by the philosopher Denis Diderot.

Rousseau's two most important political writings are *The Discourse on the Origins of Inequality* (1755) and *The Social Contract* (1762), both of which we shall examine in detail. After Rousseau's death, his writings had a significant influence on the French Revolution, the slogan of which was "Liberty, Equality, and Fraternity." We will also explore these three values in the ideas of Rousseau. The chapter concludes by addressing contemporary ideas within democratic theory, such as deliberative democracy and voting.

Why Is There Inequality?

Two central themes are at the foreground of Rousseau's political philosophy:

1. Man is by nature good, but he is corrupted and depraved by society.
2. The authority of the state is compatible with the freedom of the individual.

The first of these two themes is addressed in the *Discourse on the Origins of Inequality*. Like a medical examiner, Rousseau diagnoses what he sees as the social pathology of his time. He distinguishes between different types of inequality. There is *natural* inequality, which is the inequality that arises

---

1. Maurice Cranston, *Jean-Jacques: The Early Life and Work of Jean-Jacques Rousseau 1712–1754* (Chicago: University of Chicago Press, 1982), 266.

from the differences in strength and cognitive capacities among human beings. These types of inequalities are not what concern Rousseau. His concern is with the type of insidious inequality that erodes the health of a political community: *political* inequality. This is the idea that some people are suited to rule over others. Rousseau does not believe political inequality is part of humanity's natural condition, and thus it must be explained before we can hope to derive a feasible antidote to the ills of inequality.

Living during an era of stark inequality in eighteenth-century France, the contrast between the opulent life prospects of the French aristocracy and the destitution of the average peasant deeply troubled Rousseau. Like Hobbes and Locke, Rousseau invokes an account of life in the state of nature, canvassing a philosophical history of humanity. He paints a portrait of humanity in broad strokes, highlighting what he sees as the catalysts that created the inequality of his day. By doing so Rousseau believes we can gain clarity on what our political aspirations ought to be with respect to a better possible political future, a future governed by the *general will*.

Rousseau posits two contrasting motivations that can dominate human psychology: *amour de soi* (helpful, natural self-love, such as self-preservation or self-esteem) and *amour propre* (harmful, artificial self-love, such as vanity or pride). Rousseau describes these motivations as follows:

> Love of oneself is a natural sentiment which moves every animal to be vigilant in its own preservation and which, directed in man by reason and modified by pity, produces humanity and virtue. Egocentrism [*amour propre*] is merely a sentiment that is relative, artificial and born in society, which moves each individual to value himself more than anyone else, which inspires in men all the evils they cause one another, and which is the true source of honor.[2]

---

2. Jean-Jacques Rousseau, *Discourse on the Origins of Inequality* [1755], in David Wootton, *Modern Political Thought: Readings from Machiavelli to Nietzsche* (Indianapolis: Hackett, 2008), 371–426, 424.

For Rousseau, *amour de soi* is a morally laudable motivation and is what drives human behavior in the state of nature, before any socialization has taken place. Rousseau's state of nature is not the Hobbesian state of "war against all." Driven by *amour de soi* we simply seek to have our basic needs met for self-preservation. However, there are difficulties in the state of nature, and to overcome these adversities we are compelled to seek out cooperation with other humans. For example, tall trees create the problem of picking fruit from them. Other animals compete with us for food and pose a threat to our own survival. To survive in the state of nature we must remain physically fit, and we use our intelligence to design weapons for hunting as we realize we are superior to other animals. We can fish and catch animals in traps we make. We realize that cooperation with others can be beneficial, for example, hunting in groups. However, we are still driven by our own self-preservation at this early stage of socialization. To illustrate this point, Rousseau provides the example of a stag hunt, which resembles the coordination problem we already encountered with the prisoner's dilemma in chapter 4:

> Were it a matter of catching a deer, everyone was quite aware that he must faithfully keep his post in order to achieve this purpose; but if a hare happened to pass within reach of one of them, no doubt he would have pursued it without giving it a second thought, and that, having obtained his prey, he cared very little about causing his companions to miss theirs.[3]

A number of developments begin to shape humans into social beings, gradually replacing the motivation of *amour de soi* with *amour propre*. For example, we enter into family relationships, our cognitive abilities develop further, we create new commodities, we have more leisure time, and so on. We also develop language, which is a significant part of human development in Rousseau's account of the transition from life in the state of nature to civil society. Despite their advantages, these types of developments give rise to vanity, pride, and war. Rousseau contends that the arts and sciences arise, not to achieve moral aims (e.g., to cultivate epistemic

---

3. Rousseau, *Discourse on the Origins of Inequality*, 396.

and moral virtue), but rather to pursue materialistic goals and quell our idle curiosity. Rousseau remarks:

> As long as they applied themselves exclusively to tasks that a single individual could do and to arts that did not require the collaboration of several hands, they lived as free, healthy, good and happy men so far as they could be according to their nature, . . . but as soon as one man needed the help of another, as soon as one man realized that it was useful for a single individual to have provisions enough for two, equality disappeared, property came into existence, labor became necessary. Vast forests were transformed into smiling fields which had to be watered with men's sweat, and in which slavery and misery were soon seen to germinate and grow with the crops.[4]

The creation of private property corrupts our noble motivation in the state of nature. Humans are only moved to claim "This is mine!" when they see themselves in competition with others, and the inevitable outcome of this social convention is conflict. Rousseau claims:

> The first person who, having enclosed a piece of land, took it into his head to say *this is mine* and found people simple enough to believe him, was the true founder of civil society. What crimes, wars, murders; what miseries and horrors would the human race have been spared, had someone pulled up the stakes or filled in the ditch and cried out to his fellow men: "Do not listen to this impostor. You are lost if you forget that the fruits of the earth belong to all and that the earth itself belongs to no one!"[5]

In contrast to Hobbes, Rousseau does not believe humans are innately motivated by greed or predisposed toward conflict. We are by nature good. But it is our eventual socialization—through the creation of the family, the acquisition of language, the rise of the arts and sciences, and the introduction of private property—that facilitated the shift in our motivations,

---

4. Rousseau, *Discourse on the Origins of Inequality*, 399.
5. Rousseau, *Discourse on the Origins of Inequality*, 395.

so that eventually *amour de soi* gave way to *amour propre*. *Amour propre* is the constant comparison with others, the obsession that drives humans to acquire more and engage in conflict with others.

From his observations of the nineteenth-century France he experienced, Rousseau believed his contemporaries were motivated by vanity and pride. Rousseau's account of human psychology may still have plausibility today, with the prevalence of social media and the desire to get likes, and followers, and to establish social capital within the viral social universe. Given that humans have become social animals driven by *amour propre*, what does Rousseau propose as a solution to this predicament? After providing a diagnosis of the creation and persistence of inequality, Rousseau turns to the project of offering some prescriptions to remedy this predicament in *The Social Contract*. We cannot be "unsocialized" or return to the state of nature and *amour de soi*. Instead, hope involves shifting toward democratic governance.

The Social Contract

In *The Social Contract* Rousseau famously declares, "Man is born free, and everywhere he is in chains." The key to casting away the chains of living under the tyranny of nineteenth-century monarchy and *amour propre* is the "general will." The sovereign of a political community expresses its will in laws and proclamations (e.g., "thou shall not steal"). When the sovereign is a monarch, the sovereign's will is expressed through royal edicts. The only way the authority of the state can be compatible with the freedom of the individual, argues Rousseau, is when the sovereign's will is equated with the general will. The latter must both (1) *come from all* and (2) *apply to all*. The second of these conditions is the easier to unpack first.

To claim that the law must apply to all means that no one is above the law. The general will must apply to everyone. By itself, this requirement is compatible with rule by monarchy. As king, I could simply declare, "Everyone shall pay the king a tax of five dollars per week." This law could apply to myself, in that I am required to pay myself five dollars a week, which will be easy to do if all the subjects must also pay me every week. So condition (2) by itself is only a necessary, but not sufficient, condition of the general will.

The first requirement of the general will contains the most radical democratic expression of Rousseau's political aspirations: the law must *come* from all. The proclamations from royal edicts fail this requirement. The laws I decree as king only come from me (and my advisors); they do not come from all. Rousseau's general will expresses the ideal that everyone is the author of the law, and this is what makes political authority compatible with individual autonomy.

In *The Social Contract* Rousseau makes the statement, which is often seized upon by his critics to claim that Rousseau actually championed totalitarianism rather than democracy, that being compelled to obey the general will is only "forcing someone to be free."[6] In his 1943 essay "Rousseau and Totalitarianism," for example, Robert Nisbet portrays Rousseau as an intellectual forerunner of the twentieth-century totalitarian state. Nisbet describes totalitarianism as follows:

> The totalitarian order is unique in modern history in that it first blurs, then obliterates the distinction between society and state; it is the state of the undifferentiated mass; undifferentiated, that is, in any except the political sense. Social differentia whether vertical or horizontal have been abolished, and the whole of human population is contained in an organization that begins and ends with the state.[7]

Rousseau's claim that obeying the general will is only forcing someone to be free is construed as totalitarian by Nisbet, because he believes it entails that "the individual lives a free life only within his complete surrender to the omnipotent state."[8] But Rousseau can be defended against such an extreme reading by noting that we commonly distinguish between two selves: our rational versus impulsive self. Let us consider the example of setting the alarm in the morning to illustrate this distinction.

---

6. Jean-Jacques Rousseau, *The Social Contract* [1762], in Wootton, *Modern Political Thought*, 427–87, 434.

7. Robert A. Nisbet, "Rousseau and Totalitarianism," *Journal of Politics* 5, no. 2 (1943): 93–114, 96–97. Also see J. L. Talmon, *The Origins of Totalitarian Democracy* (London: Secker & Warburg, 1952), 96–97.

8. Nisbet, "Rousseau and Totalitarianism," 101.

Suppose I want to wake up early tomorrow morning to start reading some political philosophy to make headway on an upcoming assignment. I set the alarm on my phone for 6:00 a.m. The next morning at 6:00 a.m., my phone begins ringing loudly and I, still in a sleep-deprived state, pick up the phone and throw it into the hallway. While still sleepy I might construe the alarm as an unwelcome and intrusive invader that has disturbed my precious sleep. But *I* was the person who set the alarm. On the previous evening I *precommitted* myself to waking up early to get some work done.

The alarm sounding is really my "rational self" telling my "sleepy self": "You really want to wake up and get some work done!" When sleepy, I am not the best version of myself. The rational me set the alarm, knowing that sleepy me might struggle to wake up. So it is the rational me that is forcing myself to wake up. And that is similar to the idea Rousseau is expressing when he says the general will forces us to be free. It represents what we really want when in the proper frame of mind (i.e., not simply thinking short-term or just about our narrow self-interest).

One way of trying to pin down what Rousseau means by the general will is to contrast it with what he calls "the will of all," expressed in the following passage:

> There is often a great deal of difference between the will of all and the general will; the latter considers only the general interest, whereas the former considers private interest and is merely the sum of private wills. But remove from these same wills the pluses and minuses that cancel each other out, and what remains as the sum of the differences is the general.[9]

To make this example more concrete, let us consider it in relation to an issue of environmental policy. Suppose a political community faces an ecological risk (e.g., pollution or climate change) that can only be abated if everyone adopts some stringent changes, such as recycling and reducing carbon emissions. If we consider this predicament from only the perspective of a person's particular will, that is, their own self-interest, they would claim that what they want is for other people to take on more burdensome

---

9. Rousseau, *The Social Contract*, 437.

obligations so that the environmental risks could be mitigated, but without any obligation falling on them personally (it is rational to want to free ride off the sacrifices of others). The problem is if each person reasons this way, we end up with the "sum of particular wills" which prescribes, in our example, that "everyone else should make some sacrifices for the benefit of the environment." But then nothing would be achieved. However, if we take away the pluses and minuses of the sum of particular wills, we find what remains is a common ground no one could reasonably reject: that everyone should take on some degree of responsibility so that the collective goal of mitigating the environmental risks can be achieved. The particular will is the expression of our own self-interest. The general will is the expression of our commitment to the common good. Rousseau believes it is this communal motivation that should be expressed in the sovereign's will.

What does the general will require? At the most basic level, it is democratic governance. This is what makes Rousseau such an important thinker in the Western canon. We have to recall that in the eighteenth century there were no established democracies; the idea of democratic government was simply an aspiration that Rousseau was theorizing about (the glory days of the Athenian experimentation with democracy had been extinguished more than two thousand years earlier). Therefore, the ideas about democracy he develops will differ from the actual democratic institutions and practices that end up emerging in Western democracies a century after Rousseau.

The type of democracy that Rousseau envisions is not a representative democracy, which is the type of democracy that Western democracies ended up adopting. Representative democracy is a political system dominated by political parties, where citizens elect representatives who are then charged with the duty of crafting the laws and public policies that govern a country. Rather than laws being made in a legislative body by elected representatives, Rousseau believes that (only male) citizens should themselves make the decision about which legislation should be enacted in popular assemblies. Thus Rousseau is envisioning democracy on a small scale, with a few thousand people versus tens or hundreds of millions.[10]

---

10. Some commentators have argued that other parts of Rousseau's writings suggest his views on representation and democratic principles are not as straightforward as

Furthermore, while Rousseau believes it is desirable that all (men) take part in creating legislation, he is not in favor of all executing such legislation. This would risk corruption. Instead, the most experienced and competent citizens will be elected to apply the law in specific cases, governing for the interests of all. Thus some scholars suggest the best way to characterize Rousseau's position is that he endorses a democratic form of *sovereignty* but not a democratic form of *government*.[11] The sovereign is the supreme authority, composed of all.

To ensure people are deliberating and voting in accordance with the general will (rather than just their own particular will), Rousseau makes a number of proposals that seek to bring out the best in humans, while minimizing the risks of the worst in our nature. Like Plato, Rousseau believes that education is important. It can help solidify the social bonds that are necessary to ensure the general will is expressed by democratic decision-making. In *Emile*, for example, Rousseau elaborates on his vision of the ideal education of a young boy from infancy to adulthood. Civil religion is another formative influence that inculcates civic virtue in people, as it reinforces belief in a benevolent deity, the idea that the just will be rewarded and the unjust punished, and the sanctity of the social contract itself.

Rousseau also defends state censorship, an issue that raises concerns of authoritarianism. In Book 4, chapter 7, of *The Social Contract* Rousseau clarifies what role he believes state censorship should play (i.e., upholding public morality rather than dictating it):

> Just as the declaration of the general will takes place through the law, the declaration of the public judgement takes place through the censorship. Public opinion is the sort of law whose censor is the minister, and which he only applies to particular cases, after the example of the prince.

---

some parts of *The Social Contract* imply. See Richard Fralin, *Rousseau and Representation* (New York: Columbia University Press, 1978).

11. See Christopher Bertram, *Routledge Philosophy Guide Book to Rousseau and "The Social Contract"* (New York: Routledge, 2003).

Thus the censorial tribunal, far from being the arbiter of the people's opinion, is merely its spokesman, and as soon as it deviates from this opinion, its decisions are vain and futile.[12]

The criticism that Rousseau's envisioned state is invoking the type of censorship typical of a totalitarian regime, or at least authoritarian government, is (at least partly) deflated when attention is given to the actual example Rousseau provides. Rousseau is not proposing that the state censor all dissenting opinions, ensuring the authority of the state can go unchallenged. Instead, Rousseau provides an example of the king of France upholding the popular opinion that the practice of using "seconds" in duels was cowardly. At the time in France it was common to engage in duels when two parties were in conflict with each other, when at least one party felt the other had insulted them. But rather than actually fighting their own battle with a sword, many affluent Frenchmen would use "seconds," the practice of retaining others to fight their duels for them. It is of course easier to challenge many people to a duel when you yourself will not be putting your life on the line. So this practice of using seconds meant that many young men died a premature death for trivial reasons. When a royal edict declared that the using of seconds was cowardly, Rousseau claims that this simply reinforced the public morality of the majority of people. However, when earlier royal edicts were made claiming that all dueling was itself cowardly, this was not shared by the general public and thus was not taken notice of. The censor tribunal Rousseau has in mind is therefore given the responsibility of upholding the public morality rather than acting paternalistically by proclaiming what is moral and imposing that on the general population.

This response is unlikely to ease those concerned with this aspect of Rousseau's argument. Fear of the tyranny of the majority is a standard reason why liberals want to ensure there are constraints, in the form of constitutional protections, placed on majority rules. Just because the majority of people consider certain beliefs, expressions, or actions to be a threat to common morality does not legitimate a censorial tribunal to enforce this morality on others. Many exclusionary practices stemming from religious

---

12. Rousseau, *The Social Contract*, 481.

intolerance, racism, and sexism have been supported by majorities. The prospect of censorship tribunals to enforce the public morality runs the risk that there could be significant harms imposed on minorities who disagree with or challenge what the majority considers the conventional morality of the collective to be.

Economic Inequality

In addition to democratic governance, and ensuring people identify with the collective as a whole through education, the civil religion, and censorship, Rousseau also proposes limiting the amount of economic inequality between citizens. Here are two comments pertaining to this concern:

> Do you therefore want to give constancy to the State? Bring the two extremes as near to each other as possible. Tolerate neither rich men nor beggars. These two estates, which are naturally inseparable, are equally fatal to the common good. From the one come the fomenters of tyranny, from the other the tyrants.
>
> . . .
>
> No citizen should be so rich as to be capable of buying another citizen, and none so poor that he is forced to sell himself.[13]

To have a shared sense of community and collective destiny, the gap between the rich and poor in society cannot be too large. Rousseau's concerns for the socially corrosive effects of economic inequality remain apt for democracies in the twenty-first century. More contemporary "communitarian" authors like Michael Sandel, for example, have highlighted the negative effects of the growth of economic inequality within the United States. In *Democracy's Discontent* Sandel argues that the rapid rise in economic inequality in the 1970s in the United States undermined the spirit of friendship self-government requires. When there exists a large gap between the rich and poor, they no longer share their collective fates. The affluent, for example, have little reason to be concerned for the quality

---

13. Rousseau, *The Social Contract*, 448.

of public services like affordable housing, decent public education, and universal health care when they can privately purchase these services for themselves. Sandel contends:

> As affluent Americans increasingly buy their way out of reliance on public services, the formative, civic resources of American life diminish. The deterioration of urban public schools is perhaps the most conspicuous and damaging instance of this trend. Another is the growing reliance on private security services, one of the fastest growing occupational categories in the 1980s. So great was the demand for security personnel in shopping malls, airports, retail stores, and residential communities that by 1990 the number of private security guards nationwide exceeded the number of public police officers.[14]

In "Rousseau's Critique of Economic Inequality" Frederick Neuhouser argues that Rousseau's argument against inequality, especially economic inequality, stems from inequality's tendency to create two evils: unhappiness and the loss of freedom. With respect to the threat that inequality poses to human happiness, Neuhouser claims:

> Rousseau's idea ... is that substantial disparities in wealth make it difficult for social members to satisfy one specific, fundamental longing that plays a major role in human happiness, the desire, derived from amour propre, to achieve a recognized standing for others. One problem is that in societies marked by inequalities in wealth, especially societies whose public culture regards income as an indicator of status or worth, being at the bottom of the economic scale is commonly experienced as humiliating, making it difficult for the recognitive desires of the worse off to be satisfied.[15]

---

14. Michael Sandel, *Democracy's Discontent* (Cambridge, MA: Belknap Press of Harvard University Press, 1996), 332.

15. Frederick Neuhouser, "Rousseau's Critique of Economic Inequality," *Philosophy and Public Affairs* 41, no. 3 (2013): 193–225, 204–5.

Rousseau believes economic inequality threatens freedom because, for Rousseau, to be truly free is to act in accordance with the general will. However, when there is a polarization between the rich and poor, a real threat emerges that the poor will be dependent on the will of the rich rather than the general will. That threat can result in domination rather than freedom.

The Mysterious Lawgiver

By characterizing the status quo of nineteenth-century French culture in such a problematic light—basically a society governed by *amour propre*—Rousseau faces the predicament of explaining how we can transform the (admittedly) nonideal reality into something more closely approximating what the ideal or desired political community prescribes. In other words, what is the transformative link between the here and now and the more desirable future? The critic might argue that Rousseau, like other social contract theorists, faces the difficulty of plausibly describing how his political aspirations can be reasonably achieved given that the shortcomings he has gone to great lengths to explain are so omnipresent in the status quo.

Rousseau's proposed solution to this transition from a society ruled by *amour propre* to one governed by the general will is that an ideal legislator (a figure of superior intelligence) is needed to transform us into moral beings. This lawgiver would shape the institutions that in turn shape the people. Once this is done, the general will can come into existence and the society and people will all flourish.

This ideal lawmaker, about whom Rousseau provides scant details, sounds similar to Plato's appeal to rule by philosopher kings and queens. If only we could identify such wise and infallible leaders, then we might not even need democracy at all—just permit those with the skills and competence to govern for the common good to be at the helm indefinitely.

Here are the details Rousseau provides about the mysterious lawgiver:

> Discovering the rules of society best suited to nations would require a superior intelligence that beheld all the passions of men

without feeling any of them; who had no affinity with our nature, yet knew it through and through; whose happiness was independent of us, yet who nevertheless was willing to concern itself with ours; finally, who, in the passage of time, procures for himself a distant glory, being able to labor in one age and find enjoyment in another. Gods would be needed to give men laws.[16]

This part of Rousseau's argument is subject to many pressing problems and objections. Is it even possible for such persons to exist? Rousseau himself admits that "Gods would be needed." Even if someone did emerge, claiming to have such competence and motivation, how could we be sure they are genuine and worthy of our trust? Perhaps, when given the opportunity to influence laws, they will shape them toward their own personal advantage over the laudable collective goals that Rousseau believes they will pursue. Finally, Rousseau's argument for democratic governance was predicated on the assumption that no one is superior to others, and thus meant to govern over others. Yet the claim that a mysterious lawmaker is needed to help put us on the right path sounds very unequal. The dilemma is that Rousseau has painted such a dire picture of the status quo, and the grip *amour propre* has over our psychology, that it seems unlikely the fallible and flawed human beings in such a predicament could actually escape it.

To his critics, Rousseau's appeal to a mysterious lawmaker sounds like a pie-in-the-sky solution to the pressing practical problems that Rousseau described in his political writings. Thus, like many other political theorists, Rousseau fails to adequately explain how the gulf between the problematic here and now and the desired future can be overcome. Despite this, Rousseau's ideas had a significant impact on the aspirations of the French revolutionaries who sought to redress the inequalities inherent in the hierarchal system of rule by the French monarchy.

---

16. Rousseau, *The Social Contract*, 442.

The French Revolution: "Liberty, Equality, and Fraternity"

Rousseau died in 1778, eleven years before the storming of the Bastille and the start of the French Revolution. His ideas about equality and democratic government had a significant influence on the French Revolution, a period of prolonged popular uprisings that reflected the fragile stability of French society in the late eighteenth century. This fragility was, at least in part, the result of a polarized, deeply divided society with, on the one hand, the vulnerable masses of peasants struggling to meet their basic material needs, and, on the other hand, the aristocratic class which enjoyed the opulence such a political system afforded it. In 1794 Rousseau's remains were actually moved from their original burial spot to the Panthéon in Paris. The motto of the French Revolution was "Liberty, Equality, and Fraternity." We shall examine these three political values as they relate to Rousseau's ideas.

Liberty is a core political value in Rosseau's work, and two important distinctions can be drawn that clarify Rousseau's understanding of liberty, as well as his position relative to other political thinkers who invoke the value of freedom. These two distinctions are:

1. Rousseau's distinction between natural freedom versus civil or moral freedom.
2. The distinction between positive versus negative freedom.[17]

The first of Rousseau's conceptions of freedom is the freedom people enjoy in the original state of nature, when governed by *amour de soi*. In the state of nature our freedom was only constrained by our own (physical and cognitive) powers and by other animals. There were no laws that constrained our freedom, nor moral duties to others that we had to fulfill. However, the loss of natural freedom is not something we should now lament, as the transition into the social being in civil society offers us a new type of civil or moral freedom. This is the freedom that is realized when we live according to the general will. Rousseau remarks:

---

17. Isaiah Berlin, "Two Concepts of Liberty," in *Four Essays on Liberty* (London: Oxford University Press, 1969), 118–72.

This passage from the state of nature to the civil state produces quite a remarkable change in man, for it substitutes justice for instinct in his behavior and gives his actions a moral quality they previously lacked. Only then, when the voice of duty replaces physical impulse and right replaces appetite, does man, who had hitherto taken only himself into account, find himself forced to act upon other principles and to consult his reason before listening to his inclinations.[18]

Moral freedom, for Rousseau, is obedience to a self-prescribed law. This is the idea we encountered earlier, that being compelled to obey the general will is only forcing someone to be free. But if it is a self-prescribed law, why would we need to be compelled to obey it? One way of understanding Rousseau's stance on this is that there will (inevitably) be occasions where we are mistaken about what the general will prescribes. For example, suppose the popular assembly is voting on a particular policy measure. I vote in favor of the policy because I genuinely believe that the policy will be conducive to the common good. However, the majority of people vote against the policy, and do so from their assessment of what is genuinely in the interests of the common good versus just their own self-interest. In this case I accept the will of the majority, understanding that the rejection of the policy was what the general will actually was. I do not see the will of the majority as contravening my liberty, because moral freedom entails my living in accordance with what the general will is.

In his famous 1958 inaugural lecture as the Chichele Professor of Political Theory at Oxford University, Isaiah Berlin delivered a lecture titled "Two Concepts of Liberty."[19] This was during the Cold War, and Berlin conjectured that the world was witnessing the clash of two ideologies between the "free world" and the authoritarian regimes of the Soviet bloc in Eastern Europe. Berlin argued that there were two concepts of liberty or freedom: positive and negative. Negative freedom is the conception of freedom typically invoked in contemporary liberal societies, which equates freedom with freedom from noninterference. Thus negative

---

18. Rousseau, *The Social Contract*, 434.
19. Berlin, "Two Concepts of Liberty."

liberty is promoted when the state refrains from interfering in the religious beliefs, political expressions, or sexual orientation of the citizenry. A society that respects negative liberty will be pluralistic given that people will have diverse opinions, values, and traditions that constitute their conception of what the good life is. The main proponent of negative liberty is the nineteenth-century English philosopher John Stuart Mill, who we will examine in great detail in chapter 10.

By contrast, Berlin defined positive liberty not as the absence of constraints but as the *presence* of something, such as self-mastery or self-determination. This ideal of positive liberty is evident not only in Rousseau's defense of democracy but also in Karl Marx's critique of capitalism and his aspirations for a postcapitalist society in which the self-determination of all (rather than just the capitalist class) can be realized.

Within political philosophy there has been much debate about the relative merits of the negative and positive conceptions of liberty. Those defending negative liberty emphasize the importance of constraining state interference in our choices and decisions, for it is the potentially tyrannical state that represents the biggest threat to individual liberty. But to its critics, negative liberty is an insufficient ideal of true freedom. If a capitalist society resists implementing public policies that would provide a guaranteed level of basic material well-being for its population because such a safety net would be construed as interfering with freedom, can we really say that those living in poverty are truly free? The proponents of positive liberty subscribe to the ideals of self-government and/or self-determination and thus can maintain that certain types of government interference (e.g., to mitigate market vulnerabilities or limit economic inequality) are necessary for promoting the positive freedom of all. The champions of negative liberty believe that the life prospects of the population are better served when the state allows individual persons to live free lives, for such autonomous choices are more likely to result in improvements to the welfare of all than the strategy of entrusting the government to implement ambitious paternalistic policies (as these often fall short of achieving their desired ends).

Equality

From both the *Discourse on the Origins of Inequality* and *The Social Contract*, it is evident that a foundational concern in Rousseau's political writings is equality and inequality. The inequality that existed in eighteenth-century France, between the opulent life enjoyed by the monarchy and the bleak life prospects of the peasantry, was not "natural." An elite few are not destined to govern over the masses. According to Rousseau, inequality originated with the transformation in our motivations for self-preservation in the state of nature to the vanity and greed of the contemporary society, a transformation aided by the creation of private property, the acquisition of language, and the rise of the arts and sciences.

For Rousseau, moral and political equality ought to be the basis of a social contract that rejects rule by the monarchy and instead empowers citizens to determine the laws by which they are bound. The realization of rule by the general will epitomizes this ideal of political equality. Despite the revolutionary political aspirations of Rousseau's writings, there is one obvious blind spot in his call for democracy. The equality he envisions is only extended to men. In *Emile*, for example, where Rousseau describes the education a boy requires to grow up to be an autonomous agent, he describes (in Book 5) the aspirations for women as follows:

> Nature herself has decreed that woman, both for herself and her children, should be at the mercy of man's judgement.

> Worth alone will not suffice, a woman must be thought worthy; nor beauty, she must be admired; nor virtue, she must be respected. A woman's honour does not depend on her conduct alone, but on her reputation, and no woman who permits herself to be considered vile is really virtuous. A man has no one but himself to consider, and so long as he does right he may defy public opinion; but when a woman does right her task is only half finished, and what people think of her matters as much as what she really is. Hence her education must, in this respect, be

different from man's education. "What will people think" is the grave of a man's virtue and the throne of a woman's.[20]

Rousseau unwittingly accepted the sexual inequality of his own time: the patriarchal view that women are naturally passive and weak and their primary duty is in the domestic realm as wife and mother. While he possessed the insight to challenge some of the inequalities prevalent in his own time, alas, Rousseau was blind to one of the most persistent forms of inequality: sexual inequality. And this then severely constrains the democratic aspirations of Rousseau's argument. Genevieve Lloyd explains this predicament as follows:

> On the one hand, Rousseau insists that living in the opinion of others is the root of oppression, the origin of pernicious inequalities between human beings, the source of misery, the deprivation of freedom. Any form of social institution that depends on it is, by that token, a corrupt social institution. Yet, he seems to insist with equal vehemence, this very living in the opinion of others is natural to women. Here it is not the mark of nature gone sour, but rather how things ought to be. There is, it seems, paradoxically, a "factitiousness" of women based in nature itself.[21]

Sexism will be the target of the feminist critique advanced by thinkers like Christine de Pizan, Mary Wollstonecraft, and Anna Cooper. We shall address this point in greater detail in chapter 8, when we consider the so-called nature versus nurture debate.

Fraternity

The third value in the motto of the French Revolution is "fraternity," a value that encapsulates the ideas of community and solidarity. Rousseau's political philosophy aspires to transcend the individualism that often dominates contemporary political discussion and debate. "Each of us

---

20. Jean-Jacques Rousseau, *Emile* [1762], trans. B. Foxley (London: Dent, 1911), 328.
21. Genevieve Lloyd, "Rousseau on Reason, Nature and Women," *Metaphilosophy* 14, nos. 3–4 (1983): 308–26, 314.

places his person and all his power in common under the supreme direction of the general will."²² Rather than asking "What can the government do to promote my self-interest?" Rousseau's vision of democratic governance, framed around the idea of the general will, requires each person to adopt the collective perspective of asking what is the common good for society as a whole. Rather than simply electing political leaders that will best represent our personal interests when they form a ruling government, Rousseau envisions that we would directly decide on the laws of the community.

Democratic Theory Today

Many of the themes from Rousseau's political writings still dominate contemporary debates in political philosophy. In this concluding section I will canvass three such topics:

1. What is democracy?
2. Why vote?
3. Deliberative democracy

The first question—"What is democracy?"—has received many different answers. We typically associate democracy with *majority rules* and having an *equal vote*. But in practice a democracy entails a lot more than this. A king might proclaim that the masses can vote on whether taxes will be raised by 5 or 10 percent, with everyone having an equal vote on the question and the majority vote winning, but that would not satisfy our convictions that the outcome was in some way genuinely "democratic."

Furthermore, there are good reasons for conceptualizing democracy as involving more than simply a particular type of government. To be sustained over time, democracy also requires a particular type of *culture*—norms of openness (e.g., the freedom to question and criticize authority), inclusivity, and civility (e.g., listening to one another and resolving disagreement via dialogue and compromise versus violence or deception and manipulation). One of my favorite accounts of democracy (and one

---

22. Rousseau, *The Social Contract*, 432.

of the most concise) comes from the twentieth-century pragmatist philosopher John Dewey, who claimed that democracy is a form of social experiment and the "name for a life of free and enriching communion."[23] As an experiment, democracy enables us to harnesses human intelligence to solve problems because it is "primarily a mode of associated living, of conjoint communicated experience."[24]

A more expansive account of democracy is provided by the political scientist Robert Dahl, who identifies five opportunities a decision-making process must satisfy to be called "democratic":

1. Effective participation.
2. Equality in voting.
3. Gaining enlightened understanding.
4. Exercising final control over the agenda.
5. Inclusion of adults.[25]

Why Vote?

Rousseau's ideal of the general will stands in sharp contrast to other accounts of democracy and voting behavior championed by some political scientists. As we noted in chapter 3 on Aristotle, in 1957 Anthony Downs published a very influential book titled *An Economic Theory of Democracy*, in which Downs argued that it is *irrational* to vote. And if it is irrational to vote, it must also be irrational to become informed about politics. Downs invoked rational choice theory (RCT), an influential school of thought that assumes individuals act rationally to satisfy their preferences. When faced with a set of options, rational actors will pursue the course of action that imposes the smallest burden but yields the highest reward in terms of preference satisfaction. In market behavior this is pretty straightforward in that consumers will prefer to pay lower prices

---

23. John Dewey, *The Public and Its Problems* (New York: Henry Holt, 1927), 184.
24. John Dewey, *Democracy and Education*, in *The Middle Works of John Dewey, 1899–1924*, vol. 9, ed. Jo Ann Boydston (Carbondale: Southern Illinois University Press, 1980), 93.
25. Robert Dahl, *On Democracy* (New Haven, CT: Yale University Press, 2000), 38.

for products of similar quality. It would be irrational to prefer to pay a higher price for the same product. Rational actors employ a cost-benefit calculation before acting.

When applied to the act of voting in an election, Downs argued that the voter incurs a certain cost in voting—taking the time to go to the polling station, waiting in line to vote, and so on—but has no expected benefit given that one's vote is very unlikely to make the difference to the outcome of an election among millions of voters. Consider, for example, the typical voter—we will call her Sarah. Suppose Sarah has a preference for presidential candidate X to win the upcoming election. Sarah likes X's political platform. The principles and policies the candidate proposes to use as a guide for their term as president strikes Sarah as the correct priorities to inform the presidential office. These policies are ones Sarah believes would help hardworking families such as hers. However, like most people, Sarah lives a very busy life. She has a full-time job and school-aged children, is active in her community, and so on. The election is tomorrow—should Sarah vote?

According to Downs's rational choice analysis, Sarah will incur a guaranteed (not overly burdensome but not trivial) *cost* with voting. She might have to drive twenty miles across town and wait in line to vote, which means taking time out of her busy workday or time with her kids after school. All of this will not likely bring her any benefit. Her one measly vote will not determine the outcome of the presidential election. Thus Downs concludes it is not rational for Sarah to vote. If it is not rational for Sarah to vote, it follows that it is also not rational for Sarah to take the time to learn about the political parties, platforms, and so forth. Thus it seems that the only truly rational people, at least in large-scale elections where millions of votes will determine the outcome, are apathetic nonvoters who are disengaged from the voting process.

Deliberative Democracy

Downs's analysis of rational choice informed a more general vision of democracy known as the "aggregative model of democracy." This model of democracy can be summarized as follows:

Individuals in the polity have varying preferences about what they want government institutions to do. They know that other individuals also have preferences, which may or may not match their own. Democracy is a competitive process in which political parties and candidates offer their platforms and attempt to satisfy the largest number of people's preferences. Citizens with similar preferences often organize interest groups in order to try to influence the actions of parties and policy-makers once they are elected. Individuals, interest groups, and public officials each may behave strategically, adjusting the orientation of their pressure tactics or coalition-building according to their perceptions of the activities of competing preferences.[26]

In the 1990s political philosophers began to reject the aggregative model of democracy and invoke instead the ideal of "deliberative democracy," which shares many of the political aspirations of Rousseau's political writings. Deliberative democrats do not conceive of voting as market behavior, as rational choice theory presumed. They instead emphasize norms of reciprocity and public reason. Amy Gutmann and Dennis Thompson, for example, argue that the principle of reciprocity entails that "citizens owe one another justifications for the mutually binding laws and public policies they collectively enact."[27]

For deliberative democrats, the democratic process is a *transformative* process. It goes beyond people simply expressing their preferences and voting for parties and candidates that promise to satisfy those preferences. By participating in dialogue and debate with one another, the preferences we hold can themselves be revised or abandoned. Perhaps through dialogue and debate I come to realize that the public policies I thought were the most important to implement are not that important, or even that they may be harmful.

Deliberative democracy faces one of the same challenges as Rousseau's defense of democratic sovereignty: the problem of large scale. Rousseau's

---

26. Iris Marion Young, *Inclusion and Democracy* (Oxford: Oxford University Press, 2000), 19.

27. Amy Gutmann and Dennis Thompson, "Deliberative Democracy beyond Process," *Journal of Political Philosophy* 10, no. 2 (2002): 153–74, 156.

popular assemblies might sound attractive for a relatively small political community of a few thousand people, but it will not be viable for millions of people to be so actively involved in deciding the laws of their community. Likewise, the ideal of deliberating together and meeting the demands of reciprocity might sound viable and attractive for smaller deliberative bodies, such as the jury in a criminal court proceeding. The same could be argued for the deliberation of local politics in a townhall meeting where the town's policies may be formatively shaped by the input of local residents' discussion and debate. But how can millions of people deliberate together? Michael Walzer raised this point and argued that "deliberation is not an activity for the demos. . . . 100 million of them, or even 1 million or 100,000 can't plausibly 'reason together.'"[28]

The democracies of the world today face many pressing challenges, such as the quality of their media, voter apathy, and the divisive politics that often pits factions of society against one another. Rousseau's arguments concerning inequality, fraternity, and the general will, arguments that influenced the French Revolution after Rousseau's death, remain active, topical issues for the democracies of the twenty-first century to address. Rousseau's democratic aspirations were predicated on the particular view of moral psychology he invoked, concerning the motivations of *amour de soi* and *amour propre*. A project for democratic theory today is to take the latest empirical insights concerning the prosocial and biased perceptions and actions we all share, and to theorize how democracies can forge ahead to bring out the best in our nature and minimize the worse within us.

---

28. Michael Walzer, "Deliberation, and What Else?," in *Deliberative Politics: Essays on Democracy and Disagreement*, ed. Stephen Macedo (Oxford: Oxford University Press, 1999), 58–69, 68.

CHAPTER 7

Conservative Political Thought

Conservatism is an influential and significant political perspective that is important to understand and critically engage with. In this chapter we shall explore a diverse range of historical thinkers and topics to help elucidate the central political convictions of conservatism. One challenge with characterizing conservatism as a political ideology or belief system is that many conservatives would contend that it does not constitute a "political theory," at least not in the way that the term is often used when describing certain political orientations or commitments. In his essay "On Being Conservative," for example, the English philosopher Michael Oakeshott argues that conservativism is not a creed or doctrine, but rather a *disposition*:

> To be a conservative is to be disposed to think and behave in certain manners; it is to prefer certain kinds of conduct and certain conditions of human circumstances to others; it is to be disposed to make certain kinds of choices.[1]

Oakeshott's characterization of conservatism may frustrate many for its overt ambiguity: "think and behave in certain manners," "prefer certain kinds of conduct," and "disposed to make certain kinds of choices." To which one might reasonably retort: "Think in *which* manner?" "Prefer *which kinds of conduct?*" "Disposed to make *which kinds of choices?*" But like the virtue ethics tradition, conservative political thought is not something that provides the concrete moral code of utilitarianism, or the prescriptive aspirations of Rousseau's vision of democracy or Marx's predictions concerning the eventual transformation of capitalism into communism.

---

1. Michael Oakeshott, *Rationalism in Politics and Other Essays* (Indianapolis: Liberty Fund, 1991), 407.

Instead, conservativism denotes a particular set of sentiments or orientation toward political life and human affairs. There are nuanced differences between different types of conservative thinkers, but one methodological insight they share is that they see the past, the present, and the future as inexorably linked.

Conservatives maintain that we cannot think sagely about how to navigate through the challenges of the future without some intimate knowledge of what has worked, and what has not worked, in the past with respect to making headway against such challenges. The past, for conservatives, represents important lessons that should not be ignored. Thus (sage) change and progress are *piecemeal* and *gradual* and achieved through the exercise of practical insight and judgment versus radical or abrupt change. The latter is typically motivated by utopian or unbridled aspirational thinking.

John Kekes describes conservatism as a political morality, the fundamental aim of which "is to conserve the political arrangements that have shown themselves to be conducive to good lives."[2] Conservatives orient their analysis of political life from a position that tends to emphasize the positives in the status quo, and a skepticism or apprehension about political aspirations and prescriptions that are predicated on weak foundations. Kekes contends that conservativism "denies that the reasons for or against particular political arrangements are to be derived from a contract that fully rational people might make in a hypothetical situation; or from an imagined ideal society; or from what is supposed to be most beneficial for the whole of humanity; or from the prescriptions of some sacred or secular book."[3]

There is a fascinating psychological literature on the extent to which political ideologies that emphasize tradition and stability (conservativism) versus innovation and progressive change (liberalism) may reflect different personality traits.[4] A rapidly growing body of empirical evidence documents a multitude of ways in which liberals and conservatives

---

2. John Kekes, "What Is Conservatism?," *Philosophy* 72, no. 281 (1997): 351–74, 351.

3. John Kekes, "What Is Conservatism?," 353.

4. See, for example, B. Verhulst, L. J. Eaves, and P. K. Hatemi, "Correlation Not Causation: The Relationship between Personality Traits and Political Ideologies," *American Journal of Political Science* 56, no. 1 (2012): 34–51.

differ from each other. Jost et al., for example, have argued that a "specific set of social–cognitive motives are significantly related to political conservatism."[5] Resistance to change and more accepting attitudes toward inequality, for example, are political convictions typically associated with conservatism. Jost et al. also contend that political conservatism exists because it is a political belief system (like other belief systems) that can "satisfy various psychological needs."[6] When environmental stimuli present uncertainty and fear and threats, epistemic motives like "uncertainty avoidance" or "dogmatism, intolerance of ambiguity," coupled with existential motives like "loss prevention" and "terror management," and ideological motives like "group-based dominance," can lead many to endorse political conservatism's resistance to change and tolerance of inequality.

Haidt and Graham argue that conservatism is best understood from an anthropological perspective that conceives of the moral domain in a broad fashion.[7] The world's many moralities, they contend, are predicated on the following five foundations: (1) harm/care; (2) fairness/reciprocity; (3) ingroup/loyalty; (4) authority/respect; and (5) purity/sanctity. Persons with liberal convictions tend to orient their political perspectives and actions around the first two foundations, harm/care and fairness/reciprocity. By contrast, Haidt and Graham argue the intuitions of political conservatives are predicated on all five foundations. Many liberals will of course see the sentiments of in-group loyalty, deference to authority, and appeals to purity as morally suspect or problematic because they can lead to intolerance and a rigid mode of thinking that impedes substantive change. But viewed through their anthropological perspective, Haidt and Graham encourage us to see that human cultures possess a diverse array of moral foundations, and those with a broader moral perspective will see the political landscape differently than liberals who appeal only to two (harm/care and fairness/reciprocity) of the five moral foundations.

---

5. J. T. Jost, J. Glaser, A. W. Kruglanski, and F. J. Sulloway, "Political Conservatism as Motivated Social Cognition," *Psychological Bulletin* 129, no. 3 (2003): 339–75, 366.

6. Jost, et al., "Political Conservatism as Motivated Social Cognition," 369.

7. Jonathan Haidt and Jesse Graham, "When Morality Opposes Justice: Conservatives Have Moral Intuitions That Liberals May Not Recognize," *Social Justice Research* 20, no. 1 (2007): 98–116.

Edmund Burke

If there is any historical figure who is typically hailed as the founder of conservative political thought it is the eighteenth-century Irish-born political thinker and politician Edmund Burke (1729–97). Born in Dublin, Burke was elected as a member of Parliament for Bristol in 1774. He was deeply involved in the political events of his day and gave influential political speeches as a parliamentarian.

Burke would perhaps reject the label that he was a "political theorist." He is probably bettered characterized as a political *practitioner* rather than a theoretician. Burke does not advance a vision of government that is predicated on some abstract moral values such as those typical of the social contract tradition or utilitarianism. Instead, Burke addresses specific societal and political predicaments (e.g., both the American and French Revolutions, private property, etc.), and does so in a manner that reaffirms traditional values in new or changing circumstances.

Burke is interested in both the American Revolutionary War (1775–83) and the French Revolution (1789–99). The latter is the focus of Burke's most influential political writing, *Reflections on the Revolution in France*, published shortly after the storming of the Bastille, a prison in Paris. Burke worries that revolutionary tendencies could spread to the rest of Europe. The *Reflections* is written in the form of a letter addressed to a Frenchman named Depont. Burke expresses concern that enthusiasm for the French Revolution is spreading, informing radicalism within Great Britain. In particular Burke is worried that his contemporaries in England could become entranced by revolutionary idealism. Richard Price, for example, was a contemporary of Burke's who gave a sermon to the Revolution Society and espoused the idea that the legal basis of political rule was founded on a principle of popular choice. In *Reflections* Burke condemns the French Revolution as a cavalier and dangerous development, a state of affairs made possible because its advocates discarded and devalued custom and heredity in favor of an abstract appeal to ideals of freedom and equality. Radical breaks with the past, argues Burke, are inherently dangerous because they forfeit the wisdom of the past and replace it with the folly of idealized aspirations about the future.

For Burke and other conservative thinkers, society is best conceptualized as a *partnership* among the living, the dead, and future generations. The radical change represented by the French Revolution, which challenged the legitimacy of the monarchy and the church and demonstrated disdain for the right to private property, meant there was no viable constraint on the tyranny of mob rule that emerged and threatened to devolve society into anarchy. Conservatives are quick to point out that, even though the status quo has its shortcomings, things could easily degenerate into an even worse situation. Burke believed this was the case with the French Revolution, describing the revolutionaries as "deluded," "stupid," and "savage," and the king of France as an innocent victim. The open atheism of French revolutionaries terrified Burke; he described it as "the most horrid and cruel blow that can be offered to society."[8]

Inequality, according to Burke, is both natural and beneficial. This appeal to a natural hierarchy has also been invoked by other thinkers discussed in this book, such as Plato and Aristotle. Plato did not think the average person was capable of governing competently, for they lack the epistemic and moral virtues needed to pursue the truth and govern in the interests of the common good. Burke had a similarly elitist view. Burke's appeal to the virtues of heredity and hierarchy might appear less offensive to our twenty-first-century sensibilities when we consider that, in the historical context of eighteenth-century Europe, most people were illiterate and religion provided a sense of shared community and motivation for living a moral life. Atheism was thus perceived by Burke as a threat to the security and stability of human communities because he did not believe it could constitute a feasible alternative to the social cohesion offered by religion.

With respect to private property and inequality, Burke remarked: "The characteristic essence of property, formed out of the combined principles of acquisition and conservation, is to be *unequal*."[9] Why would Burke suggest that the essence of property is for it to be unequal? For example, consider three individuals who each possess the same amount of wealth at time T1. Let us suppose each person has $500 of wealth in total. So at T1

---

8. Edmund Burke, "Speech on a Bill for the Relief of Protestant Dissenters," in *The Works of the Right Honourable Edmund Burke* (London: F. C. & J. Rivington, 1812), 22–40, 38.

9. Edmund Burke, *Reflections on the Revolution in France* [1789–90], in David Wootton, *Modern Political Thought: Readings from Machiavelli to Nietzsche* (Indianapolis: Hackett, 2008), 502–21, 512.

the distribution of wealth among the three individuals is one of *equality*: $500, $500, $500. However, over the course of the following year each person makes different decisions regarding what to do with their $500, and life influences their fortunes in different ways.

The first person, whom we can call "Impulsive Ivan," quickly spends all $500 to upgrade his kitchen to the luxury kitchen he always wanted. The second person, "Prudent Petra," invests half of the money ($250) in her low-interest savings account in the bank (which earns her $8 in interest) and uses the remaining $250 to pay off her student debt from her time at university. The third person, "Gambling Gary," invests the whole $500 in the stock market, and fortunately for him, the stocks double in value to $1,000 by T2. After a year the equal distribution of T1 ($500, $500, $500) had been transformed to the *unequal distribution* of T2 ($0, $258, $1000). Such inequality is inevitable, Burke would argue, as people will make different decisions about what to purchase and when, or about investing, and so forth. Burke does not believe that property is something that could or should be managed to ensure equality of outcomes. Aspiring for equality would actually leave everyone worse off, argues Burke:

> Believe me, Sir, those who attempt to level, never equalise. In all societies, consisting of various descriptions of citizens, some descriptions must be uppermost. The levellers therefore only change and pervert the natural order of things; they load the edifice of society, by setting up in the air what the solidity of the structure requires to be on the ground.[10]

Defenders of Burke could argue that Burke's insights have some validity when applied to many twentieth-century communist movements that had promised to realize greater economic equality, such as those of Joseph Stalin in the Soviet Union and Mao Zedong in China. Rather than leveling their societies into an equal distributive outcome, both implemented disastrous policies that brought economic ruin (e.g., starvation and death) to millions of people.

---

10. Burke, *Reflections on the Revolution*, 511.

Libertarianism

There are some affinities between Burke's conservative critique of equality and a planned economy, and the libertarianism of the philosopher Robert Nozick and the Austrian economist Friedrich Hayek. Nozick argues against appeals to any "patterned distributive outcome" of wealth and income because he believes "liberty upsets patterns."[11] He illustrates this argument with an example concerning Wilt Chamberlain. Standing at over seven feet tall, Chamberlain was a famous American basketball player and one of the most dominant players during his era (1960s and early 1970s). Nozick asks us to consider a society where wealth and income are initially distributed equally. Egalitarians will maintain that the initial distribution (D1) conforms with what they take to be a "just distribution" of wealth and income. But imagine now that in this equal society there is a professional basketball league with a player like Wilt Chamberlain. Chamberlain is the best player in the league and can easily sell out the tickets to any home games. His strong bargaining advantage enables him to negotiate a deal with his current team that he would receive twenty-five cents from the price of each ticket of admission. Because the owners want to retain Chamberlain on their team, they agree to this. Having him on the team will sell more tickets, and thus net a larger profit even with twenty-five cents per ticket going directly to Chamberlain.

The basketball season starts, and the fans happily attend the home games, each time dropping twenty-five cents of their admission price into a special box with Chamberlain's name on it. By the end of the season one million fans attend his home games, and this yields him an income of $250,000, which makes Chamberlain significantly wealthier than anyone else. The initial equal distribution in D1 is now transformed into the unequal distribution of D2 at the end of the basketball season. The Wilt Chamberlain example illustrates Nozick's libertarian argument that "liberty upsets patterns." If people are free, they will inevitably engage in activities that will upset any patterned distribution (such as equality).

Hayek criticizes socialist ideals that presuppose implementing a "planned economy," as this contravenes what Hayek takes to be the "spontaneous order" of communities. The latter are the product of the voluntary

---

11. Robert Nozick, *Anarchy, State, and Utopia* (New York: Basic Books, 1974).

activities of individuals and thus are not intentionally designed by any social planner. In his postscript to *The Constitution of Liberty* titled "Why I Am Not a Conservative," Hayek notes that he did not consider himself a conservative (though there are many areas of overlap between the Burkean criticism of appeals to equality and Hayek's libertarian critique of appeals to social justice). Hayek claims that conservatism is "a legitimate, probably necessary, and certainly widespread attitude of opposition to drastic change." He went on to express what he took to be the fatal shortcoming of conservatism as a political ideology:

> It is that by its very nature it cannot offer an alternative to the direction in *which* we are moving. It may succeed by its resistance to current tendencies in slowing down undesirable developments, but, since it does not indicate another direction, it cannot prevent their continuance. It has, for this reason, invariably been the fate of conservatism to be dragged along a path not of its own choosing. The tug of war between conservatives and progressives can only affect the speed, not the direction, of contemporary developments.[12]

That said, Burke did champion political arguments that sought to articulate in which direction society ought to be moving. This is perhaps most evident by his contrasting stances on the French and American Revolutions.

Burke on the American and French Revolutions

In the second half of the eighteenth century, both America and France had revolutions. Both invoked political ideals such as freedom, equality, and democracy and sought to emancipate citizens from the oppression of historical, hierarchal arrangements. One might expect that Burke, as a conservative, would oppose both revolutions in favor of the political status quo and tradition of his day. But Burke's conservatism is much more complex and nuanced than this. While he opposed the French Revolution, he

---

12. Friedrich Hayek, *The Constitution of Liberty* (Chicago: University of Chicago Press, 1960), 397, 398.

was actually supportive of the American Revolution. What explains his different stances on these two revolutions of the late eighteenth century? This is a point of contention among scholars of Burke.

One common answer highlights the fact that the rights at stake in the American Revolution were very different from the moral interests championed to justify the French Revolution. In *Thoughts on the Cause of Present Discontents* we see Burke take an empathetic and charitable stance when it comes to interpreting the societal unrest of the people, something he believes is often symptomatic of serious shortcomings of the ruling government:

> I am not one of those who think that the people are never in the wrong. They have been so, frequently and outrageously, both in other countries and in this. But I do say, that in all disputes between them and their rulers the presumption is at least upon a par in favour of the people. Experience may perhaps justify me in going further. When popular discontents have been very prevalent, it may well be affirmed and supported, that there has been generally something found amiss in the constitution or in the conduct of Government. The people have no interest in disorder. When they do wrong, it is their error, and not their crime. But with the governing part of the state, it is far otherwise. They certainly may act ill by design, as well as by mistake.[13]

Burke goes on to suggest that the masses only rise, at least in most cases, when their sufferings are unbearable, and that they are seldom wrong in their feelings of public misconduct. Many commentators contend that, for Burke, the American Revolution was justified because it was an attempt to attain the rights that Englishmen already enjoyed in England, so it was actually a revolution to attain *traditional* rights that were being denied to the American colonists. Thus, by this reading, there is no inconsistency in Burke's conservativism when he supports one revolution but not the other. The American Revolution sought to establish traditional rights for the American colonies and was thus provoked by the British monarchy.

---

13. Edmund Burke, *Thoughts on the Cause of Present Discontents*, ed. F. G. Selby and LL. D. Bombay (London: Macmillan, 1951), 6.

In contrast, the French revolutionaries appealed to abstract political ideals and showed disdain for tradition and custom (e.g., religion and private property).

But this explanation does not fully explain why Burke took opposing stances on these two revolutions. Burke saw the American Revolution in a sympathetic light, casting his criticisms on the British government rather than the revolutionary Americans. Yet just a few decades later Burke criticized the French revolutionaries as "deluded," "stupid," and "savage," and the king of France as an innocent victim. Why did Burke not see the discontent of the French peasantry as an indication that the French monarch was mismanaging their role as political leader, given that, as Burke admitted a few years earlier, people have no interest in political disorder and are seldom wrong in their feelings of public misconduct?

In "Constructing Communities: Edmund Burke on Revolution" Jeff Spinner argues that Burke takes different stances on the American and French Revolutions because he was addressing two different types of communities, and from different perspectives. When analyzing the American Revolution, Burke is concerned with what is in the best interests of England. Burke worried that a continued war with America distorted and distracted the ambitions of the British Empire.[14] Making peace with America would help strengthen England. By contrast, if the revolution in France were successful, Burke did not believe there would be a stable nation left, as the pillars sustaining French culture (i.e., the clergy, monarchy, and property) and society would have been toppled.

Spinner contends that Burke did not believe America would be easily defeated. America's love of liberty was unprecedented, which meant that it would have to be continually conquered. Furthermore, Burke believed that America was an innovative experiment showing promise that it possessed the ability to improve on old institutions. But just because this social experiment might be successful in America did not mean it would also be successful in France. Burke saw "the poor and miserable working class as a permanent fixture of Europe."[15] In contrast, the American economy was in the more fortunate position that it could expand the new frontier when people were faced with economic adversity. But in France

---

14. Jeff Spinner, "Constructing Communities: Edmund Burke on Revolution," *Polity* 23, no. 3 (1991): 395–421, 398.

15. Spinner, "Constructing Communities," 416.

the only solace was religion. Burke also believed Americans were better educated.[16]

Finally, Spinner notes that geography was particularly relevant to Burke's analysis of the different communities impacted by the American and French Revolutions. America was much more isolated than France, so the risks of pursuing an innovative social experiment in America were not likely to apply in other European countries. France, however, was interconnected in important ways to the rest of Europe, especially England. Thus Burke was concerned that the revolutionary sentiments of the French would be transposed to England and other European countries. The harms of the misguided French Revolution were substantial, in Burke's eyes. That revolution threatened the stability of all of Europe.

Hegel and the "Ethical Life" Thesis

The Prussian philosopher Georg Hegel (1770–1831) also advances a conservative political philosophy in his book *The Philosophy of Right* (published in 1821). Born in Stuttgart, Hegel studied theology at university and went on to hold various academic appointments. In *The Philosophy of Right* he addressed a number of themes central to conservative political theory (such as the family and private property) and emphasized the ethical and practical importance of existing cultural norms and practices versus abstract ethical principles such as the categorical imperative of Immanuel Kant (1724–1804). The latter prescribed that the demands of morality could be deduced by the exercise of our reason, giving rise to one form of Kant's categorical imperative, namely, "act only in accordance with that maxim through which you can at the same time will that it become a universal law."

Kant's moral methodology is deficient, argues Hegel, because it requires us to conceptualize the moral landscape in a contrived and inefficacious fashion, stripping away all the contingent factors (e.g., our desires and socially embedded duties and identities) that make living a moral human life even feasible. Hegel refers to this as the "empty formalism objection." In *The Philosophy of Right* Hegel argues that all that is left for duty, when

---

16. Spinner, "Constructing Communities," 415.

construed in Kant's abstract method of the universal categorical imperative, is "abstract universality, and for its determinate character it has identity without content or the abstractly positive, the indeterminate."[17]

Instead of advancing a moral ethic predicated on the abstract reasoning of the Kantian categorical imperative, Hegel's ethic takes more seriously our embedded social nature. "Hegel's theory of ethical life derives our ethical duties from social relationships and institutions."[18] The foundational concept of Hegel's political theory is known as the ethical life (*Sittlichkeit*) thesis, which maintains that norms consist in nothing other than the duties and virtues embedded in the central institutions of modern social life. For Hegel these institutions include (1) the family, (2) civil society, and (3) the state. The family is important for sentiment and affection, as it promotes love and trust among family members. Civil society is the domain in which individuals pursue their own self-interests (e.g., as a consumer in the market), though as an unintended consequence of such action we actually benefit the common good (e.g., by spending and consuming we help grow the economy, which provides employment for others, etc.). Finally, the state, through its laws and policies, helps provide a community of mutual recognition.

To illustrate the ethical life thesis, consider the following moral dilemma. After a long, busy week at work, Tired Thomas feels that he could really enjoy flying away to a sunny, tropical resort to enjoy a week of rest and relaxation. However, Tired Thomas is also a parent, with parental responsibilities, which include caring for his children and making sure they safely arrive at school each day, especially next week as they have some important school exams. Taking a family vacation at this time is simply not feasible. But imagine if Tired Thomas said to himself: "Maybe I can just fly away, by myself, for a short vacation to enjoy two or three days in the sun!" Not sure if taking his vacation is ethical, Tired Thomas, a devoted Kantian, contemplates what guidance Kant's categorical imperative might provide and asks: "Would I will the following maxim to become a universal law: 'Parents should abandon their parental responsibilities when

---

17. *Hegel's Philosophy of Right*, trans. T. M. Knox (Oxford: Oxford University Press, 1967), 89.

18. Allen Wood, *Hegel's Ethical Thought* (Cambridge: Cambridge University Press, 1990), 158.

they feel a strong desire to enjoy a solo holiday'?" By contrast, Hegel's ethical life thesis contends that appealing to such abstract reasoning is both unnecessary and ill advised, because the appropriate norms are embedded in the institution of the family.

While we might empathize with Tired Thomas and his desire for a vacation, being a parent entails making personal sacrifices for one's children. While a solo trip might, in certain situations, be permitted (even obligatory), Tired Thomas's situation is not such a circumstance. He should either wait to take a family vacation with his children (when the school term is over) or make plans for another family member to help cover his parental duties so he could take a vacation. But he is not morally permitted to just abandon his parental duties for a vacation. A moral agent does not need to appeal to Kant's categorical imperative to know that such actions are morally wrong. Parental duties and responsibilities are embedded in the institution of the family and provide the appropriate moral guidance for such deliberations. This is how Hegel's ethical life thesis functions. Moral guidance comes from the social institutions of modern society, not from the abstract, rational deductions of a moral agent in solitude. This Hegelian sentiment resonates with many contemporary conservative thinkers, hence the priority they place on family, religion, and tradition when it comes to diagnosing current societal predicaments as well as their potential resolution.

There are some obvious limitations and problems with Hegel's appeal to the ethical life thesis. Firstly, there may be times when our duties conflict. For example, there may be a parental duty but also an employee duty (e.g., working overtime on weekends, eroding time with one's family), and when our duties conflict, simply appealing to these institutions and identities does not help us resolve or adjudicate these trade-offs and conflicts. Second, the institutions of modern society often have embedded within them morally problematic beliefs and practices. The family, as we shall see with feminist thinkers such as Mary Wollstonecraft in chapter 8, has embedded norms of gender inequality that place unfair expectations and burdens on females—for example, treating daughters differently than sons in terms of their educational opportunities, or invoking norms that impose more unpaid, domestic work on mothers than fathers. So invoking Hegel's ethical life thesis has problematic implications, because it exemplifies the "status quo" bias that critics of conservativism often condemn.

The most conservative implication of Hegel's stance is perhaps most evident in the following passage from *The Philosophy of Right*, which implies that moral progress is not only infeasible but also unnecessary.

> To comprehend what is, this is the task of philosophy, because what is, is reason. Whatever happens, every individual is a child of his time; thus philosophy too is its own time apprehended in thoughts. It is just as absurd to fancy that a philosophy can transcend its contemporary world as it is to fancy that an individual can overleap his own age, or leap over Rhodes. If his theory goes beyond the world as it is and builds an ideal one as it ought to be, that world exists indeed, but only within his opinions, an unsubstantial element where anything you please may, in fancy, be built.[19]

The claim that "what is, is reason" implies a stringent status quo bias in favor of whatever societal duties and responsibilities happen to exist. Even Hegel himself, in his own historical context, championed specific reforms in Prussia, such as trial by jury and public criminal trials. So the ethical life thesis is not meant to function as an unyielding constraint on evolving societal norms, though its critics have argued that Hegel's conservatism leaves little room for the possibility that "what is" could be transformed into "what could/ought to be."

Washington and Black Conservatism

In chapter 9 we will examine Black political thought, covering a diverse array of thinkers and topics such as Frederick Douglass on slavery, W. E. B. Du Bois on racial inequality, Martin Luther King Jr. on nonviolent protest, and Frantz Fanon on colonialism. Black political thought covers a wide range of viewpoints (including those of Black conservatives), methodologies, concerns, and collective prescriptions. In this section we limit our focus to one prominent Black American conservative thinker: Booker T. Washington (1856–1915). In *Black Conservatism: Essays in Intellectual and*

---

19. *Hegel's Philosophy of Right*, 11.

Political History, Peter Eisenstadt notes two limitations that are involved in characterizing Black conservatism. First, any general characterization of Black conservatism will not be true of all parts of Black conservatism. Second, identifying any core values, insights, judgments, or societal prescriptions as defining Black conservativism will inevitably capture things that many non-Black conservatives also espouse. Thus Eisenstadt concludes that "categories of political thought are at best tenuous."[20]

The central political insights and judgments typical of Black conservative thought, which we shall see Washington exemplify, focus on feasible, piecemeal progress and reform (versus radical change or revolution), especially when it comes to the issue of racial inequality. While Washington "rejected white racist denigrations of African-Americans and championed self-help, education, morality, entrepreneurship, and hard work,"[21] his Black conservatism emphasized positive aspects of the status quo while eschewing utopian or overidealized aspirational thinking. "Black conservatism must be examined within the context of American history; it cannot be understood as an isolated phenomenon."[22]

Like Frederick Douglass, Washington was born into slavery, without knowledge of when he was born or who his father was (though he heard rumors his father might have been a white man who lived on a nearby plantation). Washington's mother was the plantation cook. Washington never attended school while enslaved, and he could not recall any time his family sat down to eat dinner together. In *Up from Slavery* Washington remarks:

> On the plantation in Virginia, and even later, meals were gotten by the children very much as dumb animals get theirs. It was a piece of bread here, a scrap of meat there. It was a cup of milk at one time and some potatoes at another. Sometimes a portion of our family would eat out of a skillet or pot, while some one else

---

20. Peter Eisenstadt, ed., *Black Conservatism: Essays in Intellectual and Political History* (New York: Garland, 1999), x.

21. Henry Lewis Suggs, "The Washingtonian Legacy: A History of Black Political Conservatism in America, 1915–1944," in Eisenstadt, *Black Conservatism*, 81–82, 82.

22. Suggs, "The Washington Legacy," 81.

would eat from a plate held on the knees, and often using nothing but hands with which to hold the food.[23]

In contrast to Douglass's description of the persistent conflict between enslaver and enslaved, Washington notes that, despite its obvious oppression and inequality, there still existed some common humanity and respect between enslaved persons and enslavers. Washington claims that, "as a rule, not only did members of my race entertain no feelings of bitterness toward the whites before and during the [Civil] war, but there are many instances of Negroes tenderly caring for their former masters and mistresses who for some reason had become poor and dependent since the war."[24] Washington's experience can be contrasted with that of Douglass, who repeatedly noted the harshness and inhumanity of the relationships between enslavers and the enslaved. At the end of the Civil War, slavery was abolished and Washington was freed. In *Up from Slavery* Washington recalls the impression he had of white people's reaction to slavery being abolished in the South. His sense was that their sadness arose "not because of the loss of property, but rather because of parting with those they had reared and who were in many ways very close to them."[25]

Washington rejected the view that slavery was beneficial to whites and harmful to Blacks. He believed slavery was harmful to *both* enslavers and enslaved persons.

> The hurtful influences of the institution were by no means confined to the Negro. This was fully illustrated by the life upon our own plantation. The whole machinery of slavery was so constructed as to cause labour, as a rule, to be looked upon as a badge of degradation, of inferiority. Hence labour was something that both races on the slave plantation sought to escape. The slave system on our place, in large measure, took the spirit of self-reliance and self-help out of white people. My old master had

---

23. Booker T. Washington, *Up from Slavery* [1901], ed. William Andrews (Oxford: Oxford University Press, 1995), 5.

24. Washington, *Up from Slavery*, 8.

25. Washington, *Up from Slavery*, 10.

many boys and girls, but not one, so far as I know, ever mastered a single trade or special line of productive activity.[26]

Because Washington's political outlook places such a high valuation on self-reliance and work habits, he contends that when freedom came for Black Americans, there was, at least in certain respects, more equality of opportunity than one might presume. Washington believes former slaves were most disadvantaged in "book learning and property." But when it came to the mastery of some handicraft, and a willingness to labor and do so without shame, Black enslaved persons had an advantage over most white enslavers. For many of the latter, argues Washington, the institution of slavery, and its eventual abolition, left them without the skills and aptitude needed to be self-reliant. The critic might contest the emphasis Washington places on "self-help" in this context, as doing so may threaten to marginalize the gravity of the harms slavery inflicted on Black Americans by implying that "it was not all bad, since it fostered a strong work ethic and self-reliance."

Elsewhere in *Up from Slavery* Washington acknowledges that slavery did impose significant inequalities on Black enslaved persons, though again the concern is framed through his distinctly conservative political ethic. For example, Washington notes that slavery had a significant negative impact on the influence of ancestry for Black Americans, noting that many whites would criticize Black youth for their "moral weakness" and compare them with white youth. But such comparisons are unfair, argues Washington, because they ignore the reality that most Black people had little substantive ties with their families over time. Washington had no memory of his own grandmother. He explains the significance this alienation from familial ties had on moral behavior as follows:

> The very fact that the white boy is conscious that, if he fails in life, he will disgrace the whole family record, extending back through many generations, is of tremendous value in helping him to resist temptations. The fact that the individual has behind and surrounding him proud family history and connection serves as

---

26. Washington, *Up from Slavery*, 10.

a stimulus to help him to overcome obstacles when striving for success.[27]

This strong emphasis on family remains a foundational conviction of conservatism in the late twentieth and early twenty-first centuries. The family and individual effort and achievement, rather than proactive government intervention/assistance, are considered the real keys to success for Black (and other) conservative thinkers.

Angela Lewis has noted that "black conservatives show great respect for Western civilization, its culture, and its institutions."[28] In particular Lewis notes that entrepreneurship, rather than direct activism in the political system, was entrenched in American Black conservative thought.

> Capitalism is seen as an advantageous tool for blacks because it gives everyone who can master its ways an equal opportunity for success. . . . The number and diversity of black-owned business in America before the Civil War also demonstrates entrepreneurship among blacks. For example, in the early 1800s blacks flourished in real estate, construction, manufacturing and transportation. Many black businesses also employed whites. A Philadelphia abolitionist and entrepreneur, black conservative James Forten, was a living example of the possibilities business ownership could bring to blacks.[29]

Washington also emphasizes the importance of entrepreneurship in *Up from Slavery*. He recounts the many times he had written to the industrialist and philanthropist Andrew Carnegie requesting funding to erect a new library building. He did this for ten years. Carnegie eventually replied to his persistent requests, agreeing to donate the $20,000 requested to build the new facility. Washington claims that "strict business methods go

---

27. Washington, *Up from Slavery*, 21–22.

28. Angela K. Lewis, "Black Conservatism in America," *Journal of African American Studies* 8, no. 4 (2005): 3–13, 4.

29. Lewis, "Black Conservatism in America," 5.

a long way in securing the interests of rich people."[30] Washington found that the most effective strategy was to request small donations from people of moderate wealth versus relying on large donations from the wealthiest. Interwoven into Washington's strategy of relying on philanthropy was an appeal to Christian ethics. Religion typically plays a foundational role in the outlook of conservative ethics and political theory.

Education was also a key formative aspiration of Washington's Black conservatism. After the US Civil War many southerners rejected the idea that Black Americans should receive formal education. In the Reconstruction period Washington was an influential advocate for equality of opportunity for education. In "The Atlantic Exposition Address" Washington highlights the importance of education, though he adds nuance to what type of education is most important:

> Our greatest danger is that in the great leap from slavery to freedom we may overlook the fact that the masses of us are to live by the productions of our hands, and fail to keep in mind that we shall prosper in proportion as we learn to dignify and glorify common labor and put brains and skill into the common occupations of life; shall prosper in proportion as we learn to draw the line between the superficial and the substantial, the ornamental gewgaws of life and the useful. No race can prosper till it learns that there is as much dignity in tilling a field as in writing a poem. It is at the bottom of life we must begin, and not at the top. Nor should we permit our grievances to overshadow our opportunities.[31]

For Washington, industrial education versus an elitist educational framework was the key to the economic integration and success of Black Americans in the industrial era of the late nineteenth and early twentieth centuries. "From the perspective of Washington and other proponents, ...

---

30. Washington, *Up from Slavery*, 113.

31. Booker Washington, "The Atlantic Exposition Address," in *Up from Slavery* (New York: Dover, 1995), 107.

such an education represented a win-win situation.... It served not only to build character; it prepared [B]lacks for a practical life."[32]

Did Washington believe that Black enfranchisement was desirable and would help accelerate the cultural transition to a more equitable society? Washington's stance on this issue is not a simple yes or no answer. In "The Atlantic Exposition Address," he explicitly states that any law that permits an ignorant and poverty-stricken white man to vote but prevents a Black man in the same situation from voting is unjust. In principle he supports universal suffrage, but he believed the circumstances of the southern states at the time were such that some exclusions needed to remain in place, either in the form of an educational or property test, or a combination of the two. But such exclusions must apply to both white and Black voters. "Though Washington supported literacy tests for voters, he publicly urged that such tests be applied fairly, and he signed petitions to state legislatures to oppose bills that would disenfranchise [B]lacks unfairly."[33] Washington's conservative stance on this issue is seen, by his critics, as an accommodation of, or at least acquiescence to, the exclusionary practices of the Jim Crow era. Many would challenge Washington's presumption that nonpolitical change would be sufficient to inspire the kind of political change needed to make substantial progress against racial inequality in America in the late nineteenth and early twentieth centuries.

The Conservative Temperament in Public Policies

The dispositions of conservativism are often characterized as having a status quo bias.[34] A presumption in favor of the status quo is not something conservatives are necessarily unwavering about, but because the status quo is sometimes settled upon via the experience and wisdom of past generations, it is not something conservatives believe should be easily cast aside, and certainly not for the pursuit of abstract and unrealistic political

---

32. Christopher Bracey, *Saviours or Sellouts: The Promise and Peril of Black Conservatism, from Booker T. Washington to Condoleezza Rice* (Boston: Beacon, 2008), 19.

33. Bracey, *Saviours or Sellouts*, 20.

34. Geoffrey Brennan and Alan Hamlin, "Conservative Value," *Monist* 99 (2016): 352–71, 352.

aspirations and ambitions. Our political imagination can conjure up more desirable future states of affairs, but that does not mean we will improve our current situation by striving to realize such ideals. Conservatives often argue that the risks that we will actually make things worse, not better, are tangible.

In *Reflections on the Revolution in France*, Burke describes the significant and nimble intellectual task of being disposed to preserve but also possessing the ability to improve and reform as follows:

> At once to preserve and to reform is quite another thing. When the useful parts of an old establishment are kept, and what is superadded is to be fitted to what is retained, a vigorous mind, steady persevering attention, various powers of comparison and combination, and the resources of an understanding fruitful in expedients are to be exercised; they are to be exercised in a continued conflict with the combined force of opposite vices, with the obstinacy that rejects all improvement and the levity that is fatigued and disgusted with everything of which it is in possession.[35]

Oakeshott describes the foundational temperament of conservative thought as one that enjoys "what is available rather than wish for or look to something else: to delight in what is present rather than what was or may be."[36] He continues by noting that conservatives prefer "the familiar to the unknown," "the tried to the untried," "fact to mystery," "the actual to the possible," "the near to the distant," "the sufficient to the abundant," and so forth. The default setting for conservatives is thus one that is resistant to, or at least skeptical of, progressive social policies that may threaten to disrupt existing social institutions or the benefits of the status quo. Oakeshott argues that "innovation entails certain loss and possible gain, therefore, the onus of proof, to show that the proposed change may be expected to be on the whole beneficial, rests with the would-be innovator."[37]

---

35. Edmund Burke, *Reflections on the Revolution in France*, ed. L. G. Mitchell (Oxford: Oxford University Press, 1993), 169.

36. Oakeshott, *Rationalism in Politics*, 408.

37. Oakeshott, *Rationalism in Politics*, 411.

Understanding that conservatives begin from a mindset of "loss aversion" and skepticism about the potential benefits of social or technological innovation can help explain many of the contemporary disagreements that arise between progressives and conservatives, from issues like same-sex marriage and the welfare state to climate change and genetic engineering. I will briefly canvass how these diverse policy issues often face opposition from conservatives who have adopted the temperament Oakeshott articulates.

The family is a long-established social institution, and one that conservatives place a high priority on protecting. In the late twentieth and early twenty-first centuries many countries in the world moved in the direction of extending legal recognition of marriage to include same-sex couples. According to the Human Rights Campaign,[38] there are thirty-six countries in the world where same-sex marriage is legal, including Canada, Colombia, Finland, Spain, Taiwan, the United Kingdom, the United States, and Uruguay. The most compelling and commonly invoked argument for extending the legal recognition of marriage to include same-sex couples is an appeal to *equality*. Ralph Wedgwood articulates this argument as follows:

> The basic rationale for marriage lies in its serving certain legitimate and important interests of married couples. But many same-sex couples have the same interests, which marriage would serve in essentially the same way. So restricting marriage to opposite-sex couples is a denial of *equality*. There is no way of justifying this denial of equality without appealing to controversial conceptions of the good (such as the moral superiority of heterosexuality or the procreative family); and it is a basic principle of *liberalism* that the state should not promote, or justify its actions by appeal to, such controversial conceptions of the good. So the institution of marriage ought to be reformed as to allow same-sex couples to marry.[39]

---

38. HRC Foundation, "Marriage Equality Around the World," Human Rights Campaign, https://www.hrc.org/resources/marriage-equality-around-the-world, accessed February 19, 2024.

39. Ralph Wedgwood, "The Fundamental Argument for Same-Sex Marriage," *Journal of Political Philosophy* 7, no. 3 (1999): 225–42, 225.

There are many aspects of this equality-based argument for granting same-sex marriage that conservatives contest. The liberal premise that the government should not promote a conception of good (often referred to as a principle of *neutrality*) is one conservatives reject. For example, the contemporary conservative political theorist Robert George, in *Making Men Moral*, champions the perfectionist tradition of Aristotle and Saint Thomas Aquinas to argue that sound politics and good law are concerned with helping people live moral lives.[40] So part of the disagreement between some defenders and critics of same-sex marriage concerns the broader issue of what the legitimate functions of government are. There are more specific disagreements concerning the pros and cons of granting same-sex couples the same legal rights as opposite-sex couples.

Historically the status quo for legal recognition of marriage was only applied to opposite-sex couples. Following Oakeshott's sentiment that one ought to prefer the "familiar to the unknown" and worry that "innovation can result in losses," many conservatives thus oppose, or have serious reservations about, extending the legal rights of opposite-sex couples to same-sex couples. But what kinds of risks could extending the legal recognition of marriage to same-sex couples actually entail? What are the potential harms? Are those concerns empirically valid, or are they baseless fears or expressions of prejudice? To the critics of conservatism, especially the conservative opposition to same-sex marriage, a status quo bias toward tradition with respect to marriage is predicated on sexual prejudice versus empirically informed considerations of the actual likely benefits and harms of innovation in marriage laws.[41]

Fiscal conservatives often oppose the redistributive aspirations of socialism or even the welfare state on the grounds that such government interventions are predicated on the untried, the mysterious, or the unknown versus the traditional, actual, and tried ways of mitigating

---

40. Ralph George, *Making Men Moral: Civic Liberties and Public Morality* (Oxford: Clarendon Press, 1995).

41. See, for example, J. van der Toorn, J. T. Jost, D. J. Packer, S. Noorbaloochi, and J. J. Van Bavel, "In Defense of Tradition: Religiosity, Conservatism, and Opposition to Same-Sex Marriage in North America," *Personality and Social Psychology Bulletin* 43, no. 10 (2017): 1455–68.

poverty. Philanthropy and mutual aid among local community members, for example, have a long history of helping ameliorate some of the vulnerabilities of human suffering. Rather than supporting the welfare state and its ambitious aspirations of providing affordable housing, health care, education, and a livable income for all, many conservatives often champion the efficiency of smaller government and lower taxes, enabling businesses to hire more workers, which then enables workers to develop the virtues of self-sufficiency versus risk the poor becoming dependent on government assistance for their material needs.

The critics of conservatism maintain that its tendency to eschew government intervention in favor of highlighting the potential benefits of private property and market capitalism is predicated on a highly selective focus on the positives of the latter, and an unjustified skepticism about the former. Many countries in the world have implemented strong welfare-state protections for many decades. For example, Scandinavian countries such as Denmark, Sweden, and Norway are often recognized as exemplars that invest seriously in welfare-state initiatives to help provide a safety net for their society's most vulnerable. Many conservative pundits, in American politics for example, eschew comparisons with such countries, labeling them as "communist" or "socialist" failed experiments, or invoking American "exceptionalism" for why they would not be as successful in the American context (e.g., claiming that the United States is a much larger and more diverse country).

Black conservatives like Thomas Sowell and Booker T. Washington emphasize what they consider to be the actual and tried solutions to poverty and inequality, such as cultivating self-reliance rather than overtly political (e.g., civil disobedience) or statist solutions to racial inequality. In *Affirmative Action around the World: An Empirical Study*, Sowell argues that affirmative action or group preference policies have not had the empirical consequences their proponents believed they would have. The justification for such policies, in university admissions and the job market, is that this would help abate the effects of racial inequality. But the philosophical justification that such policies will help promote equality is incongruent with the actual impacts of such policies, contends Sowell. Unintended and undesired consequences have resulted from such policies. For example, Sowell notes that preferential policies have resulted in some members of the nonpreferred group redesignating themselves as part of the preferred group (e.g., Indigenous). He contends that this has occurred not only in the United States and Australia—where group preferential policies led to an increase in the number of people who used mixed ancestry to redesignate themselves—but also in China, Indonesia, Malaysia, and India. Sowell remarks:

> The spread of benefits from group to group not only dilutes those benefits—especially when more than half the population of the country becomes entitled to them, as in both India and the United States—it can also make the initial beneficiaries worse off after the terms of the competition are altered. For example, in the United States, where hiring and promotions decisions are subject to review by government agencies investigating discrimination, objective criteria may be used increasingly by employers for legal self-protection, even if the relevance of these criteria to the job is questionable. If these criteria are met more often by one of the preferred groups than by another—if white women have college degrees more than black men, for example—then one preferred group may be no better off, on net balance, than if the preferences did not exist. It is conceivable that they can be worse off.[42]

Critics of Sowell's argument, such as James Sterba, have taken issue with both the (im)precision of Sowell's definition of affirmative action and the adequacy of the prescriptions he draws from his empirical analysis of countries with very different histories, policies, and laws. Sterba defines affirmative action as "a policy of favoring qualified women or minority candidates over qualified men or nonminority candidates with the immediate goals of outreach, remedying discrimination, or achieving diversity, and the ultimate goals of attaining a color-blind (racially just) and a gender-free (sexually just) society."[43] Sterba contends that the affirmative action policies pursued by Sri Lanka and Nigeria, which involved

---

42. Thomas Sowell, *Affirmative Action around the World: An Empirical Study* (New Haven, CT: Yale University Press, 2004), 11–12.

43. James Sterba, "Review: Completing Thomas Sowell's Study of Affirmative Action and Then Drawing Different Conclusions," *Stanford Law Review* 57, no. 2 (2004): 657–93, 659.

the politically dominant groups enacting preferences for themselves (in Sri Lanka it was the Sinhalese over the Tamil minority, and in Nigeria it was the Hausa-Fulani over the Ibo tribe), do not give rise to empirical generalities that can yield sage prescriptions or insightful illuminations into affirmative action within America.

Is the conservative's inclination "to delight in what is present rather than what was or may be" illustrative of wisdom and a patient and considerate temperament? Or, on the contrary, is it symptomatic of an uncreative and unimaginative disposition that rationalizes the status quo and undermines the innovative thinking needed to transform societies and culture to a more equal future? How a political theory interprets both the past and present can have a dramatic impact on how it orients its aspirations for the future. The diverse historical political thinkers covered in this book are illustrative of the different ways political philosophers and thinkers have contemplated these issues.

Understanding the conservative disposition and temperament can also be instructive in helping explain the different stance many take on one of the most pressing societal challenges of the twenty-first century: *climate change*. Many conservatives are resistant to taking aggressive or costly collective action (e.g., "net zero," which means reducing greenhouse gas emissions to as close to zero as is feasible) to combat the harmful effects of climate change. As a political disposition that tends to focus on the near over the distant, it is not surprising that many take this perspective. For the conservative, it may seem more prudent and desirable to focus on increasing economic growth and prosperity now, which can help societies adapt to future climate change, versus forfeiting those benefits in the hopes that it will abate the risks of climate change. Climate change policies that aspire to intentionally alter the climate are often characterized by conservative opponents as the untried versus the tried.

The conservative status quo bias need not be construed as one highly reliant on utilizing energy that emits high levels of greenhouse gases. Some conservatives champion the development of new, cheaper forms of energy. But the prospect of undertaking some experimental form of "geoengineering," for example, such as stratospheric aerosol injection—which would involve the deployment of particles in the stratosphere to enhance reflection of incoming solar radiation[44]—is one that many conservatives would resist. It is a risky experiment that could result in unintended adverse outcomes, even potentially catastrophic consequences. As Oakeshott argues, for conservatives the onus of proof (of safety and efficacy) is on those championing innovation. The sage and safe temperate, argues Oakeshott, is the one that pursues "small and slow changes" to "large and sudden."[45] But this creates a serious problem when there is an urgency to redress the significant harms of global warming.

Conservative political thought encompasses a diverse array of thinkers, topics, and concerns. The weight that society ought to place on tradition and experience, versus progressive aspirations and appeals to reason, is a debate that continues to consume contemporary political life. To its critics, conservative political thought may appear as an archaic political temperament that often impedes redressing the injustices of the past and present. To its defenders, the conservative temperament is considered a vital salve to the often idealistic aspirations of those inclined to cavalierly disregard the importance of the wisdom of the past.

---

44. P. W. Keys, E. A. Barnes, N. S. Diffenbaugh, J. W. Hurrell, and C. M. Bell, "Potential for Perceived Failure of Stratospheric Aerosol Injection Deployment," *Proceedings of the National Academy of Sciences of the United States of America* 119, no. 40 (2022), e2210036119.

45. Oakeshott, *Rationalism in Politics*, 410.

CHAPTER 8

Feminist Political Thought

At various stages of this book we have highlighted the omission of the voices, experiences, and interests of women within the traditional canon of the history of Western political philosophy. From Plato's discussion of the Guardian class of his ideal society to Rousseau's differential treatment of the education of boys and girls, the inequality between men and women remained a marginalized topic of concern for most of the traditional, canonical political thinkers typically taught to undergraduates in political theory and philosophy courses for the past half a century. But the composition of the canon has been both scrutinized and revised in recent years, thanks in part to the increased prominence of feminist political philosophy and a more inclusive historical view of past thinkers. For example, in a recent volume on the social and political philosophy of Mary Wollstonecraft, the editors remark:

> Anyone glancing through the course reading lists at most universities, or browsing the bookshelves in an academic bookstore, might reasonably conclude that philosophy was something that was written historically only by men. . . . As the influence of feminist thinking has reshaped so much of the philosophical enquiry . . . this has allowed us to reassess, as well as rediscover, the unforgotten input that women have had.[1]

In *The Racial Contract* Mills describes an "epistemology of ignorance" that pervades the canon of Western political philosophy. This epistemology perpetuates cognitive distortions that blind us to social realities such as racial inequality. Furthermore, as Weiss notes, there is a gender

---

1. Sandrine Bergès and Alan Coffee, eds., *The Social and Political Philosophy of Mary Wollstonecraft* (Oxford: Oxford University Press, 2016), 2.

equivalent of Mills's point. Historically the narrative of what constituted the canon of Western political philosophy excluded female, as well as nonwhite political thinkers and philosophers.[2] So it is not surprising that, among traditional canonical (white, male) philosophers, concerns about the existence and persistence of patriarchy and racial inequality have been (alarmingly) absent. In this chapter we attempt to at least partially redress this "epistemology of ignorance" by covering three different female political thinkers, and doing so in a fashion that also permits us to integrate feminism with concerns for racial equality. The latter is also addressed, more substantively, in the chapter on Black political thought, and, to some extent, in the discussion of Black conservatism in the previous chapter.

This chapter will examine three important historical feminist thinkers: the Italian-born poet and writer Christine de Pizan (1364–1430), the English liberal feminist Mary Wollstonecraft (1759–97), and the American Black feminist Anna Cooper (1858–1964). Engaging with these historical feminist thinkers will also permit us to examine other topics related to contemporary feminist political theory, such as the slogan "The personal is political," gender representation in democratic politics, the ethics of care, and intersectionality.

Christine de Pizan on Misogyny

Born in Venice in 1364, Pizan moved to France as a child and remained there for the rest of her life, living mostly in Paris. France during the fourteenth century was a feudal society, hierarchal and religious. Pizan was born during a period of great economic instability and insecurity, exacerbated by famines, prolonged military conflict with England (the Hundred Years War [1337–1453]), incompetent governance, and popular uprisings.

Married at age fifteen, mother to three children (the third died at a young age) and a widow by age twenty-five, Pizan was a fierce critic of the social and political life of France during her lifetime. She is often considered a "first" in at least two noteworthy respects. Pizan is regarded "as the

---

2. Penny A. Weiss, *Canon Fodder: Historical Women Political Thinkers* (University Park: Pennsylvania State University Press, 2009), 31.

first person in France, male or female, to have earned a living by her pen."[3] She is also considered the first feminist, at least in the Western tradition of political thought. In her book *The Second Sex*, twentieth-century philosopher Simone de Beauvoir describes Pizan as the first woman who took up her pen to defend her sex.[4]

Pizan's writings address the oppression of women and confront the misogynistic culture that she witnessed and experienced in her day-to-day life. Commenting on the way men perceived women as inferior, Pizan remarks: "One day, a man criticized my desire for knowledge, saying that it was inappropriate for a woman to be learned, as it was so rare, to which I replied that it was even less fitting for a man to be ignorant, as it was so common."[5] In addition to an insightful intellect, Pizan also possessed a sharp sense of humor.

> She was a woman in a man's world, an Italian at a French court, the daughter of a civil servant in a world structured by social class. The quintessential outsider, she wrote a dozen political treatises that dared to instruct the ruling classes on how to govern themselves and their kingdoms. Her corpus of political works includes five works designed to educate the male ruling class, commonly known as mirrors for princes, two works expressly for princesses and a treatise on warfare.[6]

Similar to Julia Annas's critical engagement with Plato's *Republic* (see chapter 2) and Plato's proposal that women could be philosopher rulers, some have questioned how far Pizan's arguments go in terms of embodying a consistent and robust emancipatory feminist ethic.[7] Like ancient

---

3. Tracy Adams, "Christine de Pizan," *French Studies* 71, no. 3 (July 2017): 388–400, 388.

4. Simone de Beauvoir, *The Second Sex*, trans. H. M. Pashley (New York: Knopf, 1953), 128.

5. Christine de Pizan, "L'Avision Christine," in *The Writings of Christine de Pizan*, ed. Charity Cannon Willard (New York: Persea, 1994), 16.

6. Kate Langdon Forhan, *The Political Theory of Christine de Pizan* (New York: Routledge, 2002), vi.

7. See, for example, Sheila Delany, "'Mothers to Think Back Through': Who Are They? The Ambiguous Case of Christine de Pizan," in *Medieval Literary Politics: Shapes of Ideology* (Manchester: Manchester University Press, 1990), 88–103.

Greece, medieval Europe was a historical context where aspirations for the legal and political equality of all, either men or women, were beyond the scope of political imagination. But like all the historical thinkers we address in this book, whose ideas were shaped and limited by their time and geography, it is important to understand that their critical engagement with the challenges and predicaments of their own time will not always align with our twenty-first-century moral sensibilities and political aspirations. Furthermore, we will not have time to survey Pizan's voluminous contributions to poetry and political thought.

In defending Pizan as a champion of women, Brown-Grant argues that Pizan's achievement lay "not in her anticipation of the strategies which later feminists would employ, but rather in her critical engagement with the dominant ideology of her day."[8] The dominant ideology of her day was misogyny. In the first chapter of Book I of *The Book of the City of Ladies*, Pizan describes how she became motivated to write the book. She describes coming to the realization that, in all the books she had read, men portrayed women in damning terms. She remarks: "It is all manner of philosophers, poets and orators too numerous to mention, who all seem to speak with one voice and are unanimous in their view that female nature is wholly given up to vice."[9] Pizan, portraying herself as the central character of the book, also named Christine (hereafter referred to as Christine, meaning the character in the book), describes how she began to examine her own behavior, and that of the women she knew, and she found no evidence for the negative view of female nature and the habits that men attributed to women in their writings. Christine notes her thoughts on trying to make sense of this predicament with her theological belief in an all good and powerful deity:

> With a deep sigh, I called out to God: "Oh Lord, how can this be? Unless I commit an error of faith, I cannot doubt that you, in your infinite wisdom and goodness, could make anything that wasn't good. Didn't you yourself create woman especially and endow her with all the qualities that you wished her to have? How could you

---

8. Rosalind Brown-Grant, introduction to Christine de Pizan, *The Book of the City of Ladies*, trans. Rosalind Brown-Grant (London: Penguin, 1999), xxxv.

9. Christine de Pizan, *The Book of the City of Ladies*, 6.

possibly have made a mistake in anything? Yet here stand women not simply accused, but already judged, sentenced, and convicted! I just cannot understand this contradiction."[10]

Christine then recounts how her prayers were answered, as the three daughters—Reason, Rectitude, and Justice—appear and speak to her, informing her that she is to build a sturdy and walled city open only to women of virtue, those worthy of praise with a good reputation. "To those lacking in virtue, its gates will remain forever closed."[11] The function of this city of virtuous women is to protect them from those who would attack them.

> The female sex has been left defenceless for a long time now, like an orchard without a wall, and bereft of a champion to take up arms in order to protect it. Indeed, this is because those trusty knights who should by right defend women have been negligent in their duty and lacking in vigilance, leaving womankind open to attack from all sides. It's no wonder women have been the losers in this war against them since the envious slanders and vicious traitors who criticize them have been allowed to aim all manner of weapons at their defenceless targets.[12]

Women cannot rely on men to protect them, argues Pizan. Christine describes how Lady Reason appears and explains to her that Nature does not slander women; rather, such slander comes from men. But such slander is not part of a deity's wishes. Lady Reason explains the multitude of reasons why men are misogynistic: some men have criticized women out of good intentions—to prevent those men who have fallen for depraved women from doing so—but in the process have attacked all women; some other men attack women out of sin—they are overwhelmed with sheer envy, or have "bitter and twisted minds" and take delight in slandering others, or they mimic the literary techniques of writers who

---

10. Christine de Pizan, *The Book of the City of Ladies*, 7.
11. Christine de Pizan, *The Book of the City of Ladies*, 11.
12. Christine de Pizan, *The Book of the City of Ladies*, 11.

came before them, perpetuating the slander against women. But Lady Justice does not characterize all men in this negative light. She remarks:

> Yet, thank goodness, not all old men are full of depravity and rotten to the core like a leper. There are many other fine, decent ones whose wisdom and virtue have been nourished by me and whose words reflect their good character, since they speak in an honourable and sober fashion. Such men detest all kinds of wrongdoing and slander. Thus, rather than attacking and defaming individual sinners, male or female, they condemn all sins in general. Their advice to others is to avoid vice, pursue virtue and stick to the straight and narrow.[13]

Having been widowed at a young age, Pizan was personally aware of how society marginalized the needs and status of women. As a widow "she tried to recover her husband's unpaid salary, the sums of money owed to him, and the principal of funds invested with an unscrupulous merchant for her children's futures."[14] Her personal experiences as a mother and widow inform her political theory.

The economic prospects and social status of a woman in the late Middle Ages living in Europe was linked to her husband (who was considered her legal guardian). With high rates of mortality caused by risk factors such as infectious disease, it was not uncommon for married women with children to become widows at some point in their lives. Widows were particularly vulnerable because they would not receive equal treatment by the law in protection of the family property and wealth after the husband passed. Thus Pizan argues that widows ought to be considered a vulnerable group.

> When advising widows, Christine uses forceful terminology to describe the injury and domination widows are bound to encounter on account of their sex. . . . Christine treats widows as a marginalized group who should be protected by the law and by contemporary legislation. She argues that certain rights are

---

13. Christine de Pizan, *The Book of the City of Ladies*, 19.
14. Forhan, *Political Theory of Christine de Pizan*, 15.

also applicable outside legal proceedings and the courtroom. The right to defend oneself against oppression is based on the shared humanity of all women and all men.[15]

The virtue of justice, for Pizan, had to have a procedural component, an Aristotelian sentiment that was prevalent in the Middle Ages. The subservient treatment of women in both the legal arena and society more generally meant that the administration of procedural justice was compromised. Like Pizan, the feminist political theorist Mary Wollstonecraft also emphasized the unequal treatment women received, especially in education, and their economic dependency on men and the institution of marriage.

Wollstonecraft and "Nature versus Nurture"

Mary Wollstonecraft was born in 1759 in London, England. Understanding some of her personal background will help explain why she addresses the concerns she does, such as the importance of education, and love and friendship in marriage. Like Hobbes and Locke, Wollstonecraft lived through a time of turbulent political upheaval, and she traveled in France during the French Revolution. Her ideas were shaped by the historical context in which she was living, a context that was deeply patriarchal. While European countries in the eighteenth century were hierarchical along lines of social class (e.g., nobility and peasantry), they were also hierarchical among lines of both race (which provided a justification for the transatlantic slave trade) and sex. Women were considered subservient to men, as was evident in formal political decision-making (an elite position, and one predominately occupied by men), societal attitudes about marriage and the family (e.g., that a woman should marry, become a mother, and maintain a household), and education.

Wollstonecraft left home at age nineteen, after having been raised in a troubled family household. In eighteenth-century England women were

---

15. Ilse Paakkinen, "Rights and Needs: Widows as a Protected Group in Christine de Pizan's Thought," in *Rights at the Margins: Historical, Legal and Philosophical Perspectives* ed. Virpi Mäkinen, Jonathan Robinson, Pamela Slotte, and Heikki Haara (Leiden: Brill, 2020), 150.

expected to marry, as there were very few occupations available to women. This financial dependency on men was detrimental to both women and men, as well as the relationships between them, argues Wollstonecraft. She contends that god had given all humans (male and female alike) the power to reason, but society only permitted boys to receive the education necessary to cultivate the dispositions and virtues of independence and reason.

As a teacher Wollstonecraft was able to witness firsthand the different educations young boys and girls received. Her own turbulent personal life, which included her father squandering the family inheritance, her having a daughter out of wedlock with the American Gilbert Imlay, and her attempted suicide when he left her, provided her with insight into the dysfunction of patriarchal marriage and family life. At age thirty-eight Wollstonecraft married the philosophical anarchist William Godwin. She died that same year while giving birth to their daughter Mary Wollstonecraft Godwin (better known later as Mary Shelley, author of the book *Frankenstein*).

Wollstonecraft found the inequalities of her time and culture deeply problematic, in particular the inequality between men and women. As with the defense of the divine right of kings, most of Wollstonecraft's contemporaries simply assumed that the inequalities between men and women were natural rather than being socially created and morally indefensible. Wollstonecraft was aware that this problem of a moral blind spot to the pervasiveness of gender inequality extended to both women and men of her time. "The oppressed women fail to see the appeals of equality and liberty; they are not capable of doing so because their reason is underdeveloped or atrophied."[16]

Engaging with Wollstonecraft as a political theorist brings to the fore one of the most contested debates in the social sciences, the so-called nature versus nurture debate. Males and females share many common characteristics (both can love; both get angry; both require food and shelter; both can reason, etc.). But they also have some differences. Some of those differences are explained by biology (defined here as sex differences),

---

16. Sandrine Bergès, "Why Women Hug Their Chains: Wollstonecraft and Adaptive Preferences," *Utilitas* 23, no. 1 (2011): 72–87, 79.

but many other differences are caused by the culture and laws of society (defined here as gender differences).

To differentiate along lines of sex is to identify specific biological differences—both internal and external bodily characteristics—between male and female, though the classification is more complex than this binary distinction.[17] Biological sex and how it relates to gender is more complicated than having XX or XY chromosomes, or being born with gonads or ovaries. *Transgender* is an umbrella term that describes people who identify with a gender that is incongruent or different from the sex assigned to them at birth; *nonbinary* describes those who feel their gender identity is outside or in between male and female identities (e.g., a person who experiences both identities or neither).[18]

Many different scientific disciplines study the binary sex differences among different species, focusing on things like physical differences (e.g., appearance, size, strength), behavioral differences (e.g., aggression, mate selection), and biochemical differences (e.g., hormonal and genetic differences). In peacocks, for example, there are observable physical differences between males and females in size and in the colors of their plumage. There are also behavioral differences, as only male peacocks spread their wings and dance in an attempt to attract female mates.

When it comes to humans, there are also observable biological differences between sexes. Male humans are, on average, larger than females. On average males also have a lower vocal frequency and stronger grip strength than females. Males are typically also more violent and have a lower life expectancy. Males possess both X and Y chromosomes and can remain fertile from puberty to at least the ninth decade of life. These biological differences of sex can be influenced by environment, but they are not determined by culture as gender identity is.

Gender is a *social construction*—though, as Judith Lober notes, "gender is so pervasive that in our society we think it is bred into our genes."[19]

---

17. The Editors, "This Is Not a Women's Issue," *Scientific American*, September 2017, 30.

18. G. Spizzirri, R. Eufrásio, M. C. P. Lima et al., "Proportion of People Identified as Transgender and Non-binary Gender in Brazil," *Scientific Reports* 11, no. 2240 (2021), 11176.

19. Judith Lorber, *Paradoxes of Gender* (New Haven, CT: Yale University Press, 1994), 13.

Gendered stereotypes concerning identities like "masculine" and "feminine," for example, are created and perpetuated by culture. While biology may determine who can and cannot give birth to offspring, culture influences who can and cannot take parental leave from their career after the child is born. Similarly, societal attitudes also influence the typical division of unpaid work within the home, such as cooking and cleaning. If young boys and girls are taught that some work is typically done by females (e.g., "feminine" = child-rearing and domestic chores) and other work by males (e.g., "masculine" = work outside the house and voting), then this will influence the norms and laws of society. Patriarchy persists because of this interdependent dynamic between societal attitudes and formal legal and political institutions.

It is this nature versus nurture debate concerning gender that Wollstonecraft seeks to undermine in the eighteenth century. It is culture, not biology, that causes gender inequality. The education young girls receive (or do not receive) growing up, for example, influences the societal roles that will be real options for them later in life as adults. For Wollstonecraft and other feminist philosophers, the family is a *political* institution, and as such political values such as equality ought to apply to that institution and the relationships involved between husband and wife, and between parents and children. Marriage should be a form of friendship between two people, entailing free choice, equality, and mutual respect. But the traditional view of the family, of which Wollstonecraft is very critical in the eighteenth century, actually created poor wives and dangerous mothers because it did not facilitate the rational development of women. Instead it encouraged women to be superficial by emphasizing so much the preoccupation with their physical beauty—to attract the attention of men—rather than their own development as a well-rounded person.

In the eighteenth century women had to get married to a man to attain some level of economic security, prestige, and influence in society (and sadly this is still true in many parts of the world today). In effect, women in such circumstances are economically dependent on men. In England in the eighteenth century very few occupations were available to women. Being a teacher, like Wollstonecraft, was one exception. This meant that marriage was a relationship of necessity for most women, but not for men.

Gender inequality is also reflected in the phrases often used to describe the difference in societal attitudes about men and women and their relationship status or sexual behavior. A single man can be described as a "bachelor," whereas a single woman can be described with the negative connotation of a "spinster." A promiscuous man might be referred to as a "player" or "stud," in contrast to the derogatory terms commonly used to describe a woman who engages in the same behavior. These different social expectations and norms meant that marriage was a choice for men, but an economic necessity for women.

The source of the inequalities between men and women stemmed, argues Wollstonecraft, from the different education they received from a young age. Females were trained in what she describes as the "art of pleasing": learning how to flirt, display outward obedience, and emphasize their external beauty. Females were taught to always seek the attention of men, a consuming preoccupation that, when taken to its logical conclusion, contends Wollstonecraft, only created unfaithful partners. A system that encouraged flirtation, a fixation on external beauty, and gaining the attention of men creates alluring mistresses rather than women who could be equal partners in marriage.

By contrast, males are raised to be rational and independent. Women were not allowed to develop their rational potential, and instead were treated as trivial creatures concerned only with physical appearance. In effect, women were treated as children themselves, and thus not competent to raise their own children. In *A Vindication of the Rights of Woman* Wollstonecraft argues:

> Taught from their infancy that beauty is woman's sceptre, the mind shapes itself to the body, and, roaming round its gilt cage, only seeks to adorn its prison. Men have various employments and pursuits which engage their attention, and give a character to the opening mind; but women, confined to one, and having their thoughts constantly directed to the most insignificant part of themselves, seldom extend their views beyond the triumph of the hour.[20]

In chapter 5 on John Locke we addressed Carole Pateman's argument against consent-based views that focused only on political obligation and the state, but ignored what goes on within the family. If political

---

20. Mary Wollstonecraft, *A Vindication of the Rights of Woman with Strictures on Political and Moral Subject* (London: J. Johnson, 1792), 39.

inequality among citizens is objectionable, then surely the arbitrary use of power by husbands over their wives and children must also be objectionable. Yet liberalism remained silent on the inequality within the family. Wollstonecraft aspires to redress this neglect by emphasizing the importance of power within the family.

In *A Vindication of the Rights of Woman* Wollstonecraft notes that she considers independence as "the grand blessing of life, the basis of every virtue."[21] Women living in England during the eighteenth century, denied access to adequate education and employment opportunities, lacked independence and generally had to marry if they hoped to attain some financial security and social prestige. For Wollstonecraft the concern for broader political independence, such as the independence French revolutionaries sought from the arbitrary rule of monarchs during the French Revolution (started in 1789), parallels the feminist concern for the use of arbitrary force within the family.

In "Freedom as Independence: Mary Wollstonecraft and the Grand Blessing of Life," Alan Coffee argues that freedom as independence is an essential ingredient in successful and flourishing relationships in three respects. First, it is an egalitarian tool for all persons, regardless of sex, in all aspects of life—the personal domain (family) as well as economic and political domains. Second, "independence is a flexible ideal that allows for both sexes to interact and participate socially on differentiated terms that reflect their respective outlooks and interests."[22] Third, to ensure social independence can be maintained in the future it is imperative that both men and women can provide input into the societal arrangements.

The Personal Is Political

Wollstonecraft's emphasis on the importance of power within the family became an integral element of twentieth-century feminism, encapsulated in the motto "The personal is political." In *Justice, Gender, and the Family* the feminist Susan Moller Okin provides a concise analysis of how the personal is political.[23]

---

21. Wollstonecraft, *A Vindication of the Rights of Woman*, 5.

22. Alan Coffee, "Freedom as Independence: Mary Wollstonecraft and the Grand Blessing of Life," *Hypatia* 29, no. 4 (2014): 908–24, 910.

23. Susan Okin, *Justice, Gender, and the Family* (New York: Basic Books, 1989).

First, Okin argues that power dynamics exist within the family, thus making it political. When the institution of marriage treats a woman as the property of her husband, for example, this permits him to wield power over her. This might entail inflicting physical, emotional, or sexual abuse on his wife without any fear of criminal repercussions, or being the sole authority for familial decisions regarding finances and other matters.

Second, the family is the result of political decisions. Laws concerning marriage and divorce were enacted and enforced by deliberative bodies that did not include the fair representation of women. Historically such laws were shaped by hierarchical (e.g., monarchial) and religious authorities. While women were equal stakeholders in the institution of marriage, in that its laws and norms impact both their lives and those of their husbands, women were not consulted, let alone permitted to shape or veto, the patriarchal practices and laws adopted in the world's cultures. All such political decisions were made only by men.

Third, Okin argues that "the personal is political" in that domestic life is where most of our early socialization takes place. Wollstonecraft emphasizes this point by drawing attention to the "art of pleasing" that young girls were taught from a young age. Girls were "taught from infancy that beauty is woman's sceptre." In contrast, boys were raised with a wide spectrum of employment opportunities and pursuits available to them. The traits of "masculine" and "feminine" are often inculcated in the socialization that takes place within the family. Sons are encouraged to be assertive and independent, pursuing their goals and life ambitions. Daughters, meanwhile, are encouraged to learn how to acquiesce to others (especially men) and focus primarily on the goals of marriage and having and raising a family.

The fourth way in which Okin argues "the personal is political" is that the division of labor within most families raises psychological as well as practical barriers against women in all other spheres. The prospects for women becoming elected or chosen as politicians, judges, news anchors, and so on are influenced by how women are perceived in such a culture. A culture where women are not considered equals to men is one where women will face significant barriers, even if only informal ones, to succeeding in such professions. If the traits of being rational and impartial are characterized as distinctively male traits, for example, then women will have a difficult time being elected as a politician or appointed as a judge.

Political Representation

To redress the corrosive legacy gender inequality has had on democratic institutions and practices (e.g., political parties and elections), many countries have adopted gender quotas for political parties as a way of accelerating women's political participation. The idea of representative government is that the interests of all should be represented by the elected officials. But if most or all of the politicians are male, when approximately 50 percent of the population is female, such a political process cannot be described as genuinely inclusive and representative.

Countries have adopted different measures to redress the problem of low female political representation, depending on both the specifics of their election process and the degree of gender inequality prevalent in the society. For example, in countries that have among the highest levels of gender representation within their elected political representatives (such as Sweden and Norway, both with approximately 45 percent of parliamentary seats held by women), they have relied on voluntary political party quotas. Other countries have legislated gender quotas or adopted reserved seats. Angola, Brazil, Mexico, and South Africa, for example, all have legislated candidate quotas, and Sudan, Niger, and Afghanistan have reserved seats. Afghanistan's 2004 Constitution stipulates that seats in the Lower House are to be reserved for women so that there are at least two women for each of the thirty-four provinces.

Jane Mansbridge states that the case for gender quotas rests on three distinct arguments:

1. an argument that descriptive representation is substantively and symbolically important, even necessary, for the descriptively represented group and for the polity as a whole;
2. an argument that a group's lower than proportional representation in a representative assembly has been caused by some form of inappropriate discrimination against that group; and
3. an argument that quotas are the most effective way in practice to achieve descriptive representation.[24]

---

24. Jane Mansbridge, "Quota Problems: Combating the Dangers of Essentialism," *Politics and Gender* 1, no. 4 (2005): 622–38, 622.

One line of concern that Mansbridge addresses concerning gender quotas comes from what she calls "essentialism": "the conviction that the individuals represented through quotas have some essential traits that help define them and that render them unable to be represented adequately by those without such traits."[25] If the argument for gender quotas was predicated on essentialism, as opposed to the aspiration to redress the inappropriate discrimination of the group from representative assemblies, it would face the objection that it imposes rigid identity markers that could make the idea of a representative democracy conceptually incoherent.

For example, if men are said not to be capable of representing the interests of women because they do not have the same lived experiences as women, how can politicians with more education be said to represent the interests of those with lower levels of formal education? Taken further, this essentialist line of reasoning might ask if we could expect elected representatives who are Christian to genuinely represent the interests of atheists or Muslims. Extended further, it could be applied to sexual orientation, race, disability, and so on. The essentialist reasoning thus threatens the very notion of "representative democracy."

Mansbridge responds to this objection by arguing that gender quotas should be instituted without encouraging essentialism. "The belief that there is some 'essence' of womanness or femininity, blackness or negritude, that members of the group have and that is not accessible to an outsider, reinforces group stereotypes from both without and within."[26] She continues: "The best way to fight the reification of essentialism that quotas inevitably suggest is to reinforce constantly the ways in which the great differences in existing systems of representation derive from historical and structural biases."[27] In other words, the justification for adopting gender quotas has more to do with overcoming the exclusionary legacies of patriarchy than it does with claims that only other members of a particular group can be said to authentically represent the interests of that group.

Still, some feminists have argued that there are important differences between men and women, especially with respect to their moral

---

25. Mansbridge, "Quota Problems," 623.

26. Mansbridge, "Quota Problems," 630.

27. Mansbridge, "Quota Problems," 633.

orientations. The psychologist Carol Gilligan makes this argument in her influential 1982 book *In a Different Voice*,[28] which we shall now consider.

The Ethics of Care

Carol Gilligan is an American psychologist who studied with the psychologist Lawrence Kohlberg. Kohlberg developed his insights from the child development psychologist Jean Piaget. Piaget was one of the first psychologists to systematically study human cognitive development. For Kohlberg, moral development "is understood as a movement to higher more abstract and universal moral principles which regulate the moral thinking and action of the individual."[29] In the early stages of our moral development, Kohlberg contends that we simply internalize the morality imposed on us by authority figures. We learn that certain actions, like those that contravene the wishes of our parents or a teacher, bring about the negative consequences of punishment. Conversely, behaviors that comply with the directives of others sometimes bring the rewards of praise. During this preconventional stage of our moral development, morality is purely instrumental (egoism). We identify things as morally "bad" when they bring about negative consequences for us through punishment. And the same is true about good actions and their rewards.

Kohlberg's next level of moral development involves our shifting from self-interest to relationships with other people and social systems. During this stage of moral development we internalize the rules of various groups and the government and adopt a broader perspective than just our own self-interest. We can see certain behaviors and actions as good or bad from this social system perspective. Finally, Kohlberg maintains that our understanding of morality is developed at a more abstract level, one that goes beyond just our society. This principled level of moral

---

28. Carol Gilligan, *In a Different Voice: Psychological Theory and Women's Development* (Cambridge: Harvard University Press, 1982).

29. Iordanis Kavathatzopoulos, "Kohlberg and Piaget: Differences and Similarities," *Journal of Moral Education* 20, no. 1 (1991): 47–54, 47.

development, though a stage of development some never attain, allows us to see morality as universal in application, removed from our understanding of our own society.

Gilligan's argument is developed in response to what she sees as the problems with Kohlberg's (and Jean Piaget's) account of moral development. Gilligan notes that after spending a decade listening to people talk about morality and themselves, she noticed that people spoke in two different voices or modes of describing the relationship between self and other. More specifically, Gilligan argues that she observed in women a distinctive mode of thinking about relationships and morality, a mode of thinking that was not represented in the psychological theorizing by Kohlberg and Piaget. Gilligan critiqued these developmental psychologists and others for equating male development with child development. According to Gilligan, male and female psychological perspectives are different. The male moral orientation is a justice-based ethic typically framed in terms of right, fairness, and obligation. The justice-based orientation typical of males, claims Gilligan, stems from a life orientation that prioritizes individuation and the separateness of persons.

The male-oriented mode of moral reasoning Gilligan describes is arguably most apparent in the most prominent twentieth-century theory of justice, John Rawls's theory of "justice as fairness."[30] Rawls advances an account of justice that attempts to overcome what he considers the major shortcoming of the collectivist perspective of utilitarianism: its failure to recognize the "separateness of persons." That means that justice dictates that individuals have rights, and that these rights cannot be violated, even when such violations would improve the overall welfare of society. The main theoretical device Rawls employs to canvass the details of his account of justice as fairness is a hypothetical choice situation called "the original position." This is a choice position where the contracting parties are denied basic information about their identity (e.g., social class, natural talents, sex, etc.) and decide on the principles to govern society's basic institutions by asking which principles would maximize their level of what Rawls calls "primary goods" (e.g., rights and liberties, income and wealth) in this original position.

---

30. John Rawls, *A Theory of Justice* (Cambridge, MA: Harvard University Press, 1971).

Presenting the male mode of moral reasoning as "the" impartial or defensible mode of moral reasoning devalues what Gilligan contends is the feminine mode of moral reasoning. The latter moral mode of reasoning, "which reflects the cumulative knowledge of human relationships, evolves around a central insight, the self and others are interdependent."[31] *The ethic of care* is thus a mode of reasoning oriented toward contextuality and empathy for others, in contrast to Rawls's emphasis on "mutual disinterest," rights, impartiality, and universality.

Some feminists have been cautious to embrace Gilligan's gendered distinction between the ethic of justice and care because it risks reinforcing gendered norms. For example, in a patriarchal society women are burdened with a greater share of unpaid domestic labor in the home (e.g., caring for children, an aging parent, etc.), a practice that might be reinforced by appealing to an ethic of care that maintains it is simply part of female nature to be more compassionate and caring than men. There is also skepticism about how distinct the moral types of personality Gilligan canvasses are, at least along gendered lines, and perhaps conceptually as well. Finally, some feminists have resisted the tendency to reduce feminism, and the experience of women, to one unified voice. This has led to the rise of intersectionality, which we now turn to as we consider the ideas of the American Black feminist Anna Cooper.

Anna Cooper

Anna Cooper (1859–1964) was born in North Carolina to a mother who had been enslaved. Like both Christine de Pizan and Mary Wollstonecraft, Cooper was well aware of the ills of the social inequalities—both racial and gender inequalities—that existed in her time. In her book *A Voice from the South* Cooper gives expression to life experiences that were typically ignored and marginalized in the United States after the Civil War. Cooper maintains that the exclusion of people because of their sex, race, or class eroded the sense of community that is foundational to a

---

31. Carol Gilligan, *In a Different Voice: Psychological Theory and Women's Development* (Cambridge, MA: Harvard University Press, 1982), 74.

healthy society. Thus she believes it is imperative that the voice of those on the margins of society should be amplified, which she does in her own political writings.

Cooper was a strong advocate for the education of Black women and spent her life as a teacher and principal. She received her PhD, with a thesis on the topic of slavery, from the Sorbonne in Paris at age sixty-seven. In the section of *A Voice from the South* titled "Has America a Race Problem; If So, How Can It Best Be Solved?" Cooper identifies two types of peace. The first type of peace is achieved through suppression and domination by eliminating one faction. Cooper draws an analogy between peace among intimate partners in the family to show how even in our primary relationships, unhealthy types of peace can be manifest. She remarks:

> A harmless looking man was once asked how many there were in his family. "Ten," he replied grimly; "my wife's a one and I am a zero." In that family there was harmony, to be sure, but it was a harmony of a despotism—it was the quiet of a muzzled mouth, the smouldering peace of a volcano crusted over.[32]

In this type of marriage the husband has no voice, and any peace such a relationship has achieved is only at the expense of the oppression of the husband. We can extrapolate from this example of an intimate relationship to society as a whole. When the voice and interests of one group in society are marginalized, because of their race or gender, this is also symptomatic of suppression and domination.

The second, authentic and lasting, way of achieving peace, argues Cooper, is through "the proper adjustment of living, active forces." This peace is achieved through the motivation of hope and the vision and realization of equality. Like Wollstonecraft, Cooper believes that important political parallels can be drawn between the relationships within the family and those in society more generally. Domination must be abated in both domains.

---

32. Anna Julia Cooper, *A Voice from the South* [1892] (Bolton, ON: Graphyco, 2020), 85.

Cooper asks the question "Who are Americans?" The common answer, she replies, is one of exclusion. She notes the attitude common among her contemporaries in the late nineteenth century:

> America for Americans! This is the white man's country! The Chinese must go, shrieks the exclusionist. Exclude the Italians! Colonize the Blacks in Mexico or deport them to Africa. Lynch, suppress, drive out, kill out! America for Americans![33]

Cooper argues that conflict in America was there from the very beginning. There has always been one party, race, or belief contending for supremacy in America. One group is identified as the "home group" and another group as "the strangers." Cooper notes that it is the Indigenous peoples of America that have the strongest claim to being called "Americans":

> The red men used to be the owner of the soil,—but they are about to be pushed over into the Pacific Ocean. They, perhaps, have the best right to call themselves "Americans" by law of primogeniture. They are at least the oldest inhabitants of whom we can at present identify any traces. . . . The fact is this nation was foreordained to conflict in its incipiency. Its elements were predestined from their birth to an irrepressible clash followed by the stable equilibrium of opposition. Exclusive possession belongs to no one. There was never a point in history when it did.[34]

This last point stands in sharp contrast to the idealizing assumptions of John Locke's theory of the social contract, especially the initial acquisition of property. Rather than highlight a counterfactual history of initial property acquisition, Cooper's political theory takes *real history* seriously, along with its conflict and injustices. A genuinely civil society is thus antithetical to the supremacy of any one group or faction. The interests of all must be considered. As Cooper puts it: "All interests must be consulted, all claims conciliated."[35] Cooper's political theory abates the

---

33. Cooper, *A Voice from the South*, 93.
34. Cooper, *A Voice from the South*, 93.
35. Cooper, *A Voice from the South*, 93.

type of "epistemology of ignorance" that Charles Mills (1997) contends has pervaded white political philosophy. While Rousseau and Locke both appeal to equality in their political writings and aspirations, their political imagination could not transcend the grips of the sexism and racism of their time.

Intolerance and inequality are impediments to the realization of an inclusive and equal society. Cooper thus argues for an inclusive vision of democratic governance, one that transcends the exclusionary practices of classism, racism, and sexism.

> Where a hundred free forces are lustily clamoring for recognition and each wrestling mightily for the mastery, individual tyrannies must inevitably be chiselled down, individual bigotries worn smooth and malleable, individual prejudices either obliterated or concealed.... The will of the majority must rule because no class, no family, no individual has ever been able to prove sufficient political legitimacy to impose their yoke on the country.[36]

Like Rousseau's appeal to the general will and democratic rule, Cooper rejects the legitimacy of a political community predicated on exclusionary historical hierarchies. But her diagnosis of these inequalities is much more expansive than that posited by Rousseau. Racial and gender biases and discrimination, and not simply those stemming from social class, also undermine the ideals of democratic self-government.

In *Canon Fodder: Historical Women Political Thinkers* Penny Weiss argues that, for Cooper, there are three impediments, or locations of resistance, to equality and community.[37] The first source of resistance is psychological: our fear of change. In the late nineteenth century the prospect of women entering universities and the workforce was met with fear and resistance as this presented a radical break from the traditional beliefs people had about the role of women. Likewise, in the twentieth century many other societal attitudes were challenged, such as segregation on buses, in pools, and in education; interracial marriages; and same-sex marriage. To make progress on each of these issues, people had to overcome their fear about what such

---

36. Cooper, *A Voice from the South*, 93–94.

37. Weiss, *Canon Fodder*, 94.

changes might entail. In chapter 7 we examined conservatism in greater detail and considered why theorists like Edmund Burke championed giving a primacy to tradition and custom over progressive ideals.

A second location of resistance that Cooper identifies is society's admiration of the dominant masculine traits epitomized in bullies and prizefighters over feminine traits such as being lovers of mercy. The latter are considered weak, argues Cooper. This domination of masculine qualities constrains the transformative potential of the current political landscape because democratic community requires a concern with aiding those currently marginalized in society.

Finally, the third location of resistance that Weiss notes in Cooper's writings is the resistance that resides within women themselves. Cooper argues that even though society is patriarchal, women do have power—often wielded in ways that further undermine equality. White women, for example, often wield power to more deeply entrench racial and social divisions. An affluent white woman might look down on other women, such as a servant the family employs to prepare meals and clean the house, because of their race and/or social class. Such prejudices must be overcome if substantive progress toward a more equal future is to be realized. Cooper's insight about the ways in which different forms of inequality are interdependent, such as those that arise from race, gender, and class, has become a central feature of contemporary feminist analyses that employ the concept of intersectionality.

Intersectionality

One critical framework of contemporary feminist political theory is known as intersectionality. This approach was first employed by Cooper and then refined and named by more contemporary feminist scholars such as Kimberlé Crenshaw. "Intersectionality was introduced in the late 1980s as a heuristic term to focus attention on the vexed dynamics of difference and the solidarities of sameness in the context of antidiscrimination and social movement politics."[38] In her seminal 1989 paper on the topic,

---

38. Sumi Cho, Kimberlé Williams Crenshaw, and Leslie McCall, "Toward a Field of Intersectionality Studies: Theory, Applications, and Praxis," *Signs* 38, no. 4 (2013): 785–810, 787.

Crenshaw invokes intersectionality as a metaphor for understanding the ways in which disadvantage and inequality can compound themselves.[39] This creates obstacles that might not be fully understood by normative theories and frames that ignore interdependency.

Crenshaw invokes an analogy of traffic at an intersection to illustrate why identities like race, class, and gender ought not to be treated as distinct categories when examining discrimination. Crenshaw asks us to imagine the traffic as discrimination. On one street the traffic might be congested because of sexual discrimination. On another street the congestion could be caused by racial discrimination. Now imagine a Black woman at the intersection of these different forms of discrimination. An approach that tries to tackle each of these types of discrimination separately will overlook the realities facing Black women since they must contend with the intersection of different types of discrimination. Any solution that adopts the frame of a single-lane solution will fail to mitigate the intersecting disadvantages Black women face with respect to discrimination.

This intersectional analysis has been applied more broadly to societal problems and oppression. Consider, for example, health and the case of HIV/AIDS. For the year 2020, the World Health Organization estimates that approximately 1.5 million people acquired HIV and 680,000 people died from HIV-related causes.[40] HIV is transmitted via the exchange of certain bodily fluids (such as blood, breast milk, semen, and vaginal secretions) from an infected person. Sharing needles during drug use and unprotected sex can increase the risk of HIV transmission. While everyone is potentially susceptible to HIV infection, some groups are at a higher risk than others. A single-axis framework for preventing the risks of HIV would categorize risks into discrete categories, like sexual orientation (e.g., gay and bisexual men versus heterosexuals), sex, race/ethnicity, substance abuse, and so on. But some people may fall into more than one of these categories. For example, prisons are a high-risk environment for HIV transmission for many reasons. They are crowded, have poor health

---

39. Kimberlé Williams Crenshaw, "Demarginalizing the Intersection of Race and Sex: A Black Feminist Critique of Antidiscrimination Doctrine, Feminist Theory, and Antiracist Politics," *University of Chicago Legal Forum* 1 (1989): 139–67.

40. "HIV and AIDS," World Health Organization, July 13, 2023, https://www.who.int/news-room/fact-sheets/detail/hiv-aids.

care, and are often plagued by drug use and unprotected sex. If persons from disadvantaged social classes or ethnic groups are incarcerated in higher numbers, that means members of those groups will also face higher risks of HIV transmission. The background sociolegal culture of a society can have a profound influence on the health inequalities between different groups. Adopting an intersectional lens helps bring to the fore the interdependence of a number of complex social determinants of health.

In *Harsh Justice* the legal scholar James Whitman explains how the stringent American retributivist policies of the so-called war on drugs of the 1970s, which led to a highly disproportionate number of Black men being incarcerated, were entrenched in cultural features of American civil, religious, and political life. In addition to factors like racism and fierce Christian beliefs, Whitman argues that the divergence between American and continental European approaches to punishment over the past number of decades reflects the different patterns of egalitarian social status they have pursued in punishment and patterns of resistance to state power.

Whitman contends that continental Europe had, prior to becoming democratic polities, a tradition of treating upper- and lower-class offenders differently. This *inegalitarianism* in the treatment of wrongdoers reflected the hierarchy embedded in Europe prior to the Enlightenment. Wrongdoers from the common class would be routinely subjected to degrading punishment (e.g., mutilation, shaming, etc.) and were effectively perceived and treated as slaves. In contrast, wrongdoers from the nobility and members of higher societal standing would not be subjected to these same degrading measures. As this hierarchy in Europe began to unravel over the nineteenth and twentieth centuries, the application of criminal justice moved in the direction of treating all like upper- rather than lower-class offenders. Thus continental Europe pursued a "leveling up" approach to criminal punishment. This approach meant that punishment in these countries was pursued in a manner that is more compatible with *human dignity*.

In Germany, for example, criminal justice must be consistent with the "principle of normalcy" enshrined in the third paragraph of the Code of Punishment. This principle prescribes that prison life is something that should approximate outside life as closely as possible. Thus prisoners' dress must resemble clothes people wear in the outside world; they must avoid dress that imposes a degradation of status (e.g., stripes or other symbols that brand offenders). In France prisoners are not required to wear any uniforms. Furthermore, in both France and Germany the principle of normalcy also extends to offenders the privileges of the social welfare state and legal protections of their dignity (e.g., privacy).[41]

In contrast, criminal justice in the United States entails *disenfranchisement* measures that strip inmates of the right to vote.[42] Democratic rights are thus regarded as entitlements that wrongdoers forfeit by breaking the law. Part of criminal punishment involves stripping inmates of these basic democratic rights, treating them as less than full citizens. This can be contrasted with France and Germany, where criminals are encouraged to vote. Participation in democratic governance has long been considered an effective tool in the moral development of the populace.

An intersectional analysis of the impact of relational power and privilege is advanced by Nandita Sharma in her examination of "how immigration and carceral controls created racialized and gendered categories of people denied access to the mythical institutions of liberal democracy: liberty, fellowship, and equality."[43] While slavery was officially abolished in the United States in 1865, the government utilized incarceration as a tool to ensure the former slaves continued to be disadvantaged because of their race.

Like the criminal justice system, immigration control measures can also reflect the racist and exclusionary sentiments of a host country. Sharma notes that the first US immigration control law was passed in 1875: the Page Act, which limited entry for Chinese coolies[44] and women deemed by state inspectors to be brought for "lewd and immoral purposes." These racist exclusionary measures were further amplified with the better-known Chinese Exclusionary Act of 1882, which suspended

---

41. See James Q. Whitman, *Harsh Justice: Criminal Justice and the Widening Gap between America and Europe* (Oxford: Oxford University Press, 2003), esp. 87–88.

42. This is a matter of state legislation, so there is variation in the severity of this element of punishment.

43. Nandita Sharma, "States and Human Immobilization: Bridging the Conceptual Separation of Slavery, Immigration Controls, and Mass Incarceration," *Citizenship Studies* 25, no. 2 (2021): 166–87, 167.

44. "The 'coolie' system [was] the recruitment of workers, mostly men and mostly from the colony of British India or British-controlled China to work in conditions of contracted indentured servitude." Sharma, "States and Human Immobilization," 170.

immigration from a specific nationality. This exclusionary past, contends Sharma, is linked to the existence and persistence of institutional racism in both policing and criminal justice, and the exclusionary elements of immigration policy today.

With respect to how racism continues to influence immigration policies today in the twenty-first century, one could point to the efforts to remove unauthorized immigrants in the United States, which are often framed as being "racially neutral."[45] Provine notes that while immigration laws that target specific groups, such as the Chinese Exclusionary Act of 1882, are no longer used, immigration laws and restrictions permit a significant degree of discretionary decision-making concerning surveillance and enforcement, and racist sentiments influence these features of the law.[46] For example, immigrants of Mexican and African origin have been disproportionately targeted for deportation.[47] Provine points to a number of examples of ethnoracial profiling in the state of Arizona, which borders Mexico, to illustrate how the highly discretionary work of policing enables racial bias with regard to immigration. An example is Arizona's 2010 measure SB 1070 (Support Our Law Enforcement and Safe Neighborhoods Act). Provine explains some of the problematic provisions of the act:

> Among its 10 provisions, the most notable is Section 2b, requiring a police officer to ascertain the legal status of anyone he or she stops if the officer suspects that person might be undocumented. If suspicions persist, the officer must detain the individual and contact federal immigration authorities. A department's failure to enforce SB1070 is grounds for a citizen-initiated suit for damages. The law expands the powers to stop and search and offers a blueprint for other states to express their determination

---

45. D. M. Provine and R. D. Doty, "The Criminalization of Immigrants as a Racial Project," in "Between Black and White: Theorizing Racial Democracy, Crime, and Justice," ed. María Vélez, Rod K. Brunson, and Jody Miller, special issue, *Journal of Contemporary Criminal Justice* 7, no. 3 (2011): 261–77.

46. Doris Marie Provine, "Institutional Racism in Enforcing Immigration Law," supplement, *Norteamérica* 8 (2013): 31–53.

47. Provine and Doty, "Criminalization of Immigrants."

to fight unauthorized immigration by deploying municipal policy in the effort.[48]

By expanding the power to stop and search, local police are thus deployed to address unauthorized immigration, and an officer's initial suspicion that someone might be undocumented may often be predicated on ethno-racial profiling. An intersectional analysis prescribes the political theorist to pay attention to the impact both history and identity have on societal attitudes, as well as formal legal and political institutions and structures.

---

48. Provine, "Institutional Racism," 43–44.

Chapter 9

Black Political Thought

This chapter will cover a diverse array of Black political theorists, including Frederick Douglass, W. E. B. Du Bois, Martin Luther King Jr., and Frantz Fanon. Already in this book we have covered other Black political thinkers and ideas, such as Charles Mills's criticism of the social contract in chapter 5, Booker T. Washington's concern for personal responsibility in chapter 7, and Anna Cooper and Kimberlé Crenshaw's views on intersectionality in chapter 8. Any of those thinkers could potentially have been included in this chapter on Black political thought. However, the ideas and arguments championed by Black thinkers connect with many other areas of political theory and do not constitute a single, unified political perspective, so they could not all be adequately addressed in this one chapter.

Black political theorists and philosophers have offered valuable contributions to many topics, including slavery, the social contract tradition, women's education, equality, civil disobedience, and conservatism. They have also raised foundational theoretical questions for the discipline of political theory, such as intersectionality (Du Bois, Cooper, and Crenshaw), the significance of attending to real versus idealized history in normative theorizing (Mills), and how real history impacts the creation and evolution of relationships among people in an allegedly free society (Douglass, King, Fanon). These methodological and epistemological concerns will come to the fore in this chapter.

In his essay "Contours of Black Political Thought: An Introduction and Perspective," Michael Hanchard describes Black political thought as follows:

> Black political thought can be viewed as the attempt to develop a set of critical tools to help explain the political distinctiveness of black life-worlds and how this distinctiveness is structured by

a series of relations between individual and community, self and other, state and society, citizen and non-citizen, and national and multinational (or global) circumstances.[1]

This is a succinct characterization that captures the themes of the thinkers we cover in this chapter. I have chosen the specific list of thinkers and themes for this chapter because I believe doing so takes seriously the historical reality that, as the sociologist Paul Gilroy has emphasized, "racial slavery was integral to western civilization."[2] We begin with the abolitionist Frederick Douglass.

Slavery and Frederick Douglass

As noted in earlier chapters, slavery has had a long and omnipresent history in human affairs. Plato's critique of Athenian democracy did not take issue with the fact that it was built on the unjust practice of slavery. For Plato, Athenian democracy was inherently problematic because it perverted what Plato believed to be the proper hierarchical arrangement, with philosophers ruling over soldiers and workers (including women and enslaved persons). Many other hierarchical arrangements have been defended by religions, cultures, and philosophies over the previous millennia.

Historically the servitude or death of one's enemy was considered the appropriate reward for victory in battle. Societal practices such as patriarchy, colonialism, the expansion of Christianity, serfdom, the exploitation of workers, and so on were given ideological justifications and rationalizations, and many of the people living with such oppressive practices (including many of the oppressed) often did not see those practices in a critical light. This is one reason why such practices persisted for so long. A particularly insidious form of servitude is the focus of the thinkers in this chapter: *racial slavery*.

---

1. Michael Hanchard, "Contours of Black Political Thought: An Introduction and Perspective," *Political Theory* 38, no. 4 (2010): 510–36, 510.

2. Paul Gilroy, *The Black Atlantic: Modernity and Black Consciousness* (Cambridge, MA: Harvard University Press, 1993), ix–x.

The transatlantic slave trade formed part of the European Commercial Revolution; it "owed its modern form to the growth of nation states that replaced feudalism and lent their support to the trade, to the rise of towns, the broadening of commerce, the development of the merchant classes, and to new outlooks upon competition, profits and capital formation."[3] The historian Joseph Inikori argues that "the development of markets and the market economy was central to the process of socioeconomic development in the Atlantic world from the fifteenth to the nineteenth century.... The process was propelled by the plantation and mining zones located in the New World."[4]

In addition to the economic factors that drove it, the transatlantic slave trade was sustained by the religious and cultural beliefs (e.g., different moral status ascribed to whites versus nonwhites) that justified such servitude. One estimate of the total number of enslaved persons that lived, either through birth or trade, from the early seventeenth century through the latter part of the nineteenth century, is 10 million enslaved who contributed 410 billion hours of labor.[5] The writings of the abolitionist Frederick Douglass, who was born into slavery and escaped at age twenty, provide a unique perspective into the physical, psychological, and societal toll of slavery as an institution. Douglass's writings and reflections are also an effective example of the human mind's capacity for hope, resilience, and a determination to challenge and change what might feel like immutable injustice.

Douglass begins his autobiography *Narrative of the Life of Frederick Douglass* with his personal reflections on the toil of American slavery. His mother was a slave, and Douglass never met his father, although he notes it was rumored that his father may have been his white enslaver, "Captain Anthony." As the child of a mother who was enslaved, Douglass was born into slavery too. He only saw his mother four or five times in his life, and

---

3. James Rawley and Stephen Behrendt, *The Transatlantic Slave Trade: A History*, rev. ed. (Lincoln: University of Nebraska Press, 2005), 2.

4. Joseph Inikori, "Transatlantic Slavery and Economic Development in the Atlantic World: West Africa, 1450–1850," in *Cambridge World History of Slavery*, vol. 3, ed. David Eltis and Stanley L. Engerman (New York: Cambridge University Press, 2011), 650–74, 650.

5. David Hacker, "From '20. and Odd' to 10 Million: The Growth of the Slave Population in the United States," *Slavery and Abolition* 41, no. 4 (2020): 840–55.

he had no recollection of seeing her during the daylight hours when she was working. He only saw her in the evening, and she died when he was approximately seven years old. Douglass describes the few memories he has of mother as follows:

> She was a field hand, and a whipping is the penalty of not being in the field at sunrise.... I do not recollect ever seeing my mother by the light of day. She was with me in the night. She would lie down with me, and get me to sleep, but long before I waked she was gone. Very little communication ever took place between us. Death soon ended what little we could have while she lived, and with it her hardships and suffering. She died when I was about seven years old, on one of my master's farm's, near Lee's Mill. I was not allowed to be present during her illness, at her death, or burial.... Never having enjoyed, to any considerable extent, her soothing presence, her tender and watchful care, I received the tidings of her death with much the same emotions I should have probably felt at the death of a stranger.[6]

Douglass did not actually know when he was born as there was no official record of it, so he could only estimate his own age. His first enslaver, "Captain Anthony," owned two or three farms and about thirty enslaved persons. Douglass described the overseer of these farms as the drunkard and savage monster named Mr. Plummer. Plummer was an individual Douglass described as "hardened by a lifetime of slaveholding" who enjoyed whipping enslaved persons. As a child living on a plantation, Douglass would frequently awaken to the shrieks of his aunt being whipped by Plummer.

> I have often been awaked at the dawn of day by the most heart-rending shrieks of an own aunt of mine, whom he [Plummer] used to tie up to a joist, and whip upon her naked back till she was literally covered with blood. No words, no tears, no prayers, from his gory victim, seemed to move his iron heart from its

---

6. Frederick Douglass, *Narrative of the Life of Frederick Douglass, an American Slave*, ed. John R. McKivigan, Peter P. Hinks, and Heather L. Kaufman (New Haven, CT: Yale University Press, 2016), 14.

bloody purpose. The louder she screamed, the harder he whipped; and where the blood ran fastest, there he whipped longest.[7]

These formative and personal experiences of the brutality and inhumanity of slavery informed Douglass's abolitionist political philosophy. Nineteenth-century white America was a society that did not recognize Blacks as human beings worthy of equal dignity and human rights. Douglass noted that "the killing of a slave, or any coloured person, in Talbot county, Maryland, is not treated as a crime, either by the courts or the community."[8] Douglass recounts that Sundays were the only day he would have some leisure time, which he would spend in a sort of "beast-like stupor, between sleep and wake, under some large tree."[9] At times he felt tempted to take his own life or those of the many brutal overseers he had during the first two decades of his life.

Douglass recounts a beating from Mr. Covey, a farmer he was sent to work for, who had a reputation for breaking the will of enslaved persons who displayed any resistance. On one occasion, when Douglass was suffering extreme dizziness and a violent aching of his head while working in the sun, Covey struck Douglass on the head with a hickory slat to compel him to get back to work. Douglass then escaped Covey's farm and fled to his enslaver, Master Thomas, to ask for protection. But Master Thomas ridiculed Douglass for suggesting that Mr. Covey would kill Douglass, and informed Douglass that Thomas had agreed to give Covey Douglass's labor for the year. If Douglass did not return to work for Covey, responded Master Thomas, then he would whip Douglass himself to obtain his compliance. Douglass returned to Covey's farm, but when confronted by Covey, Douglass decided to fight back. He describes this as the turning point in his life:

> This battle with Mr. Covey was the turning point in my career as a slave. It rekindled the few expiring embers of freedom, and revived within me a sense of my own manhood. It recalled the departed self-confidence, and inspired me again with a determination to

---

7. Douglass, *Narrative*, 15–16.

8. Douglass, *Narrative*, 27.

9. Douglass, *Narrative*, 51.

be free. The gratification afforded by the triumph was a full compensation for whatever else might follow, even death itself. . . . It was a glorious resurrection, from the tomb of slavery, to the heaven of freedom. . . . From this time I was never again what might be called fairly whipped, though I remained a slave four years afterwards. I had several fights, but was never whipped.[10]

In *My Bondage and My Freedom* Douglass emphasizes the value of literacy, something he developed after moving to Baltimore as a young adolescent. The ability to read and write helped Douglass articulate the oppression he witnessed in slavery. It created an intense form of cognitive dissonance for the teenage Douglass.

When I was about thirteen years of age, and had succeeded in learning to read, every increase of knowledge, especially respecting the FREE STATES, added something to the upmost intolerable burden of the thought—"I AM A SLAVE FOR LIFE." To my bondage I saw no end. It was a terrible reality, and I shall never be able to tell you how sadly that thought chaffed my young spirit.[11]

At the heart of Douglass's diagnosis of the ills of slavery is the *right to self-ownership*, a moral sentiment we already explored with John Locke's liberalism. For example, in *My Bondage and My Freedom* Douglass draws a comparison between the ownership of humans and oxen:

I now saw, in my condition, several points of similarity with that of oxen. They were property, so was I: they were to be broken, so was I. Covey was to break me, I was to break them; break and be broken, such is life.[12]

While Douglass has been viewed as a progressive or reformer, Nicholas Buccola contends in *The Political Thought of Frederick Douglass*

---

10. Douglass, *Narrative*, 57.

11. Frederick Douglass, *My Bondage and My Freedom* [1855], introduction by David Blight (New Haven, CT: Yale University Press, 2014), 126.

12. Douglass, *My Bondage and My Freedom*, 170.

that the majority of scholars interpret Douglass as a classic liberal. This classical liberal reading of Douglass sees his condemnation of slavery as arising from a commitment to individual rights. Douglass's commitment to a right to self-ownership is most explicitly captured in his speech "A Friendly Word to Maryland," where he asserts that every human being is the "original, rightful, and absolute owner of his own body."[13] The predicament of racial inequality arose because of an inconsistent recognition of the demands of self-ownership. Rather than being granted the same rights as white persons, as required by the right to self-ownership, the social and legal relationship of enslaved and enslaver gives the latter "absolute power over the slave. He may work him, flog him, hire him out, sell him, and, in certain contingencies, kill him, with perfect immunity."[14]

After many years of thinking about his freedom, Douglass eventually decided to plan an escape from slavery, as he recounts in *My Bondage and My Freedom*. Douglass found life under slavery intolerable; he claimed one had to make "a thoughtless" life, one "devoid of reason," to make it a contented life. In 1836 Douglass's work was bought for the year by his temporary master Mr. Freeland. But Douglass refused to "annihilate his power of reason" and instead he "longed to have a *future*."[15] After all, a future was not something that could possibly be realized when he was bound to work for someone else's benefit. He remarked:

> My faculties and powers are not my own, but are the property of a fellow mortal, in no sense superior to me, except that he has the physical power to compel me to be owned and controlled by him. By the combined physical force of the community, I am his slave—a slave for life. With thoughts like these, I was perplexed and chafed; they rendered me gloomy and disconsolate. The anguish of my mind may not be written.[16]

---

13. Quoted in Nicholas Buccola, *The Political Thought of Frederick Douglass: In Pursuit of American Liberty* (New York: New York University Press, 2012), 2.
14. Douglass, *My Bondage and My Freedom*, 355.
15. Douglass, *My Bondage and My Freedom*, 218.
16. Douglass, *My Bondage and My Freedom*, 217.

In *My Bondage and My Freedom* Douglass provides scant details of his escape from slavery, in order to protect those who aided him. Disguised as a sailor on leave, with help from his fiancée and others, Douglass traveled by train, ferry, and steamboat to New York, where he arrived with no money. He befriended David Ruggles, a Black abolitionist and head of the New York Committee of Vigilance, an organization that helped enslaved persons achieve their freedom. Douglass went on to become a prominent abolitionist and public speaker who encouraged Americans to confront the injustices of slavery and racial inequality.

W. E. B. Du Bois

Born in 1868, W. E. B. (William Edward Burghardt) Du Bois was an African American sociologist and social philosopher. Du Bois believed one could utilize the tools of social science to study racial oppression and inequality, the central concern of his intellectual life. Du Bois received his PhD from Harvard University in 1895, and his dissertation was titled *The Suppression of the African Slave-Trade to the United States of America, 1638–1870*. A professor at the University of Georgia, he empirically examined the life circumstances of Black Americans. Du Bois's book *The Philadelphia Negro: A Social Study* (1899) examined the living conditions of more than forty thousand Black Americans living in the city of Philadelphia and involved going house to house to gather information such as the number of persons living in a household, their age and sex, their literacy, their occupation and income, and so forth. Du Bois notes this was a population plagued by societal problems like poverty (slum districts), ignorance, and crime. He argues that the predicaments facing Black Americans are different than those facing other social groups and classes:

> Many are the apprehensions and misstatements as to the social environment of Negroes in a great Northern city. Sometimes it is said, here they are free: they have the same chances as the Irishman, the Italian, or the Swede; at other times it is said, the environment is such that it is really more oppressive than the situation in the Southern cities. The student must ignore both of these extreme statements and seek to extract from a complicated mass of facts the tangible evidence of a social atmosphere surrounding Negroes,

which differs from that surrounding most whites; of a different mental attitude, moral standard, and economic judgement shown toward Negroes than toward most other folk. That such a difference exists and can now and then plainly be seen, few deny; but just how far it goes and how large a factor it is in the Negro problems, nothing but careful study and measurement can reveal.[17]

To understand why the obstacles and inequalities facing Black Americas in the late nineteenth century existed and persisted, Du Bois believed the social scientist had to attend to the different types of challenges facing Black Americans (as compared to Italian or Irish immigrants). Furthermore, the social scientist had to discard the racist assumptions of Du Bois's contemporaries who simply assumed inequalities were the result of white superiority and Black inferiority.

In chapter 18 of *The Philadelphia Negro: A Social Study*, Du Bois claims that the so-called Negro problem was an issue typically addressed in one of two ways. The first way presumed that there was a simple description about what this problem is—education, crime, occupations, and so on—and thus a simple remedy (e.g., "Train them," "Guide them"). The second way viewed the problem as hopelessly complex and intricate, offering no simple solution. Du Bois contends that both views possess some truth.

> The Negro problem looked at in one way is but the old world questions of ignorance, poverty, crime and the dislike of the stranger. On the other hand it is a mistake to think that attacking each of these questions single-handed without reference to the others will settle the matter: a combination of social problems is far more than a matter of mere addition—the combination itself is a problem. Nevertheless the Negro problems are not more hopelessly complex than many others have been. . . . We rather hasten to forget that once the courtiers of English kings looked upon the ancestors of most Americans with far greater contempt than these Americans look upon Negroes—and perhaps, indeed, had more cause. We forget that once French peasants were the

---

17. W. E. B. Du Bois, *The Philadelphia Negro: A Social Study* [1899], introduction by Elijah Anderson (Philadelphia: University of Pennsylvania Press, 1996), 8.

"Niggers" of France, and that German princelings once discussed with doubt the brains and humanity of the bauer.[18]

Du Bois's analysis of racial inequality, which attended to the actual history of American society including slavery and the Jim Crow era (versus a hypothetical Lockean state of nature), recognized the plurality of other types of inequality that coexist alongside racial inequality, such as gender inequality and socioeconomic inequality. In each of these instances structural change is necessary for individual persons, be they Black, female, or peasant, to realize freedom. In *Dusk of Dawn* Du Bois remarks:

> For long years it seemed to me that this imprisonment of a human group with chains in hands of an environing group, was a singularly unusual characteristic of the Negro in the United States in the nineteenth century. But since then it has been easy for me to realize that the majority of mankind has struggled through this inner spiritual slavery and that while a dream which we have easily and jauntily called democracy envisages a day when the environing group looses the chains and compulsion, and is willing and even eager to grant families, nations, sub-races and races equality of opportunity among larger groups, that even this grand equality has not come; and until it does, individual equality and the free soul is impossible. All our present frustration in trying to realize individual equality through communism, fascism, and democracy arises from our continual unwillingness to break the intellectual bonds of group and racial exclusiveness.[19]

Du Bois's analysis of inequality shares important similarities to the intersectional analysis of Anna Cooper, which we explored in chapter 8. Some commentators have thus considered Du Bois to be an intellectual forefather of intersectionality.[20] By adopting an intersectional lens

---

18. Du Bois, *The Philadelphia Negro*, 385–86.
19. W. E. B. Du Bois, *Dusk of Dawn: An Essay Towards and Autobiography of a Race Concept* [1940] (New York: Schocken, 1968), 137.
20. Ange-Marie Hancock, "W. E. B. Du Bois: Intellectual Forefather of Intersectionality?," *Souls* 7, nos. 3–4 (2005): 74–84.

on oppression and inequality, Du Bois is able to draw optimistic conclusions concerning the potential for groups to make headway against this oppression and marginalization. For example, Du Bois notes that while formerly enslaved persons in America were poor, they were not as poor as Irish peasants used to be. While crime was rampant in America, Du Bois argues it was not worse than the violence in Italy. The critical difference between how the vulnerabilities and inequalities of peasants in Ireland and Italy had been improved versus why they had persisted for Black Americans was that "the ancestors of the English and the Irish and the Italians were felt to be worth educating, helping and guiding because they were men and brothers, while in America a census which gives a slight indication of the utter disappearance of the American Negro from the earth is greeted with ill-concealed delight."[21]

Racial inequality is not an issue that can or should be ignored in the hopes that it will somehow simply go away. Du Bois offers the following propositions that he took to be unquestionable features of race within America:

1. The Negro is here to stay.
2. It is to the advantage of all, both black and white, that every Negro should make the best of himself.
3. It is the duty of the Negro to raise himself by every effort to the standards of modern civilization and not to lower those standards in any degree.
4. It is the duty of the white people to guard their civilization against debauchment by themselves or others; but in order to do this it is not necessary to hinder and retard the efforts of an earnest people to rise, simply because they lack faith in the ability of that people.
5. With these duties in mind and with the spirit of self-help, mutual aid and co-operation, the two races should strive side by side to realize the ideals of the republic and make this try a land of equal opportunity for all men.[22]

---

21. Du Bois, *The Philadelphia Negro*, 387.
22. Du Bois, *The Philadelphia Negro*, 388–89.

Equality of opportunity is sometimes interpreted in the minimalistic sense of the removal of formal legal barriers that discriminate and treat some as inferior. For example, during Reconstruction after the American Civil War three important constitutional amendments were passed that helped redress some of the problems of racial inequality in America by prohibiting legal forms of discrimination. The Thirteenth Amendment, passed by Congress in 1865, abolished slavery and involuntary servitude. A year later Congress passed the Fourteenth Amendment, which granted citizenship to everyone born or naturalized in the United States, and also granted everyone equal protection of the law. Citizenship was something denied to enslaved people when slavery was legally permitted. The Fifteenth Amendment, passed by Congress in 1869, prohibited denying the right to vote on the basis of race. This amendment ensured that (male) Black Americans would have the right to vote and that states could not deny that right. Women were not granted the right to vote until Congress passed the Nineteenth Amendment in 1919.

While Du Bois considered the three Reconstruction amendments important first steps toward redressing racial inequality in America, they were only necessary but not sufficient measures. After the Civil War a *racial caste* system of anti-Black discrimination evolved and persisted, causing segregation in education, unequal access to health care, higher incarceration rates among Black Americans, and so forth.

It is a mistake to think that simply abolishing the legality of slavery would constitute the genuine emancipation of Black Americans. Abolishing slavery did not mean Black Americans could realize their economic independence or have access to adequate education. In *The Souls of Black Folk* Du Bois argues:

> Not a single Southern legislature stood ready to admit a Negro, under any conditions, to the polls; not a single Southern legislature believed free Negro labor was possible without a system of restrictions that took all its freedom away; there was scarcely a white man in the South who did not honestly regard Emancipation as a crime, and its practical nullification as a duty. In such a situation, the granting of the ballot to the black man was a necessity, the very least a guilty nation could grant a wronged race, and the only method of compelling the South to accept the results

of the war. Thus Negro suffrage ended a civil war by beginning a race feud. And some felt gratitude toward the race thus sacrificed in its swaddling clothes on the altar of national integrity; and some felt and feel only indifference and contempt.[23]

The Jim Crow era persisted for decades after slavery was abolished in the United States. Jim Crow referred to a blackface minstrelsy character in the nineteenth century that depicted a stereotypical Black person. Jim Crow laws were the state and local government measures created in the late nineteenth and early twentieth centuries to segregate whites and Blacks. For example, in 1896 the landmark Supreme Court decision *Plessy v. Ferguson* upheld the constitutionality of racial segregation under the doctrine of "separate but equal." A racially mixed shoemaker, Homer Plessy, had refused to sit in a train car designated for nonwhites, as mandated by the Separate Car Act. The act was passed by the Louisiana state government in 1890 and required all railway passengers to be segregated into separate train cars based on race.

In "Unreconstructed Democracy: W. E. B. Du Bois and the Case for Reparations" Lawrie Belfour argues that Du Bois's political theory examined the willful national amnesia of post–Civil War America regarding racial injustice that impeded the realization of freedom and equality for Black Americans after the abolishment of slavery.[24] Belfour argues that for Du Bois, at least three important measures would have had to be realized (but were not) after the American Civil War in order for substantive equality to be achieved. First, economic policies were needed to ensure that the formerly enslaved were truly free. Freedom, for Du Bois, does not entail simply the "absence of state interference" (which is commonly referred to as "negative liberty"), such as prohibiting slavery. Not being enslaved does not mean people will have the opportunity to work and make sufficient income to meet their basic material needs. If the formerly enslaved had no property and few economic opportunities, then their life prospects were not substantively better than under a system of slavery. Indeed, this is why segregation policies were enacted in southern states.

---

23. W. E. B. Du Bois, *The Souls of Black Folk* [1903] (New York: Cosimo, 2007), 23.

24. Lawrie Balfour, "Unreconstructed Democracy: W. E. B. Du Bois and the Case for Reparations," *American Political Science Review* 97, no. 1 (2003): 33–44.

Such measures ensured that the inequalities created under the system of slavery would persist (despite slavery itself being abolished), as whites would have access to better education, jobs, housing, and so forth than Black Americans.

"Democratic citizenship, for Du Bois, entails at least a basic education and the economic wherewithal to live a relatively comfortable life from unearned debt."[25] Belfour notes that Du Bois pointed to the objectives of the Bureau of Refugees, Freedmen, and Abandoned Lands, or Freedmen's Bureau, such as the dispersal of abandoned lands and establishment of schools in the postwar South, which were never adequately realized because the bureau was underfunded and only lasted a few years instead of the decades that would be needed to make substantive changes to racial inequality in America.

In addition to these economic policies, Belfour argues that a second feature of Du Bois's insights into the persistence of the American racial caste system of the early twentieth century was America's failure to acknowledge the contributions of Black Americans with respect to the making of America. In post–Civil War America many whites subscribed to the belief of Black passivity, but this was not an empirically valid presupposition. Du Bois noted the gifts Black Americans had for story and song, as well as sweat, brawn, and spirit. The abolition of slavery and renewal of American democracy was not something whites alone brought into existence. Thousands of Black enslaved persons had participated in a general strike and revolted against slavery by leaving the plantations for the Union army camps. Du Bois also highlighted the role Blacks had played in creating new schools in the South, which also benefited poor whites in those regions.

The third feature of reconstructing American democracy that Belfour highlights in Du Bois's writings is a recognition of Black humanity, which was rejected by the practice of slavery as well as the segregation policies enacted after the Civil War. Black inferiority enabled segregation in schools, housing, and public transport to persist in many southern states until the middle of the twentieth century.

---

25. Balfour, "Unreconstructed Democracy," 36.

Civil Disobedience

We will now turn our focus to the ideas of a prominent civil rights activist who would become a martyr for racial equality in America after he was assassinated in 1968: Martin Luther King Jr.

Recall from our analysis of Plato's *Republic* in chapter 2 that one of the perennial problems in political theory is the alleged conflict between democracy and justice. Athenian democracy was a direct democracy, prescribing "majority rules" as the legitimate way of managing society's public affairs. Yet justice, at least according to Plato, required "everyone to do what they are best suited to do." For Plato democracy and justice are, by their very nature, oppositional/conflicting values and aspirations. Justice requires an "epistocracy," or rule by the philosopher kings and queens who possess wisdom and strive to achieve truth while resisting epistemic vice. According to Plato, democracy is rule by the ignorant, and thus the vote of the majority simply tracks what is appealing to the appetites of the masses rather than what is actually conducive to the common good.

In the twentieth century this alleged conflict between democracy and justice gave rise to debates and discussions concerning the role of civil disobedience in democracy. Rather than conceiving of democracy in the ancient Athenian terms of direct democracy, democracy (and democratic theory) in the twentieth century emerged in conjunction with liberalism (i.e., the protection of individual rights and a public philosophy of limited government), and thus the predicament of reconciling democracy and justice was often construed as the project of constitutional or liberal democracy. This vision of government permits some legitimate scope for democratic aspirations to guide public policy, but the risk of tyranny of the majority is (at least in theory) constrained by a country's constitution and its commitment to individual rights. Thus democratic rule is justified only when there is some limit imposed on the ability of majoritarian governments to violate or limit the constitutional rights and freedoms of those in the minority.

John Rawls defines civil disobedience as a "public, non-violent and conscientious yet political act contrary to law usually done with the aim of bringing about a change in the law or policies of the government."[26]

---

26. John Rawls, *A Theory of Justice* (Cambridge, MA: Belknap Press of Harvard University Press, 1971), 364.

There are two types of civil disobedience: direct and indirect. Direct acts of civil disobedience break the law the protestors are actually demonstrating against. For example, in 1955 Rosa Parks (a Black American) refused to give up her seat on a public bus to a white man, thus violating the segregation policies of Montgomery, Alabama. Parks was then arrested and fined. In Parks's case it was an act of direct civil disobedience because the law she broke was the one she was protesting: racial segregation on public transport. In cases of indirect civil disobedience, like Martin Luther King Jr.'s arrest in Birmingham in 1963, the law he broke—protesting without a permit—was not the law the demonstration was protesting. What was being protested were the policies of racial segregation. King was willing to violate the law that regulates demonstrations to raise public awareness about the injustices of racial segregation.

John Rawls argues that the three core elements of civilly disobedient action—that it be public, nonviolent, and conscientious yet political—demonstrate the protestor's sincere intention to abate the specific injustice they oppose and their fidelity to the rule of law. Unlike a revolutionary, who is intent on overthrowing a political system, civil disobedience is meant to realign the laws and policies of a democratic community to more closely match their true, core political values.

An assumption Rawls makes, though somewhat ambiguously, is that civil disobedience applies in a society that is "nearly just": a society whose political culture does take seriously the basic rights and freedoms of its citizens, but nonetheless falls short of meeting all the demands of justice. It is not meant to apply in a legal regime like Nazi Germany, for example, where the Aryan race aspirations of the Nazis were antithetical to the toleration and equality of all Germans. Rawls does not address, with any precision and detail, the issue of where mid-twentieth-century American culture, with its segregation politics (at least in southern states), fits on this spectrum between an intolerant and grossly unjust regime and a nearly just society. But his discussion of civil disobedience gives the impression that he believes America is much closer to the latter than the former. This is an issue one may wish to debate and critique Rawls on. It has significance for the requirement that protest be nonviolent, an issue we shall soon see divided Martin Luther King Jr. from Black Panther leaders like Stokely Carmichael and the decolonial theorist Frantz Fanon.

King's "Letter from Birmingham Jail" (1963)

While in prison for organizing an illegal protest (the city had obtained a court injunction against the protests) against Birmingham's segregation system, King wrote his famous "Letter from Birmingham Jail," which details his thoughts on civil disobedience. Meena Krishnamurthy argues that King's letter constitutes a form of "democratic propaganda," or "truthful propaganda aimed at promoting and fostering democratic political action by stirring the emotions."[27] She contends that the letter was written in the hopes of overcoming a significant problem facing the civil rights movement: the political inaction of white moderates. As we shall see, King was also very concerned with addressing both Black Americans who displayed complacency and simply accepted segregation as an unalterable reality and those Blacks who had become bitter and hateful and advocated the use of violence.

In his letter King details the four steps of a defensible campaign of nonviolence:

1. Collection of the facts to ascertain if injustice does exist
2. Negotiation
3. Self-purification
4. Direct action[28]

The first step—collection of the facts—requires the exercise of epistemic or intellectual virtue. Before engaging in civil disobedience there is a duty to attend to the empirical reality of the situation. Does injustice actually exist? How extensive is the injustice? Why does the injustice persist? With respect to the realities of racial inequality in twentieth-century America, King notes that lynchings—the public killings of individuals who had not received the due process of the law—of Black Americans had taken place, and the policies of state discrimination (e.g., segregation in schools and in public spaces) against nonwhites continued. The Equal Justice Initiative

---

27. Meena Krishnamurthy, "Martin Luther King Jr. on Democratic Propaganda, Shame, and Moral Transformation," *Political Theory* 50, no. 2 (2022): 305–36, 307.

28. Martin Luther King Jr., "Letter from Birmingham Jail" [1963], in *Why We Can't Wait* (New York: Signet Classics, 2000), 85–112, 87.

estimates that approximately 4,084 racial lynchings took place in southern US states between 1877 and 1950.[29] These facts of racial inequality provide a credible foundation for the claim that pressing injustices need to be addressed.

The second step in a campaign of nonviolence that King emphasizes is negotiation. King notes that the critic might argue that protestors should negotiate versus engaging in direct action like unlawful protest. His response is that direct action *is* negotiation, and he refers to the kind of creative, constructive tension Socrates spurred in his contemporaries when he challenged the beliefs of ancient Athenians:

> Nonviolent direct action seeks to create such a crisis and establish such creative tension that a community that has consistently refused to negotiate is forced to confront the issue. It seeks so to dramatize the issue that it can no longer be ignored. I just referred to the creation of tension as a part of the work of the nonviolent resister. This may sound rather shocking. But I must confess that I am not afraid of the word "tension." I have earnestly worked and preached against violent tension, but there is a type of constructive nonviolent tension that is necessary for growth. Just as Socrates felt that it was necessary to create a tension in the mind so that individuals could rise from the bondage of myths and half-truths to the unfettered realm of creative analysis and objective appraisal, so we must see the need of having nonviolent gadflies to create the kind of tension in society that will help men to rise from the dark depths of prejudice and racism to the majestic heights of understanding and brotherhood.[30]

To the critic who objects that breaking the law is always wrong, King maintains that "one has a moral responsibility to disobey unjust laws." Thus King's position on this issue differs from that of Plato in *Crito*. Recall that Socrates refuses to escape after Crito has bribed the guard. Socrates

---

29. Equal Justice Initiative, *Lynching in America: Confronting the Legacy of Racial Terror*, 2017, https://eji.org/wp-content/uploads/2005/11/lynching-in-america-3d-ed-110121.pdf

30. King, "Letter from Birmingham Jail," 89–90.

believes he is morally bound to accept the punishment because he has resided within Athens all of his life and cannot break the social contract. Of course, for Plato Socrates's death sentence does not constitute a substantial harm or injustice to Socrates, for Socrates's virtue remains intact despite the punishment. What would be unjust is for Socrates to rebuke the life of virtue he strove to achieve. In *Crito* Socrates maintains that he is morally bound to accept the fate prescribed by the outcome of the trial.

The third step King identifies for nonconflict campaigns is self-purification. King notes that before breaking any law, he had organized workshops on nonviolence, preparing the dissidents for accepting the blows they would receive while protesting without retaliating. They also had to be mentally ready to endure the ordeal of jail for the cause of opposing injustice.

The fourth and final step in a nonviolent campaign is the actual engagement in direct action. Here King emphasizes the importance of strategic thinking when considering protesting for maximal societal impact. For example, he notes that he planned their action for the Easter season as this was a major shopping period of the year. Coordinating the protests during such a time of peak economic activity would "bring pressure to bear on the merchants for the needed change."[31] King argues that moderate critics who encourage instead a slower pace of progressive change pose an even bigger threat to racial equality than those who openly espouse white supremacy:

> I must confess that over the last few years I have been gravely disappointed with the white moderate. I have almost reached the regrettable conclusion that the Negro's great stumbling block in the stride toward freedom is not the White Citizen's Councillor or the Ku Klux Klanner but the white moderate who is more devoted to order than to justice; who prefers a negative peace which is the absence of tension to a positive peace which is the presence of justice; who constantly says, "I agree with you in the goal you seek, but I can't agree with your methods of direct action"; who paternalistically feels that he can set the timetable for another man's freedom; who lives by the myth of time; and who constantly advises the Negro to wait until a "more convenient season." Shallow understanding from people of good will is more frustrating

---

31. King, "Letter from Birmingham Jail," 89.

than absolute misunderstanding from people of ill will. Lukewarm acceptance is much more bewildering than outright rejection.[32]

How defensible and effective is civil disobedience in redressing real-world injustices? To the critics who believe that it is never morally defensible to break the law, unlawful protest might be considered inherently immoral. But such a strong stance will strike many as problematic because it presumes there is always a moral duty to obey the law, regardless of how unjust the law was. Should the German citizens who were living under the Nazi regime have felt morally obligated to respect the legal regime of the Third Reich, a regime that passed antisemitic laws and arbitrarily arrested, imprisoned, and killed its opponents in concentration camps? King endorses Saint Augustine's dictum that "an unjust law is no law at all." When the law perverts the foundations of basic morality, there is no moral duty to uphold it.

Another line of criticism one might have against King's position concerns his stance on nonviolence. If a legal regime/political culture commits *injustice*, why is nonviolence the only legitimate response to take? This is an issue that divided King from other critics of racial inequality in the United States during the 1960s, such as Malcolm X and Stokely Carmichael. In his famous 1966 "Black Power" speech at the University of California, Berkeley, Carmichael made the following statements, which denote a different strategy than that advocated by King:

> We are on the move for our liberation. We are tired of trying to prove things to white people. We are tired of trying to explain to white people that we're not gonna hurt them. We are concerned with getting the things we want, the things that we have to have to be able to function. The question is, can white people allow for that in this country? The question is, will white people overcome their racism and allow for that to happen in this country? If that does not happen, brothers and sisters, we have no choice but to say very clearly, "Move over, or we're goin' to move over on you."[33]

---

32. King, "Letter from Birmingham Jail," 96–97.

33. Stokely Carmichael, "Black Power" [1966], in *The Will of a People: A Critical Anthology of Great African American Speeches*, ed. Richard Leeman and Bernard Duffy (Carbondale: Southern Illinois University Press, 2012), 295–319, 319.

Malcolm X, who contrasted his position to that of the more moderate King, did not rule out the use of violence as a potential tool for liberation. But, as James Cone has noted, it is more accurate to describe Malcolm X as a proponent of self-defense versus violence per se:

> Malcolm did not advocate violence; he advocated self-defense. He believed that the right of self-defense is an essential element in the definition of humanity. Whites have always recognized this principle for themselves but not for blacks. This kind of racist thinking infuriated Malcolm. If whites have the right to defend themselves against their enemies, why not blacks? Malcolm used provocative language to express his rage. "If you want to know what I'll do, figure out what you'll do. I'll do the same thing—only more of it." He contended that blacks should use "any means necessary" to get their freedom and whites should be prepared for "reciprocal bleeding." He did not regard such language as violent. He called it intelligence. "A black man has the right to do whatever is necessary to get his freedom that other human beings have done to get their freedom."[34]

The issue of the optimal strategy (e.g., violence or nonviolence) for combating racial inequality is also central to the next thinker we shall consider: Frantz Fanon, one of the foremost theorists of decolonization.

Frantz Fanon and Decolonial Political Theory

Addressing problems of racial inequality has been the theme of this chapter. A central focus of Douglass's writings was slavery and its violation of the right to self-ownership. For Anna Cooper (covered in chapter 8 on feminist political thought) education and a strong sense of community coupled with (like Du Bois's *intersectional analysis*) a critical engagement with the real history of the past (that is, the actual history of colonialism rather than some idealized, ahistorical Lockean "state of a nature") are all

---

34. James H. Cone, "Martin and Malcolm on Nonviolence and Violence," *Phylon* 49, nos. 3–4 (2001): 173–83, 180. Quotations from Malcolm X come from *Malcolm X Speaks*, ed. George Breitman (New York: Grove, 1965), 113, 197–98.

critical for moving toward a more equal society by redressing the societal ills of both patriarchy and racial inequality. For Martin Luther King Jr. a key strategic judgment in combatting the ills of racial inequality was to pursue a strategy of *nonviolent* protest, a middle-ground position between complacency about the realities of racial segregation and acceptance of the use of violence promoted by some Black nationalists. The last thinker we will address in this chapter on Black political thought is the West Indian political philosopher and psychiatrist Frantz Fanon (1925–61). Fanon was born on the Caribbean island of Martinique, which was under French colonial rule. Fanon's writings engage with a number of themes we explore elsewhere in this book, including the issue of violence and equality and Karl Marx's emphasis on alienation and ideology.

Fanon served in the Free Army in France during the Second World War. After the war he attended university in France and became a physician and psychiatrist. During the 1950s he worked as a psychiatrist in Algeria, which had been colonized by France in 1830. From the 1830s until 1962, "French officials maintained that Algerian territory was part of France and that Algeria's inhabitants were French,"[35] though France maintained a practice of exclusion for French Algerians for most of that time. In his clinical practice Fanon witnessed firsthand the devasting consequences colonialism imposed on those colonized. This experience led him to become involved with the Algerian liberation movement.

The Algerian liberation war was fought from 1954 to 1962, and the number of total casualties from the conflict remains an issue of debate among historians. "Comparing different censuses before and after the war, researchers have calculated that 350,000–400,000 men, women and children were killed during the conflict, representing three per cent of the Algerian population at the time."[36] Fanon's writings draw inspiration from many different sources, including his lived personal experiences as well as poetry, psychology, philosophy, and political theory. From these

---

35. Todd Shepard, *The Invention of Decolonization: The Algerian War and the Remaking of France* (Ithaca, NY: Cornell University Press, 2006), 20.

36. Natalya Vince, *The Algeria War, the Algerian Revolution* (Palgrave Macmillan, 2020), 2.

diverse sources Fanon diagnoses the social ills of colonialism and advances an anticolonial liberation political theory.

Fanon's experience as both a Black man and a psychiatrist gave him unique insight into the psychological toll colonialism imposed on the oppressed, in terms of their sense of dignity and value in a colonial world and how this impacted their health and well-being. In *The Wretched of the Earth* Fanon explicitly argues that the goal of anticolonial liberation can only be achieved via violence: "National liberation, national resistance, the restoration of nationhood to the people, commonwealth: whatever may be the heading used or the new formulas introduced, decolonization is always a violent phenomenon."[37] Why does Fanon invoke the use of violence to emancipate the colonized from the oppression of colonialism? Fanon does not appeal to the gratuitous use of violence, that is, to engage in violence for the sake of violence. Rather, Fanon argues that colonialism itself is, by its very nature, a system of violence. The oppression of the colonized cannot be sustained without the use and threat of violence. As such it is not a system that can be transformed via rational dialogue and debate. The oppressors are not going to acquiesce and end colonial oppression simply because the oppressed have pointed out that colonialism is unjust.

Because the colonizer will not voluntarily redress the harms of racial and colonial inequality, the only feasible remedy to injustice is *revolution*. Fanon's analysis thus coheres with a Marxist social analysis. Capitalism will not redress the harms of capitalism simply because the proletariat have noted that it is a social system that exploits them. The bourgeoisie will not voluntarily dismantle the social arrangement that enables them to exploit others. Instead, the only prospect for emancipation is for the proletariat to rise up and overthrow the system. Fanon applies this same Marxist reasoning to colonialism itself.

Consider, for example, apartheid in South Africa. Throughout the twentieth century the white minority in South Africa imposed policies of racial segregation and discrimination against nonwhites via apartheid legislation such as the Natives Land Act of 1913. Black landowners were forcibly removed from their land by legislation that prohibited them from owning or purchasing land. Other racist policies of apartheid in

---

37. Frantz Fanon, *The Wretched of the Earth*, preface by Jean-Paul Sartre (New York: Grove, 1963), 35.

South Africa included prohibiting interracial marriage and sexual relations. Such laws remained in effect until the 1990s, when measures like the Abolition of Racially Based Land Measures Act were passed and the anti-apartheid activist Nelson Mandela (imprisoned from 1964 to 1982) became the first Black president of South Africa in 1994. The dismantling of apartheid in South Africa was not something that enlightened white South Africans voluntarily enacted after appeals to their moral and rational conscience. However, it was also not something achieved through a strategy of violence by the oppressed. Rather, it was the culmination of decades of activism, coupled with external pressure from other countries outraged by the violence often perpetrated by the South African police to quell protests against apartheid.

One of the most violent incidents took place in 1960 and is now referred to as the Sharpeville massacre. Police shot at protestors, killing 69 people and injuring 180 more. There was rising global opposition to apartheid, and in 1962 the United Nations created the Special Committee against Apartheid. South Africa was suspended from the UN in 1974. International economic sanctions and boycotts were utilized in an effort to pressure white political elites in South Africa to end apartheid.

Fanon contends that colonial relationships are adversarial in nature and thus could not be peacefully redressed. In "Frantz Fanon and the Ethical Justification of Anti-Colonial Violence" Oladipo Fashina argues that, for Fanon, anticolonial violence is political violence in the specific context of colonial oppression. In such a context there already exists political violence on the part of the colonizer. Therefore, it would be inaccurate to frame the question of anticolonial violence in the way John Rawls, for example, frames civil disobedience when he presupposes that the society in question is "nearly just." A colonial state that imposes racial segregation and discrimination is not "nearly just"; it is a system that utilizes violence to ensure the colonized are oppressed. It is thus against the background of a society where inequality and violence already exist and are inflicted on the colonized by the colonizer that Fanon's analysis of the moral appropriateness of anticolonial violence takes place. For Fanon, anticolonial violence is the only viable antidote to the violence and inequality of colonial oppression. This violence not only includes "what the police and army do, but also harm caused by the economic structure of colonies, the total separation of the colonized from the colonizers, and the actions of government agencies."[38]

Fashina argues that there are two ways to interpret Fanon on the issue of violence: the "humanistic interpretation" and the "nonhumanistic interpretation." Humanism is the position that the following normative premises are foundational to a political theory and ethical framework:

1. Assumption of a common humanity.
2. Assumption of the intrinsic moral worth of all human beings.
3. Inference to the appropriate treatment of human beings.
4. Human dignity and intrinsic worth as the standard for the assessment of social practices and institutions.
5. Assumption of the motivational force of appeal to humanity.[39]

A humanistic interpretation of Fanon's anticolonial stance takes his invocation of anticolonial violence as a means to end the inequality between the colonizers and the colonized. The sociologist Immanuel Wallerstein[40] argues that Fanon should not be described as a postmodernist or a champion of identity politics, but rather as a thinker who invoked a humanistic public ethic. For example, Wallerstein cites the following passage from Fanon's *Black Skin, White Masks*:

> The disaster of the man of color lies in the fact that he was enslaved.
>
> The disaster and inhumanity of the white man lie in the fact that somewhere he has killed man.
>
> And even today they subsist, to organize this dehumanization rationally. But I as a man of color, to the extent that it becomes

---

38. Oladipo Fashina, "Frantz Fanon and the Ethical Justification of Anti-Colonial Violence," *Social Theory and Practice* 15, no. 2 (1989): 179–212, 181.

39. Fashina, "Frantz Fanon," 181.

40. Immanuel Wallerstein, "Reading Fanon in the 21st Century" *New Left Review* 57 (2009): 117–25.

possible for me to exist absolutely, do not have the right to lock myself into a world of retroactive reparations.

I, the man of color, want only this:

That the tool never possesses the man. That the enslavement of man by man cease forever; that is, of one by another. That it may become possible for me to discover and to love man, wherever he may be.

The Negro is not. Any more than the white man.[41]

This passage certainly supports the humanistic reading of Fanon's anticolonial political theory. Like Douglass's condemnation of slavery, Fanon's desire that "the tool never possesses the man" appears to appeal to the common humanity that whites and nonwhites share, and it is the violation of the requirement of equal recognition that colonial oppression obfuscates because it portrays the colonized as inferior to the colonizer.

The nonhumanistic reading of Fanon sees the appeal to equality and dignity as simply an expression of the white bourgeois ideology that will ensure the colonizer maintains their position as oppressor. Fashina contends that the nonhumanistic interpretation of Fanon is more defensible, though he concedes there is textual support for both interpretations. This nonhumanistic interpretation of Fanon's anticolonial political theory contends that appeals to equality are simply part of the colonial ideology. There can never be equality between colonizer and the colonized; that aspiration is merely an illusion. In *The Wretched of the Earth* Fanon explicitly takes this nonhumanistic stance when he writes:

> Bourgeois ideology, however, which is the proclamation of an essential equality between men, manages to appear logical in its own eyes by inviting the sub-men [those colonized] to become human, and to take as their own their prototype Western humanity as incarnated in the Western bourgeoisie.[42]

---

41. Frantz Fanon, *Black Skin, White Masks* [1952] (London: Pluto Press, 1986), 231.
42. Fanon, *The Wretched of the Earth*, 163.

Like Marx's stance that liberal political theory is simply a "superstructural" ideology to mask the exploitative nature of capitalism, for Fanon Western enlightenment ideals (e.g., the appeal to a shared capacity for reason and human dignity) are ideologies that mask the exploitation of colonialism. They will not lead to the emancipation of the colonized. Colonialism has created what Fanon calls a Manichean world, a system of duality thinking that pits the colonizers against those colonized. These values portray the former (i.e., European ideals) as "good" and "superior" and the latter as "evil" and "inferior." In *The Wretched of the Earth* Fanon argues:

> Decolonization is the meeting of two forces, opposed to each other by their very nature.... Their first encounter was marked by violence and their existence together—that is to say the exploitation of the native by the settler—was carried on by dint of a great array of bayonets and cannons.[43]

Fanon explicitly rejects appeals to "European universalism." He argues, if Africa is to be turned into a new Europe or America, then by all means appeal to European ideals, but if Africa is to advance forward beyond what colonial control has to offer, "we must turn over a new leaf, we must work out new concepts, and try to set afoot a new man."[44] Fanon died of leukemia at age thirty-six in 1961. The following year, Algeria was granted its independence after 132 years of French colonial rule.

---

43. Fanon, *The Wretched of the Earth*, 36.
44. Fanon, *The Wretched of the Earth*, 316.

Chapter 10

Utilitarianism

What makes an individual or collective (e.g., public policy) action the morally right choice? If a person or society is religious, the answer to this question will often be determined by reference to a religious text or some other pious authority. In the eighteenth and nineteenth centuries in England, a powerful secular answer to this question was advanced by a group of philosophers (e.g., Jeremy Bentham, James Mill, John Stuart Mill, and Henry Sidgwick) known as proponents of utilitarianism. Utilitarianism maintains that an action or policy decision is the morally appropriate course of action if it produces the most good (i.e., the "greatest happiness of the greatest number").

Utilitarianism is a specific version of what is known as a *consequentialist* moral theory. Consequentialists maintain that it is the expected *consequences* of an action that determine its moral rightness or wrongness (versus its conformity to religious commands). While consequentialists agree that the expected consequences of different options make decisions morally right or wrong, they can disagree (significantly) on the moral weight to place on different consequences. Nonetheless, the appeal of such an approach, maintain its defenders, is that it is a rational and impartial public ethic. Moral decision-making ought not to be predicated on (our biased and highly fallible) intuitions, religion, or the fears of the public, but rather on accurate empirical information and reliable data about the likely consequences of policy decisions.

For utilitarians, the specific consequences that morally matter are the maximization of happiness and minimization of pain. As we shall see in this chapter, there are important disagreements among utilitarian philosophers on issues such as defining what constitutes well-being, but what they share is the commitment to adopting a consequentialist lens for decision-making and aspiring to promote "the greatest happiness of the greatest number." In this chapter we shall focus on the two most important utilitarian philosophers: Jeremy Bentham and John Stuart Mill.

The Law and Punishment

Jeremy Bentham (1748–1832) was born in London and spent his life writing about a variety of topics in ethics, law, and politics. He was a radical critic of the status quo of his day, especially of established doctrines like natural law and contractarianism. Bentham developed novel ideas not only about ethics and happiness but also about punishment and law. He is often considered an early proponent of the legal philosophy known as legal positivism. The legal jurist John Austin (1790–1850), a contemporary of Bentham's, coined the central tenet of legal positivism with the claim "The existence of law is one thing; its merit and demerit another."[1]

Legal positivists emphasize that law is a *human* convention, rather than something provided by a supreme deity. This can be contrasted with the natural law tradition, which (at least historically) conceived of human laws as an expression of divine law. As such the natural law tradition characterized the relationship between law and morality as necessary, as Saint Thomas Aquinas (1225–74) maintained that "an unjust law is no law at all." The British common law tradition, of which Bentham was critical, placed great weight on historical precedent. It thus treated the factual antiquity of law as equivalent to providing a moral justification of the law. But Bentham refutes this point, distinguishing instead between *descriptive* and *critical* jurisprudence. The latter is determined not by historical precedents or natural law but rather by the degree to which laws advance the greatest happiness for the greatest number of people. For Bentham political obligation is predicated not on an appeal to some hypothetical social contract but rather on the principle of utility. He famously proclaimed that "talk of natural rights is nonsense on stilts."[2]

---

1. John Austin, *Austin: The Province of Jurisprudence Determined* [1832], ed. Wilfrid E. Rumble (Cambridge: Cambridge University Press, 1995), 157.

2. Jeremy Bentham, "A Critical Examination of the Declaration of Rights," in *The Works of Jeremy Bentham*, vol. 2, ed. John Bowring (Edinburgh: William Tait, 1843), 914.

Bentham is well known for his consequentialist defense of punishment and his proposal for a *panopticon* penitentiary. The panopticon prison, based on the idea of central inspection, was Bentham's proposal for the design and management of institutions like prisons. He suggested a circular building design, with the inspectors placed in the middle of the prison cells, which would allow them to watch inmates without being seen themselves. Bentham believed such a prison design would be affordable and effective in keeping contact between inmates to a minimum by making them feel they were under constant watch by the inspectors.

The primary function of punishment, according to Bentham, was deterrence. By imposing a disutility on criminal wrongdoing, Bentham believed people would have compelling reason to not contravene the law. The more severe the wrongdoing in question, the more severe the imposed punishment should be. For example, the punishment for armed robbery of a bank should be more severe than the punishment for petty theft of some fruit at the market. Bentham considered the issue of capital punishment, which was widespread in the eighteenth century, and his stance on this topic was nuanced and provisional. He recognized that incarceration and hard labor, unlike capital punishment, were forms of punishment that could be altered in the case of judicial error. Bentham also saw that the harshest form of punishment was typically applied unequally, with the poor receiving a disproportionate degree of death sentences. Bentham concluded that the death penalty was not an appropriate punishment.[3]

Hedonism and the Calculus of Happiness

In *An Introduction to the Principles of Morals and Legislation*, Bentham claims:

> Nature has placed mankind under the governance of two sovereign masters, pain and pleasure. It is for them alone to point out what we ought to do, as well as to determine what we shall do.[4]

---

3. See Hugo Adam Bedau, "Bentham's Utilitarian Critique of the Death Penalty," *Journal of Criminal Law and Criminology* 74, no. 3 (1983): 1033–66.

4. Jeremy Bentham, *An Introduction to Principles of Morals and Legislation* [1780], in David Wootton, *Modern Political Thought: Readings from Machiavelli to Nietzsche* (Indianapolis: Hackett, 2008), 576–91, 576.

For Bentham, the claim that humans seek to maximize pleasure and minimize pain is true both descriptively and normatively. That is, Bentham contends that humans actually do act (on the whole) in a fashion that seeks to bring about more happiness and less pain, *and* that doing so is morally defensible. Bentham's version of utilitarianism is thus a *hedonist* ("hedonism" is derived from the Greek word for "pleasure") doctrine. For Bentham, pain and pleasure are the only things that motivate human action, including our ethical behavior.

For example, if I am offered three different types of desserts—chocolate cake, cookies, or a bowl of fruit—I will tend to choose (as a good hedonist!) the dessert that gives me the most pleasure. For me that's the chocolate cake. However, there are times when I value other pleasures besides the enjoyment of sweet desserts. If I am worried about my health and am trying to lose weight and eat better, I might decide to go for a less appetizing dessert, like the bowl of fruit, because it has the fewest calories. Such a decision would be consistent with my desire to maximize a different type of pleasure (losing weight and promoting my health).

As a *normative* standard for individual and collective decision-making, Bentham takes the goal of the maximization of happiness to be the ultimate standard by which we should assess our options. For example, punishment can be justified on utilitarian grounds because, by attaching the pain of punishment to criminal wrongdoing, we provide compelling reasons for those tempted to break the law to refrain from doing so. While there may be short-term pleasure to be had in stealing my neighbor's sports car to go joyriding, the disutility of incarceration means that, in the long run, such an act would bring more pain than pleasure. Punishment is thus a needed corrective to those who do not reason impartially, putting their own interests ahead of the common good. Utilitarianism is not egoism; it is an impartial ethic in that "each person is to count for one and no one for more than one." When assessing how to bring about the good (i.e., pleasure) and avoid the bad (i.e., pain), we must do so *impartially*.

There are many contemporary ethical predicaments where the appeal of the principle of utility becomes evident. Consider the recent development of self-driving automobiles. The design of safety protocols for the software that decides what the automobile should do when an accident is unavoidable raises ethical concerns. For example, suppose a self-driving car is going down the street and a cat runs directly in front of the car. To avoid hitting the cat, the car would have to swerve into oncoming traffic at a speed that would make human injury and potential death highly likely. In such a scenario we may all agree that saving some human lives is preferable even if it means sacrificing the cat's life. But there are more complex scenarios, such as saving the lives of two pedestrians who are crossing the street when they should not be, instead of the life of the lone occupant of the car, or in a different scenario saving the lives of six occupants in one car instead of two occupants in another car. Should the safety protocol of self-driving cars be designed to save the greater numbers, regardless of whether some are occupants in the car or not (a utilitarian aim) or to maximize the safety of the occupants of the self-driving car over that of any pedestrians, cyclists, and occupants in other vehicles? The latter might increase car sales among individuals who want to prioritize their own safety (and that of their family members), but an impartial ethical perspective might compel us to endorse a utilitarian approach to such decision-making.

Bentham's "calculus of happiness" provides a more fine-grained metric for assessing individual and collective decision-making than simply "utility maximization." The calculus requires us to consider the following seven criteria when comparing potential pleasures and pains:

1. Intensity
2. Duration
3. Certainty/uncertainty
4. Remoteness/nearness in time
5. Fecundity (that is, the likelihood that it will be followed by sensations of the same kind)
6. Purity (the likelihood that it will be followed by opposite sensations)
7. Extent (the number of persons to whom it extends)

Suppose we are considering two potential courses of action (A or B) that could bring about pleasure. The first thing Bentham's calculus of happiness requires us to consider is the *intensity* of the pleasures in question. Some pleasures are more intense than others. If all other things are equal, we should prefer the more intense pleasure over the less intense pleasure.

If the action under consideration involves pursuing one of two courses of action that will result in pain, if all other things are equal, the less intense pain is to be preferred.

However, the intensity of pleasure or pain is only one of many factors we should consider. We must also consider the *duration* of these sensations. If action A will bring about a slightly more intense pleasure than action B, but B's pleasure has a longer duration, then that could provide reasons for preferring B over A even though it has a less intense pleasure. The more intense and long-lasting a particular pleasure, the higher it will score in the calculus of happiness.

In addition to intensity and duration, the calculus of happiness also instructs us to consider the *probability* that the pleasure or pain in question would be realized. In the real world there are seldom any guarantees that specific actions will bring about specific effects. The chance that things will go as we intend lies on a spectrum from the highly unlikely to the certain. When comparing the choice between actions A and B, the likelihood that the pleasure or pain in question would be realized is an important factor. The pleasure that could be realized in action A might be more intense and longer lasting, but if its certainty is only 1 percent, while B has a less intense and shorter but more certain pleasure (say 80 percent), that could tip things in favor of pursuing action B over action A even though the pleasure expected from B would be less intense and durable.

The fourth element of the calculus of happiness is the *remoteness* in time. Suppose actions A and B would bring pleasures that were comparable in terms of intensity, duration, and probability, but action A's pleasure would be more immediate than action B's. Then we would have reason to favor action A over action B. When all else is equal, it is better to experience a pleasure now than the same pleasure a year from now. Of course remoteness might not be decisive when the pleasures or pains in question differ in terms of the other important elements. A more intense and/or durable pleasure that is less immediate could be preferred over the realization of a less intense and/or less durable pleasure that is more immediate.

The fifth and sixth elements of Bentham's calculus of happiness compel us to consider the impact an action might have on bringing about other types of pleasures and pains. The criterion of *fecundity* draws attention to the likelihood that an action might bring about other types of pleasures versus only the initial pleasure the activity seeks to elicit. For example, spending an evening with a friend out on the town might be a pleasurable activity all by itself. But it could also bring other pleasures. Perhaps spending a relaxing evening with a friend socializing in a bustling social environment could lead to the development of new friendships or romantic connections. If particular pleasurable actions will likely bring about other pleasures, then those are factors that must also be added into the calculus of happiness.

The sixth element is *purity*, and like fecundity it considers other potential consequences from our actions, though in the case of purity we must consider the likelihood that actions might bring about the opposite impacts. Some pleasures might lead to pain, and vice versa. For example, spending an evening socializing with a good friend could be pleasurable, but it might also be expensive. The pleasure of enjoying an evening of dinner and drinks with a friend must be weighed against the potential pains of spending lots of money, or staying up late when you must get up early for work the next day. At a policy level a decision to raise the rate of income taxes will impose painful financial burdens on the citizenry, but if those new tax revenues improve health care, education, and environmental protection measures for the same population, the final calculation of pleasures and pains might justify pursuing such actions even though they impose some pains.

The final criterion of the calculus of happiness is the *extent* of people impacted by our decision. One course of action might create a great deal of intense and durable pleasure for a few people, but a different course of action could create greater happiness overall because it creates a less intense but still durable amount of pleasure for a significantly larger number of people. A slight improvement in the pleasure of 10 million people will count for more than a big boost to the happiness of only five people. Numbers matter. All else being equal, the more people impacted by the pleasure or pain in question, the more weighty the case for the course of action that yields the best results for the larger number of people.

While Bentham's calculus of happiness is an ambitious and coherent metric designed to guide our normative decision-making, trying to implement it in practice would be rife with difficulties. Not all pains and pleasures fall into the concise comparison, for example, as being more or less intense, remote, or pure. How do we compare the outcome of increased deaths from automobiles, smoking, or alcohol with the pleasure that comes from living in a society that grants us a wide range of autonomy concerning issues like mobility and what we can inhale or consume? In modern-day public policymaking, no society has pursued Bentham's calculus of happiness, but Bentham's moral reasoning did inspire what is now known as cost-benefit analysis (CBA).

CBA is proposed as a public policy decision-making rubric that requires decision-makers to conduct an analysis of the costs and benefits of different regulatory frameworks. However, proponents of CBA do not typically call it an applied version of Bentham's utilitarian ethics. Cass Sunstein, for example, defends an understanding of CBA that is "agnostic on large issues of the right and the good and that can attract support from people with diverse theoretical commitments or with uncertainty about the appropriate theoretical commitments."[5] Sunstein contends that CBA can help counteract predictable problems of individual and social cognition (e.g., selective attention, group interest, etc.). As such CBA can *enhance* (versus replace) public policy decision-making by mitigating some of the possible cognitive distortions that may arise when a more full inventory of the relevant "facts" is ignored.

When conducting a cost-benefit analysis, policymakers compare the baseline scenario of the status quo (e.g., a situation with no regulation) with the potential costs and benefits of different regulatory options. For example, if at time T1 the baseline is a policy with no environmental regulation, policymakers can construct models to estimate what the long-term impact of this nonregulation policy will be in terms of pollution over the next fifty years. They can then compare this baseline against different regulatory options, which impose different costs on polluters and different benefits in terms of pollution mitigation. Of the options under consideration, including the baseline scenario of the status quo, CBA reveals to policymakers the courses of action that yield the biggest benefits for the least cost and ensures the costs and benefits of different types of action and inaction are addressed and compared (versus ignored).

---

5. Cass Sunstein, "Cognition and Cost-Benefit Analysis," *Journal of Legal Studies* 29, no. S2 (June 2000): 1059–103, 1061.

Democracy

In addition to his contributions to legal theory and ethics, Bentham also defended democratic reform on utilitarian grounds. He believed such reform was required by the greatest happiness principle. Democratic accountability serves as an important check on the abuse of government power, as those ruling could be replaced via elections if they are not delivering laws and policies that serve the common good.

In 1817 Bentham published *Plan of Parliamentary Reform*, and his fellow utilitarian James Mill (the father of John Stuart Mill) published *Essay on Government* in 1828. To increase the accountability of government, both Bentham and James Mill were in favor of holding more regular elections (in fact, they recommended annual elections). The Septennial Act of 1775 had increased the maximal length of a term of Parliament from three years to seven years. Such an extensive term of government eroded the accountability needed to ensure the greatest happiness of the greatest number. Parliamentarians could go years without implementing policies that improved the overall well-being of the population.

By championing annual elections, Bentham and James Mill believed Parliament would be more accountable to the public. If a government delivered little or no effective change, then new members of Parliament would be elected. James Mill favored permitting incumbents to run for reelection, but Bentham was concerned that doing so could pose a threat to the health of a democracy, because the longer someone held such an office, the greater the threat of corruption and/or ineffectiveness. To ensure accountable elections were held, Bentham emphasized the importance of there being experienced and competent candidates that the electoral pool could choose from.

When it came to the right to vote, Bentham championed expanding voting rights to include women and younger people (age twenty-one and over). When adults remained disenfranchised this threatened the greater good of society because it discouraged the moral and intellectual development that enfranchisement could foster. Political participation is a way to learn about the state of public affairs, and to be motivated to elect representatives who would pursue public policies prioritizing the greatest good of the greatest number.

One final novel feature of Bentham's ethics is the treatment of non-human animals. In the last few decades the issue of the ethical treatment of animals used for farming, food, and medical experimentation has begun to receive global attention. Bentham was a moral progressive on this topic as he raised such concerns back in the eighteenth century. Utilitarianism is concerned with the well-being of *all* sentient species, not just human beings. Chickens, apes, and cattle, for example, can experience pleasure and pain. This means that the consequences of our actions must also consider the well-being of nonhuman animals. Bentham remarks:

> The day *may* come, when the rest of the animal creation may acquire those rights which never could have been withholden from them but by the hand of tyranny. The French have already discovered that the blackness of the skin is no reason why a human being should be abandoned without redress to the caprice of the tormentor. It may come one day to be recognized, that the number of legs, villosity of the skin, or the termination of the os sacrum [bone in the lower vertebral column], are reasons equally insufficient for abandoning a sensitive being to the same fate.[6]

John Stuart Mill and the Quality (Not Just Quantity) of Pleasure

The second prominent utilitarian thinker we focus on in this chapter is John Stuart Mill (1806–73), the son of James Mill. Jeremy Bentham was the godfather of John Stuart Mill, and both James Mill and Jeremy Bentham played important formative roles in John Stuart Mill's education and intellectual development. From a young age John Stuart Mill (hereafter referred to simply as Mill, not to be confused with his father, James Mill) learned to read both Greek and Latin, and he read Plato's works in the original Greek. His moral outlook was shaped by the utilitarianism of his father and Bentham. Later in his adult life Mill

---

6. Jeremy Bentham, *An Introduction to Principles of Morals and Legislation* [1780] (Oxford: Clarendon Press), 311.

noted that what was missing from his education was any emotional education, and he suffered a mental breakdown at age twenty. In his autobiography Mill credits poetry with lifting him out of the mental despair he had felt.

In 1861 Mill published *Utilitarianism*, which echoes Bentham's commitment to the principle of utility. Mill argues that "the Greatest Happiness Principle holds that actions are right in proportion as they tend to promote happiness, wrong as they tend to produce the reverse of happiness."[7] Mill actually attempted to offer a proof of the principle of utility, claiming that "happiness is desirable, and the only thing desirable, as an end; all other things being only desirable as means to that end." Mill continues:

> What ought to be required of this doctrine—what conditions is it requisite that the doctrine should fulfil—to make good its claim to be believed? The only proof capable of being given that an object is visible, is that people actually see it. The only proof that a sound is audible, is that people hear it: and so of the other sources of our experience. In like manner, I apprehend, the sole evidence it is possible to produce that anything is desirable, is that people do actually desire it. If the end which the utilitarian doctrine proposes to itself were not, in theory and in practice, acknowledged to be an end, nothing could ever convince any person that it was so. No reason can be given why the general happiness is desirable, except that each person, so far as he believes it to be attainable, desires his own happiness. This, however, being a fact, we have not only all the proof which the case admits of, but all which it is possible to require, that happiness is a good: that each person's happiness is a good to that person, and the general happiness, therefore, a good to the aggregate of all persons.[8]

---

7. John Stuart Mill, *Utilitarianism* [1861], in *Collected Works of John Stuart Mill*, vol. 10, ed. John M. Robson (Toronto: University of Toronto Press / London: Routledge & Kegan Paul, 1969), 203–59, 210.

8. Mill, *Utilitarianism*, 234.

While Bentham had a significant influence on Mill's ideas about utilitarianism, Mill believed that Bentham's commitment to hedonism required modification. According to Bentham, poetry is as good as push-pin (a child's game), if both provide the same amount of pleasure. But this was not a conclusion that Mill shared. The *quality*, and not just quantity, of pleasure mattered to Mill. In *Utilitarianism* Mill claimed that it is "better to be Socrates dissatisfied than a fool satisfied." For Mill, pleasures of the intellect rate higher than sensual pleasures.

Mill thus makes a distinction between what he calls "higher" and "lower" pleasures, a distinction that is somewhat vague but can be given clarity by invoking Mill's comparative assessment, the "informed preference test."[9] Generally speaking Mill takes the pleasures of the intellect and the morally virtuous person to be "higher pleasures"—those pleasures "of the intellect, of the feelings and the imagination, and of the moral sentiments"[10]—when compared to the pleasures experienced by persons motivated simply by the sensual pleasures like eating and drinking. The informed preference test stipulates:

> Of two pleasures, if there be one to which all or almost all who have experience of both give a decided preference, irrespective of any feeling of moral obligation to prefer it, that is the more desirable pleasure. If one of the two is, by those who are competently acquainted with both, placed so far above the other that they prefer it, even though knowing it to be attended with a greater amount of discontent, and would not resign it for any quantity of the other pleasure which their nature is capable of, we are justified in ascribing to the preferred enjoyment a superiority in quality, so far outweighing quantity as to render it, in comparison, of small amount.[11]

I have experienced the pleasure of reading philosophy and the pleasure of eating pizza. And no amount of pizza could equal the pleasure I derive from engaging with philosophy. If, according to Mill's informed

---

9. Robert Crisp, *Mill on Utilitarianism* (London: Routledge, 1997), 29.
10. Mill, *Utilitarianism*, 210.
11. Mill, *Utilitarianism*, 211.

preference test, most people who have experienced both types of pleasure have the same attitude as I, then the intellectual pleasures of philosophy are a "higher pleasure" compared to the gustatory pleasures.

If one takes a concern for the quality, and not just quantity, of pleasure to be an integral aspect of human well-being, then Mill's informed preference test will be seen as an improvement over Bentham's hedonism. However, critics may retort that the appeal of Bentham's theory is that it did not stipulate which pleasures are the most important; that is up to each individual person. Thus Mill's informed preference test could be critiqued as being somewhat elitist. Mill's tactic for ensuring the intellectual pleasures are convincingly portrayed as "higher pleasures" is to define "competent judgment" to discern that point in a manner highly likely to conform to that conclusion. The opinions of those who do not enjoy the intellectual pleasures of philosophy or poetry, for example, would not be counted in Mill's approach.

Someone defending Mill can note that Mill's argument that some pleasures are higher than others does not necessarily entail that "the quality of a pleasure automatically outweighs considerations about the quantity in which it is available."[12] Christoph Schmidt-Petri, for example, claims that Mill's informed preference test is best understood as an *epistemic* claim concerning how to know if some pleasures are higher and others are lower rather than a metaphysics of pleasure and their relations. And the epistemic test is simply a decided preference for one type of pleasure over another (even when in larger quantity) among people who have experienced both types of pleasures. But it does not follow that persons must (or should) always choose the higher pleasure over any amount of lower pleasures. Mill's position does not commit those who qualified for the informed preference test to always seek out higher pleasures. The quality of pleasure is important to Mill's utilitarianism, but so too is the quantity of pleasure.

---

12. Christoph Schmidt-Petri, "Mill on Quality and Quantity," *Philosophical Quarterly* 53, no. 210 (2003): 102–4, 102.

Mill's Liberty Principle

Mill's *On Liberty*, published in 1859, has also been influential. *On Liberty* advances one of the core political convictions of Western liberal democracies, the *liberty* (or *no harm*) *principle*. The principle stipulates the circumstances in which governments can and cannot justifiably interfere with individual liberty. Mill describes the principle:

> The object of this Essay is to assert one very simple principle, as entitled to govern absolutely the dealings of society with the individual in the way of compulsion and control, whether the means used be physical force in the form of legal penalties, or the moral coercion of public opinion. That principle is, that . . . the only purpose for which power can be rightfully exercised over any member of a civilised community, against his will, is to prevent harm to others. His own good, either physical or moral, is not a sufficient warrant.[13]

The liberty principle brings into focus the *reasons* for justifiable state interference in the liberty of individuals, and those exclude paternalistic or moralistic justifications. The state cannot justifiably interfere with our liberty in order to protect our own interests or persuade us to do the morally right action. Of course, society can attempt to persuade us to do these things through noncoercive means (e.g., education), but it cannot justifiably use the coercive power of the state to interfere with our liberty unless our actions pose a real risk of harm to others.

In the passage above from *On Liberty*, Mill invokes a distinction between actions that can be described as "self-regarding conduct" and "other-regarding conduct." When it comes to the former, actions that only adversely impact my own interests or well-being, the government should never interfere with my actions. The liberty principle is thus an *antipaternalistic* principle: it rejects paternal government interference, the idea that the state must sometimes contravene my liberty in order to protect my interests from my own harmful actions. When it comes to actions

---

13. John Stuart Mill, *On Liberty* [1859], in Wootton, *Modern Political Thought*, 592–651, 596–97.

that harm others, harm is a necessary (though not sufficient) requirement for justified governmental intervention. Just because my actions harm you, that fact alone does not mean that government intervention is justified by Mill's liberty principle. In some circumstances permitting the state to intervene actually creates more harm than it prevents, thus reducing (rather than increasing) overall utility. For example, my inconsiderate actions (e.g., breaking promises) as a friend or romantic partner could emotionally harm my friends or partner, but having the government intervene to enforce compliance with the norms of interpersonal relationships would create more disutility than utility. By contrast, having the state enforce compliance with quarantine should I test positive for a highly infectious fatal virus would create more overall benefits as it would help prevent the spread of the virus to others, thus saving lives. When state intervention to prevent harm to others is conducive to the greater good (e.g., the threat of criminal sanctions against assault and theft), the liberty principle supports state interference.

Critics of Mill often question the distinction between self-regarding and other-regarding actions. We are social beings, interconnected with others and society in intricate ways. Are any actions, especially those that harm ourselves, genuinely just "self-regarding"? Consider, for example, the case of seat belt laws. If the justification for mandating that I must wear a seat belt when driving my car is that doing so will protect me against serious injury or death if in a collision, does this not violate Mill's liberty principle? As it is my own health risks that seem to be at stake with seat belts, does driving without a seat belt not qualify as "self-regarding conduct"? Mill's stance on this issue is more nuanced than critics might presuppose. Mill concedes that many actions that might appear, on initial impressions, to be self-regarding conduct are in fact other-regarding conduct. The example Mill provides is consuming alcohol to the point of inebriation. When my getting drunk harms no one else but myself, then society and government has no justified basis for intrusively interfering with my destructive self-regarding conduct. However, if my drinking impairs my ability to safely perform my job (e.g., as a soldier) or parent (e.g., to provide and care for my children), or to repay my debts, then my actions are harming others and should be considered harmful other-regarding conduct. State interference in such cases would not contravene the liberty principle.

Returning to the issue of seat belts, in a country that enjoys public health care, the decision to drive without wearing a seat belt does have implications for the (limited) health-care resources available to others. Should I get in an accident, I would require more medical attention because I was not wearing a seat belt, and thus my actions do adversely impact the interests of others. We must either increase funding for health care through taxation or ration scarce health-care resources because of the additional demands placed on the health-care system by drivers and occupants who refuse to wear seat belts.

Thus Mill's liberty principle requires us to critically examine the extent to which our actions can adversely impact the interests of others, even those decisions or actions that might initially appear as simply "self-regarding" conduct. Furthermore, Mill believes this principle should only apply to persons who possess the developed faculties for rational decision-making. Children, for example, cannot invoke the liberty principle to object to their parents curtailing their potentially harmful decisions. A curious four-year-old child might want to stick their fork in the electric outlet to see what happens, but because they lack the knowledge of the potentially fatal danger of their action, the protective parent is justified in intervening and taking the fork away. But the government should not treat adults as parents treat children. A society governed by the liberty principle treats its citizens as rational, autonomous agents who are capable of learning from their mistakes. While we often make errors in our decisions about what is in our best interests, a benevolent government that sought to override our autonomous decision-making would likely make even more erroneous decisions, in addition to infantilizing us. Permitting us to make mistakes enables us to learn from experience. When the government acts like a protective parent, it robs us of the opportunity to learn to be reflective and adaptive. It thus impedes our development as rational, autonomous agents.

What specifically constitutes the type of harm to others that would open the door to justifiable criminal wrongdoing? Mill does not think simply offending a person or hurting their feelings meets this threshold. If I tell you that you look unattractive wearing your red shirt, and this hurts your feelings, does that count as a harm? Or what if I demand you take off the red shirt under threat that I will swing my baseball bat into your back until you comply? The former fails to qualify as a relevant harm, while the latter does qualify. But getting precision on what Mill believes constitutes harm is a source of ongoing disagreement among scholars of Mill. Some contend that harm means an injury to the vital interests of others,[14] whereas other scholars argue that harm (for Mill) means "perceptible damage experienced against one's wishes."[15] The latter includes "physical injury, forcible confinement, financial loss, damage to reputation, broken promises (contractual and others) and so on."[16]

Piers Norris Turner argues that Mill intentionally did not specify what constituted harm in his discussion of the liberty/harm principle because Mill wanted it to be construed expansively, to be equated with *bad consequences*. This suggestion provides us with a way to unify Mill's utilitarianism with his commitment to the liberty principle as an antipaternalistic doctrine. Just because my actions harm others (understood expansively to mean that they bring about bad consequences) does not mean the liberty principle sanctions governmental or societal interference with my actions. Those bad consequences are a necessary but not sufficient condition for intervention. In effect, "the purpose of the harm [or liberty] principle is only to exclude paternalistic considerations from social deliberation."[17] To arrive at a determination of when state interference *is* justified (not simply when it is *not* justified), what must be considered is the *net impact* on the good and bad consequences of specific forms of interference, compared with noninterference. Thus we should view the liberty principle as an integral part of Mill's consequential public ethic. The state should only intervene in my liberty when I harm others *and* when such intervention brings about more utility compared to noninterference.

In addition to the issue of what constitutes harm, another tricky issue concerns the *likelihood* that harm will be realized. Sometimes our actions have a high degree of certainty that harm will be inflicted on others. If I intentionally swing a baseball bat quickly toward your legs, we can expect that action to harm you. But for many actions there may only be a *probability*, indeed, even a low probability, that harm will be realized. Speeding

---

14. John Gray, *Mill on Liberty: A Defence*, 2nd ed. (New York: Routledge, 1996), 57.
15. Jonathan Riley, *Mill on Liberty* (New York: Routledge, 1998), 99.
16. Riley, *Mill on Liberty*, 98.
17. Piers Norris Turner, "'Harm' and Mill's Harm Principle," *Ethics* 124, no. 2 (2014): 299–326, 321.

in a car, for example, poses a risk of harm to others, though most times it does not result in a car accident or fatality. But the potential harm from reckless driving is significant enough—the risks are perceptible and measurable—and the liberty in question not very weighty (the liberty to "drive recklessly"). Having speed limits on how fast automobiles can drive, especially in residential neighborhoods and near schools, promotes greater utility than having none.

The risks of harm thus occur along a spectrum, from the possible (but very unlikely) to the certain. Mill acknowledges this point in the following passage concerning freedom of expression and how context can influence the risk of expressions posing a significant harm to others:

> No one pretends that actions should be as free as opinions. On the contrary, even opinions lose their immunity, when the circumstances in which they are expressed are such as to constitute their expression a positive instigation to some mischievous act. An opinion that corn-dealers are starvers of the poor, or that private property is robbery, ought to be unmolested when simply circulated through the press, but may justly incur punishment when delivered orally to an excited mob assembled before the house of a corn-dealer, or when handed about among the same mob in the form of a placard.[18]

Mill's utilitarian defense of liberty is a nuanced one. It functions with an expansive conception of harm and a flexible attitude toward what constitutes a tolerable level of risk of harm, depending on the severity of the harm and the significance of the liberty in question. Many real-life policy decisions reflect this same nuanced analysis. Consider the case of drinking and driving. If public safety was the sole concern of policy decision-making, then a country might take the view that no alcohol consumption at all should be tolerated when driving. However, such a policy would not be based on empirical evidence, as a single sip of beer will not alter one's capacity to drive safely. Public policy decisions should also give some weight to the preferences of responsible adults who might prefer the occasional glass of wine with dinner and can drive without any real risks of

---

18. Mill, *On Liberty*, 620.

impairment. Many factors must thus be considered and balanced when it comes to rules involving alcohol consumption and driving. As a person's blood alcohol content increases, it will slow a driver's reflexes and reaction time, eventually impairing their ability to drive safely. At very high levels, alcohol consumption can cause passing out, blackouts, and memory loss. When determining what level is tolerable, policy decision-makers will weigh the significance of the harm, the risk of that harm from different blood alcohol levels, and the value of the liberty in question. A priority is given to saving lives from automobile accidents over the liberty to drive when inebriated, hence the low threshold (but not simply a "theoretical" risk) typically set for legal blood alcohol levels.

Freedom of Expression and the "Marketplace of Ideas"

In chapter 2 of *On Liberty* Mill addresses freedom of thought and expression. Truth and knowledge are integral to the utility of any society, and Mill's utilitarian defense of freedom emphasizes the epistemic reality that we are all fallible. We often make mistakes about what we think the nature of reality is (e.g., does the sun revolve around the earth?), and the way to ensure we minimize the risks of predicating our lives on false beliefs is to allow for a "marketplace of ideas" where truth can emerge victorious after robust debate concerning the evidence and merits of different beliefs. Consider, for example, scientific findings. If a scientist conjectures that A causes B based on the observations of an experiment they conducted, other scientists will try to replicate the experiment to see if this conclusion can be supported. Many scientific journals have retracted the conclusions of scientific papers based on subsequent findings that the original experiment was flawed. Without permitting others to challenge such findings, science could not progress in a meaningful manner. When a theory or hypothesis can withstand the criticisms and objections raised by skeptics, it then progresses from the realm of speculative conjecture toward more firmly established scientific knowledge. Therefore, freedom of thought and expression are vital to finding truth. Without this marketplace of ideas we would not be able to effectively discern between ideas that are worthy of defending and those that should be abandoned.

At the heart of Mill's defense of freedom of expression is a faith in human rationality, that eventually we will discard false beliefs in favor of those supported by the evidence and better argumentation. This faith in human rationality enables us to weather the storm of tolerating problematic opinions, those we believe are wrong or offensive. We can have confidence that in time, such beliefs will fall out of favor because they cannot be sustained in the competitive marketplace of ideas among reflective agents. "Mill thinks that it is our deliberative capacities, especially our capacities for practical deliberation, that mark us as progressive creatures and that, as a result, the principal ingredient of our happiness or well-being must be the exercise of these deliberative capacities."[19]

The scope and limits of free speech remain an important and challenging issue for Western societies (especially on university campuses) as they attempt to grapple with issues like hate speech, cases where respecting the values of freedom and equality can come into conflict. Should speech that publicly expresses hate against specific groups of people—based on race, religion, sex, sexual orientation, and so on—be permitted? Historically these targeted groups of people have often been legally discriminated against (e.g., prohibited from employment or other societal opportunities such as education or voting), and can face continued informal discrimination (e.g., attitudes of racism, Islamophobia, antisemitism, sexism, homophobia, etc.), and thus the expression of hate against them can impede a society's ability to achieve genuine equality for all.

Contentious cases like neo-Nazis marching in Skokie, Illinois, in 1977 or, more recently, the Unite the Right rally in Charlottesville, Virginia, in 2017—which protested plans to remove a statue of Confederate general Robert E. Lee—present complex cases because they are events where the expression at stake can cause harm (e.g., inciting violence, emotional harm to the victims of historical injustices). Many landmark legal decisions over the past century have involved determining the appropriate threshold for speech to constitute an imminent serious harm to others. In the United States there is strong protection of the First Amendment, which safeguards free speech.

---

19. David Brink, "Millian Principles, Freedom of Expression, and Hate Speech," *Legal Theory* 7, no. 2 (2001): 119–57, 123.

Critics of state censorship, like Nadine Strossen, former president of the American Civil Liberties Union, have argued that strong free speech rights are an effective measure to ensure the equality of politically disadvantaged groups, like women and racial minorities. Strossen notes that the first individuals prosecuted under the British Race Relations Act of 1965, which criminalized the intentional incitement of racial hatred, were Black Power leaders.[20] Strossen contends that the enforcement of university hate speech codes has similar deleterious effects. While intended to promote the equality of disadvantaged groups, such measures can also impose risks on the very groups they were intended to protect. Thus, Strossen argues that an anticensorship stance is, overall, better for both freedom and equality.

Some commentators have argued that Mill's stance on liberty does not lead to a strong version of libertarianism opposed to the censorship of certain types of hate speech. David Brink believes that Mill's defense of liberty is ultimately predicated on the supposition that humans are progressive beings, more specifically that we possess the capacities for practical deliberation. These deliberative capacities are an integral part of our happiness. "A good human life is one that exercises one's higher capacities (i 11; ii 20; iii 1–10); a person's higher capacities include her deliberative capacities, in particular, capacities to form, revise, assess, select, and implement her own plan of life."[21]

By making Mill's concern for practical deliberation foundational to his defense of liberty, Brink builds a compelling case for censoring certain types of hate speech. Rather than treating all speech as inviolable, this approach places greater weight on the protection of expression important to the exercise and refinement of our capacity for practical deliberation. So-called "fighting words" (e.g., insulting epithets that silence others through injury and intimidation), for example, are not intended to invoke reasoned responses. They are thus not granted strong First Amendment constitutional protection and this is consistent, Brink contends, with Mill's stance on liberty. The same can be said about certain types of hate

---

20. Nadine Strossen, "Hate Speech and Pornography: Do We Have to Choose between Freedom of Speech and Equality?," *Case Western Reserve Law Review* 46, no. 2 (1996): 449–78, 466.

21. Brink, "Millian Principles," 126.

speech. "Low-value" speech, that is, speech that undermines (rather than facilitates) the exercise of practical deliberation, diminishes rather than increases human happiness. As such there are no compelling consequentialist reasons for taking a libertarian stance on an issue like hate speech as "hate speech contributes to a hostile environment that undermines the culture of mutual respect necessary for effective expression and fair consideration of diverse points of view."[22]

The potential harms of expressions of hate—such as the denial of the Holocaust, white supremacy, or transphobia—can also be exacerbated by the *medium* of communication. Communications expressed via social media, for example, have the potential to go viral and reach millions of people. Thus the social discord that online expressions of hate can incite has created many complex challenges for the regulation of such expressions on platforms such as Facebook, X (Twitter), and TikTok. How one interprets Mill's stance on liberty, as well as how one views the impacts (intended and unintended) of censorship, will influence whether one champions or critiques different types of hate speech laws and campus speech codes. Mill's defense of freedom of expression remains an important part of the debates on free speech today, over a century and a half after he published *On Liberty*.

Representative Government and the Vote

John Stuart Mill's *Considerations on Representative Government* (1861) echoes the concerns of his father (James Mill) and Bentham that the greatest happiness principle prescribes democratic reform. Mill also championed extending the right to vote to women. He was, like Edmund Burke, a political theorist who had real life experience of the political arena of his day, as Mill was elected as a member of Parliament for the city of Westminster in 1865.

Mill condemns despotism on the basis of the kind of human beings such a system creates. If citizens have no involvement in electing representatives and monitoring the business of government (because such decisions are made by unaccountable elites), the citizens may remain passive.

---

22. Brink, "Millian Principles," 141.

People will have no motivation to create a better society since they have no responsibility for bringing such a state of affairs into reality. There is no reason, in a despotic society, for citizens to educate themselves about the affairs of government. Mill proclaims: "Let a person have nothing to do for his country and he will not care for it."[23] Democratic governance is thus desirable, contends Mill, for the effects it has on our moral and intellectual development. A despotic government might be able to competently manage the affairs of society efficiently, but it will not create the active and reflective moral agents needed for the society to realize its full potential.

Mill also criticizes direct democracy, echoing Plato's concerns that it would empower the ignorant to rule. Mill claims:

> At its best, it is inexperience sitting in judgement on experience, ignorance on knowledge: ignorance which never suspecting the existence of what it does not know, is equally careless and supercilious, making light of, if not resenting, all pretensions to have a judgement better worth attending to than its own.[24]

To help improve the epistemic fitness of representative democracy, Mill favored a number of novel (but problematic) measures with respect to the right to vote. While initially preferring the secret ballot, Mill later came to support the open vote as he believed this would help guard against the danger of people simply voting out of their own narrow self-interest versus what was best for society as a whole.

Mill also supported giving extra votes to educated elites. If utilitarianism prescribes that "all counts for one, and none more than one," how can Mill also champion plural votes for the educated? There appears to be a major contradiction between Mill's commitment to participation—that is, that the government must be accountable to all via regular elections—and his commitment to ensuring a competent elite have an enhanced voice (via plural voting) in the democratic process. The plural voting proposal strikes us as a blatant violation of the impartiality entailed by the greatest

---

23. John Stuart Mill, *Considerations of Representative Government* (London: Longmans, Green, 1872), 19.

24. Mill, *Considerations of Representative Government*, 37.

happiness principle. But we must recall that Mill does not conceive of representative democracy as a system where political parties simply pander to the individual preferences of the masses by offering party platforms designed to placate their private interests.

Joseph Miller contends that there is in fact no incompatibility between Mill's commitments to participation and to competency, and that these two principles must work in harmony if they are to produce the best system of government. Miller summarizes Mill's stance on the competency issue with regard to plural voting:

> Plural voting provides that citizens receive different numbers of votes, "competent" citizens receiving more than others. Mill offers two easy tests for picking out "competent" voters: profession and education. Mill suggests votes could be allotted based on a person's employment, such that bankers, foremen, entrepreneurs and merchants would receive more votes than common labourers. Additionally, Mill proposes that better-educated citizens (e.g., those who are university graduates) should receive more votes than uneducated citizens do.[25]

For Miller, Mill's commitment to plural voting is a way to ensure that the competent can help guide the uneducated by raising the level of debate and reasoning about issues of societal concern and politics. Universal suffrage ensures political life is one of citizen participation and education, and plural voting ensures politics is not simply about people voting out of self-interest. The latter is aided by giving more weight and influence to the educated to help elevate the democratic decision-making to pursue the greatest happiness of the greatest number (and not simply class interests).

To critics, Mill's stance on plural voting may sound just as naive and elitist as Plato's endorsement of philosopher rulers. In Mill's case, why should we assume that a university education is the relevant skill set for the type of competency needed to elect suitable political representatives? Furthermore, why assume the educated class is less susceptible to the bias of class interest than the laboring class is? Few are likely to see Mill's

---

25. Joseph Miller, "J. S. Mill on Plural Voting, Competence, and Participation," *History of Political Thought* 24, no. 4 (2003): 647–67, 651.

proposal for plural voting as viable or attractive improvements to the current health of today's democracies. But Mill's concerns for education and democratic participation are nonetheless relevant and remain vital political aspirations even in the twenty-first century.

One contemporary proposal that is sympathetic to Mill's concern for the competency of democratic decision-making is one suggested by the philosopher Jason Brennan.[26] Rather than granting plural voting, Brennan argues that democracies should implement a *competency test* for voters. Historically, democratic countries have excluded people from voting for immoral reasons, including income, sex, race, and so on. Even in the twenty-first century some of the reasons people are excluded from voting are subject to criticism, such as the exclusion of younger persons, persons with cognitive impairment, and inmates.[27]

Brennan argues that there can be good reasons to exclude some people from voting by drawing an analogy between voting and jury trials. Voting, like a jury member deciding the guilt or innocence of a suspected criminal, involves the wielding of political power. In the case of jury trails in criminal law, a finding of "guilty" might result in someone's liberty being constrained. In the case of political power, a majority win for a political party might result in that party deciding to impose tax increases on some people, reduce social support programs for the vulnerable, or implement other policies that directly impact citizens. In both cases the stakes involved are high, and thus the use of that political power must be morally justified to others.

In the case of jury trails, Brennan provides some examples where we would feel that a jury member has violated the public responsibility of being a credible juror and thus should be excluded from the jury. For example, if a juror did not pay attention to the expert testimony or evidence relevant to the guilt or innocence of a defendant, or the jury

---

26. Jason Brennan, *Against Democracy* (Princeton, NJ: Princeton University Press, 2016); Jason Brennan, "The Right to a Competent Electorate," *Philosophical Quarterly* 61, no. 245 (2011): 700–724.

27. Daniel Weinstock, "What's So Funny about Voting Rights for Children?," *Georgetown Journal of Law and Public Policy* 18, no. 2 (2020): 751–71; Linda Barclay, "Cognitive Impairment and the Right to Vote: A Strategic Approach," *Journal of Applied Philosophy* 30, no. 2 (2013): 146–59; Michael Cholbi, "A Felon's Right to Vote," *Law and Philosophy* 21, nos. 4–5 (2002): 543–65.

member had a bias or prejudice against the defendant, we would not feel it would be fair to permit this jury member to participate in the deliberations concerning the defendant's guilt or innocence. A fair trial requires impartial and competent jurors. The process of jury selection attempts to weed out biased jury members.

In the case of jury trials, Brennan argues that the process must not violate what he calls the "competence principle." This principle maintains:

> It is unjust to deprive citizens of life, liberty or property, or to alter their life prospects significantly, by force and threats of force as a result of decisions made by an incompetent or morally unreasonable deliberative body, or as a result of decisions made in an incompetent and morally unreasonable way.[28]

When it comes to trial by jury, Brennan argues that people of bad epistemic and moral character should not serve on juries. This is a compelling view because the use of the coercive power of the state must be deployed responsibly, and this is compromised when the competence principle is violated. The same sentiment, asserts Brennan, should apply to the use of the political power that arises from democratic elections. Voting, like jury trials, ought to satisfy the competence principle in order for the use of political power to be morally justified. But current democratic practices do not require this; the only requirement for voting is registering when one reaches a certain age, which does not serve as an adequate proxy for epistemic and moral character (just as an age requirement alone would not be a sufficient requirement for jury selection).

Ignorant, irrational, and unreasonable voters, claims Brennan, are just as morally problematic as ignorant, irrational, and unreasonable jury members. To remedy this problem Brennan suggests imposing a voter qualification exam, in the same way a driver exam is imposed to determine who is qualified to drive an automobile. Such an exam would test relevant basic social science and knowledge about the political candidates running for office. If successful, Brennan believes this would improve the epistemic fitness of our democratic practices, as it would ensure the electoral process tracks the judgments of competent voters instead of allowing persons to

---

28. Brennan, "The Right to a Competent Electorate," 704.

vote who lack the knowledge and insight required to make responsible decisions involving the use of political power.

While one might in principle have some sympathy with Brennan's aspiration to improve the link between knowledge and democratic voting, actually implementing a voter competence requirement in today's democracies, such as the United States, is rife with challenges and problems. Which *types of knowledge* should form the basis of the competence test? And *who* should decide this? The consequences of adopting such a policy today would likely be an exacerbation of the inequality and exclusion that already exists in countries where significant portions of the population enjoy fewer opportunities for accessing higher education, or even just middle and high school education. Disenfranchisement risks marginalizing even further the interests and voices of the most disadvantaged, and this would constitute a major injustice.

The Critique of Utilitarianism

To the defenders of utilitarianism, it is a public ethic that offers many potential benefits. As a consequentialist ethic, it defines the morally relevant features of decisions by their likely impact on human well-being instead of appealing to religious doctrines or the intuitions we might have about which courses of action are morally right and wrong. Thus it offers a *rational* public ethic, one that equates successful decision-making with making competent comparisons between the likely effects of different potential courses of action we could take. Utilitarianism is also an impartial ethic, in that all count for one and none more than one.

But utilitarianism has also received a significant amount of criticism. The most influential criticism of utilitarianism came from the twentieth-century social contract theorist John Rawls in his book *A Theory of Justice*. Rawls argues that utilitarianism is a deficient public ethic because it fails to recognize what Rawls refers to as "the separateness of persons." If utilitarianism was a moral theory that applied to just one individual person, contends Rawls, then it would be a defensible decision-making ethic.

> Each man in realizing his own interests is certainly free to balance his own losses against his own gains. We may impose a sacrifice on ourselves now for the sake of a great advantage later. A

person quite properly acts, at least when others are not affected, to achieve his own greatest good, to advance his rational ends as far as possible.[29]

However, once a utilitarian ethic is applied to the choice of an *association of people* (and not just a single person), the "balancing of losses and gains" becomes inherently problematic because some of the sacrifices required to increase overall happiness might be made by individuals who do not get to enjoy the resulting greater happiness. More specifically, Rawls argues that the basic liberties (e.g., freedom of association, freedom of expression, etc.) "are not subject to political bargaining or to the calculus of social interests."[30] For Rawls, justice requires protecting the basic liberties of all, but utilitarianism treats questions of distributive justice as questions of *efficient administration.* "The nature of the decision made by the ideal legislator is not, therefore, materially different from that of an entrepreneur deciding how to maximize his profit by producing this or that commodity, or that of a consumer deciding how to maximize his satisfaction by the purchase of this or that collection of goods."[31]

In "Cost-Benefit Analysis: An Ethical Critique" Steven Kelman presents a host of examples he believes reveal the problems with utilitarianism as a public ethic, some of which echo the concerns expressed by Rawls. I will limit our discussion here to just two of Kelman's examples.

The first is a concrete example of Rawls's point about the importance of the separateness of persons. Kelman invites us to consider the following scenario:

> A wave of thefts has hit a city and the police are having trouble finding any of the thieves. But they believe, correctly, that punishing someone for theft will have some deterrent effect and will decrease the number of crimes. Unable to arrest any actual perpetrator, the police chief and the prosecutor arrest a person whom they know to be innocent and, in cahoots with each other,

---

29. John Rawls, *A Theory of Justice*, rev. ed. (Cambridge, MA: Harvard University Press, 1999), 21.
30. Rawls, *A Theory of Justice*, 25.
31. Rawls, *A Theory of Justice*, 24.

fabricate a convincing case against him. The police chief and the prosecutor are about to retire, so the act has no effect on any future actions of theirs. The fabrication is perfectly executed, so nobody finds out about it. Is the only question involved in judging the act of framing the innocent man that of whether his suffering from conviction and imprisonment will be greater than the suffering avoided among potential crime victims when some crimes are deterred? A utilitarian would need to believe that it is morally right to punish the innocent man as long as it can be demonstrated that the suffering prevented outweighs his suffering.[32]

Kelman's concern, like Rawls's, is that there can be instances where respect for "the greatest happiness of the greatest number" will result in a grave injustice. Punishing an innocent person is wrong, even in a situation where doing so might create more utility overall.

A second example Kelman considers reinforces a similar point.

> Imagine two worlds, each containing the same sum total of happiness. In the first world, this total of happiness came about from a series of acts that included a number of lies and injustices (that is, the total consisted of the immediate gross sum of happiness created by certain acts, minus any long-term unhappiness occasioned by the lies and injustices). In the second world the same amount of happiness was produced by a different series of acts, none of which involved lies or injustices. Do we have any reason to prefer the one world to the other? A utilitarian would need to believe that the choice between the two worlds is a matter of indifference.[33]

Rawls advances an account of justice called "justice as fairness," which attempts to capture the moral intuitions we have about the importance of the injustices Kelman describes in this example. To treat people fairly

---

32. Steven Kelman, "Cost-Benefit Analysis: An Ethical Critique (with Replies)," *AEI Journal on Government and Society Regulation*, January/February 1981, 33–40, 34.

33. Kelman, "Cost-Benefit Analysis," 35.

Rawls contends that the principles designed to govern society's institutions must be chosen in what he calls the "original position." This is a choice situation where everyone is treated as an equal, where the choice of principles is made behind a "veil of ignorance" so we cannot be biased to select principles that favor us based on our social class, religion, sex, or race. In such an impartial decision-making process, Rawls contends that utilitarianism would be rejected in favor of his two principles of justice, the first statement of which is:

> First: each person is to have an equal right to the most extensive scheme of equal basic liberties compatible with a similar scheme of liberties for others.
>
> Second: social and economic inequalities are to be arranged so that they are both (a) reasonably expected to be to everyone's advantage, and (b) attached to positions and offices open to all.[34]

After making its initial appearance in the early 1970s, Rawls's theory of justice dominated Anglo-American political philosophy for many decades, and still remains a very influential theory within the field. Rawls's theory inspired many other debates in contemporary political philosophy and has also been the subject of intense criticism itself.

---

34. Rawls, *A Theory of Justice*, 53.

CHAPTER 11

Marx and the Critique of Capitalism

Few thinkers in the history of political philosophy have had (for better or worse) the real-world influence that the German philosopher Karl Marx had in the twentieth century. Born in 1818 in what was then Prussia, Marx studied philosophy and wrote his PhD thesis on the ancient Greek philosophers Democritus and Epicurus. Marx worked as a journalist, and from 1843 to 1845 he lived in Paris where he met his lifelong collaborator, Friedrich Engels. Many European countries (e.g., France and the German-speaking states) experienced revolutions in 1848, brought about by major societal transformations taking place in the early nineteenth century:

> Europe had experienced a major transformation. There were two elements in this. First, there was the onset of industrialization together with urbanisation, initially in Britain, later in Belgium, and later still in France and Germany. Second, there was the growth of population in the countryside, which not only supplied a ready-made army of migrants for towns, but also placed great strain on the resources of the poorest sections of the rural population. These two major social and economic developments set into motion the long-term strains that contributed so much to the causes of the 1848 revolutions.[1]

The *Communist Manifesto* was published in 1849, with Marx and Engels famously declaring, "The history of all hitherto existing society is the history of class struggles." Regarded as a radical threat, Marx was expelled from the German states in 1849 and emigrated to the United Kingdom, where he continued to write about the ills of capitalism.

---

1. Peter Jones, *The 1848 Revolutions*, 2nd ed. (London: Routledge, 1991), 5.

Before engaging with Marx, we should note a number of points that make studying him quite challenging. First, there is the sheer volume of work Marx published, covering thousands of pages of text. In this chapter we will only cover a small subset of the ideas Marx advanced, though I have purposefully chosen those that I believe are most integral to Marx's contributions to political philosophy, including his accounts of historical materialism, exploitation and alienation, class, and communism.

Another challenge with studying Marx is that, like many other thinkers we cover in this book, he is often vague and ambiguous in many of the terms and concepts he employs. For the purposes of this chapter I will rely on a number of influential scholars (especially G. A. Cohen's *Karl Marx's Theory of History*) who have brought a precision to Marx's ideas that Marx did not himself provide. But when conferring this level of clarity to Marx's writings, I will be sure to include the relevant textual support from Marx so that the focus remains primarily on what he actually wrote.

A third concern is that Marx's work is studied by a diverse range of disciplines, including history, literature, economics, political science, and philosophy. Each discipline brings its own unique focus and angle (critical or sympathetic) to Marx's theories. It is important to be aware of this fact, as there is perhaps greater diversity in the scholarship on Marx than on any other thinker in the history of Western political philosophy.

The fourth issue to keep in mind is that we must carefully distinguish between the ideas and arguments actually put forth by Marx in his writings versus the revolutionary movements of political leaders who espoused "Marxism" after Marx's death. The latter include Vladimir Lenin and Joseph Stalin in the former Soviet Union and Mao Zedong in China. In this chapter our focus is on what Marx actually argued, not the social experiments enacted in his name after his death. The merits and demerits of Marx's arguments should not be assessed in the same manner as those of the totalitarian regimes that often invoked his ideas to justify the form of governments they pursued.

Historical Materialism: Not One Single Theory

Recall from chapter 6 that many revolutionaries had hoped the French Revolution of 1789 would lead to a much more radically egalitarian society. Yet it did not. Why not? This question is a central concern in Marx's early writings, as he attempted to establish his political philosophy on a scientific foundation rather than on simple utopian aspirations. Marx wanted to understand why the French Revolution occurred in the first place, and also why it did not fully emancipate the French population but instead simply replaced one ruling class (the monarchy) with a new ruling class: the bourgeois/capitalist class to which Marx refers as "owners of the means of social production and employers of wage labour."[2]

Marx wanted to distinguish his theorizing about politics, which he believed was from a scientific perspective, from the utopian sentiments of earlier socialist thinkers like Charles Fourier (1772–1837), Henri de Saint-Simon (1760–1825), and Robert Owen (1771–1858). Fourier was a critic of laissez-faire market liberalism and the factory system. For Fourier, work could and should be satisfying. The rise of industrialization and mass production compromised this, according to Fourier. Fourier adopted a backward-looking nostalgic view of progress, rejecting industrialization and instead longing for a return to the agrarian mode of production. The manual labor of industrialization was intolerably dehumanizing, and thus the future Fourier aspired to bring into existence was one where the basic human drives would be satisfied. This would require the way humans worked to be radically transformed.

In contrast to Fourier, Saint-Simon stressed the positive implications of technological development, such as its increased productivity and efficiency. For Saint-Simon, progress should embrace innovation and discovery, and he proposed society be ruled by "technocrats" who could harness such advances to improve the lives of all. "The categorical imperative of Saint-Simonian thought was the call to apply the scientific knowledge of competent experts to the problems of society."[3] As such his vision of utopian socialism has been described as "hierarchal socialism" or "managerial capitalism."[4] Saint-Simon believed that there were two classes in

---

2. Karl Marx and Friedrich Engels, *The Communist Manifesto* [1848], in David Wootton, *Modern Political Thought: Readings from Machiavelli to Nietzsche* (Indianapolis: Hackett, 2008), 798–815, 798.

3. Robert B. Carlisle, "The Birth of Technocracy: Science, Society, and Saint-Simonians," *Journal of the History of Ideas* 35, no. 3 (1974): 445–64, 445.

4. Riccardo Soliani, "Claude-Henri de Saint-Simon: Hierarchical Socialism?," *History of Economic Ideas* 17, no. 2 (2009): 21–39.

society—the laboring class and the management class (the industrialist)—and that an industrial ethic that organized society efficiently would best ensure that the life prospects of all were improved.

Robert Owen was a successful Welsh entrepreneur who founded a textile factory in New Lanark, Scotland. Another critic of laissez-faire capitalism, which he viewed to be a form of heartless individualism, Owen voluntarily introduced shorter working hours and safer working conditions and ended child labor in his factory. An "Owenite movement" took root in the United States in the 1820s with the establishment of communities (e.g., New Harmony, Indiana) that attempted to implement Owen's utopian ideals.

In *The Communist Manifesto* Marx sought to distance himself from the early utopian socialists, whom he believed lacked a scientific understanding of why different modes of production (e.g., agricultural versus industrial) came into existence and what the preconditions for revolution were:

> The founders of these systems see, indeed, the class antagonisms, as well as the action of decomposing elements, in the prevailing form of society. But the proletariat, as yet in its infancy, offers to them the spectacle of a class without any historical initiative or any independent political movement.
>
> Since the development of class antagonism keeps even pace with the development of industry, the economic situation, as they find it, does not as yet offer to them the material conditions for the emancipation of the proletariat. They therefore search after a new social science, after new social laws, that are to create these conditions.[5]

Marx developed a nuanced theory of history, often referred to as *historical materialism*, that makes a number of distinctive claims concerning the primacy of material life over nonmaterial life. Material life concerns how humans produce the things needed to sustain us, and nonmaterial life includes other features of our culture, such as the social

---

5. Marx and Engels, *The Communist Manifesto*, 813.

classes (e.g., serfs, proletarians, or workers) and the constitution, laws, morality, and religion of a society. The idea of the primacy of the material in Marx's theory of history is not one unified theory or thesis. Keith Graham distinguishes the following three theories in Marx's historical materialism:[6]

1. Marx's basic materialism
2. Marx's synchronic materialism
3. Marx's diachronic materialism

Marx's basic materialism is the simple claim (the truism) that humans have material needs that must be met, daily, in order for there to be a nonmaterial life (e.g., laws, art, culture, etc.). In *German Ideology* Marx succinctly explains basic materialism:

> But life involves before everything else eating and drinking, a habitation, clothing, and many other things. The first historical act is thus the production of the means to satisfy these needs, the production of material life itself. And indeed this is an historical act, a fundamental condition of all history, which today, as thousands of years ago, must daily and hourly be fulfilled merely in order to sustain human life.[7]

Basic materialism thus asserts the most obvious way in which the material aspects of life have primacy over the immaterial. In order for humans, and our civilizations, to continue over time, we must successfully meet our material demands for food, clothing, and shelter. If those needs are not met, we cease to exist. The fact that the human species is still alive today means that the different social orders that have governed human life to date (e.g., slavery, feudalism, and now capitalism) have all satisfied the conditions of basic materialism. Had they failed to do so, we would not now exist.

---

6. Keith Graham, *Karl Marx: Our Contemporary* (Hemel Hempstead, UK: Harvester Wheatsheaf, 1992).

7. David McLellan, *Karl Marx: Selected Writings* (Oxford: Oxford University Press, 1977), 165.

Marx's Synchronic Materialism

"Synchronic" means a snapshot in time, and Marx's synchronic materialism involves further claims concerning the primacy of the material. Material life, according to Marx, conditions the nonmaterial aspects of life. The classic statement of Marx's synchronic materialism is the following famous *base/superstructure* metaphor, which utilizes a number of significant concepts that will be explained in detail:

> In the social production of their life, men enter into definite relations that are indispensable and independent of their will, relations of production which correspond to a definite state of development of their material productive forces. The sum total of these relations of production constitutes the economic structure of society, the real foundation, on which arises a legal and political superstructure and to which correspond definite forms of social consciousness.[8]

To aid in understanding the above passage, I have underlined four important concepts that should be defined clearly. First, there is the concept of *the relations of production*. In *Karl Marx's Theory of History*, which provides concise analyses of all these concepts, Cohen argues that relations of production hold between two things:

(a) Person(s) and another person(s)

OR

(b) Person(s) and productive force(s)

In (a), for example, a relation of production could hold between two people, A and B. But what kind of *specific* relation must the relationship between A and B be if, according to Marx, it constitutes a "relation of production"? For example, many possible relations could potentially hold between person A and person B. Here are five possible relations:

---

8. Karl Marx, Preface to *A Contribution to the Critique of Political Economy* [1859], in Wootton, *Modern Political Thought*, 829–31, 830.

1. A is taller than B.
2. B is older than A.
3. A weighs more than B.
4. B is richer than A.
5. A and B are siblings.

But none of the above relations qualifies as an example of a *relation of production*, as none of those relations captures the specific type of relationship involved in "relations of production." A relation of production is a relationship of *effective control* (ownership). So the following relationship between A and B *is* a relation of production:

1. A is the enslaver of B.

And this could also apply to a group of people, as follows:

2. The owners of cotton plantations enslave the people that pick the cotton on those plantations.

The relationship involved in relations of production are thus relations of effective ownership (not necessarily legal, or *de jure* ownership). It might be the case that A also has legal (*de jure*) ownership (given the laws of the society they live in) over B, but what makes it a relation of production is A's *de facto* ownership over B. A has the ability to compel (under threat of punishment) B to pick the cotton on their plantation.

Second, a relation of production can also hold between a person and a *productive force*. Productive forces include the means of production and labor power. The former include instruments of production (e.g., tools and machines) and raw materials. Labor power is "the productive faculties of producing agents: strength, skill, knowledge, inventiveness, etc."[9] So a relation of production could hold (1) between A and a factory (a means of production) of which they have effective ownership, or (2) between A and a hammer (e.g., an instrument of production), or (3) between A and their labor power (if, as a proletariat, they are free to sell their labor for a wage).

---

9. G. A. Cohen, *Karl Marx's Theory of History* (Oxford: Clarendon, 1978), 32.

Now that we have covered the definitions of relations of production and productive forces, the pieces are in place to define the third of our key concepts, the economic structure (or base) of society. In the passage above from the 1859 preface, Marx states, "The sum total of these relations of production constitutes the economic structure of society, the real foundation." This means that the economic structure of a slave society is the sum total of the relations of effective ownership that hold between the enslaved and enslavers, and between enslavers and productive forces. In a slave society, the enslaved do not have effective ownership over any productive forces (means of production or their labor power). In a feudal society, where the agricultural mode of production has feudal lordships owning the property and the peasant (serf) class bound to work on this land, the raw materials (such as land) are owned by the feudal lord class, and some means of production (e.g., tools) are owned by the peasant class. However, the peasant class does not have full effective ownership over their labor as they are bound to work on the land of their feudal lord. Finally, in a capitalist society, for the first time in human history the class of producers (the proletariat) has effective ownership over their labor power (which means they can choose to sell their labor power for a wage), but in time the capitalist (bourgeois) class would come to own all the means of production (the instruments of production and raw materials). In this way Marx can refer to different historical epochs by their economic structures: slave society, feudal society, capitalist society, and the future communist society. In the latter the immediate producers are emancipated since they come to have effective ownership over both their labor power and the means of production.

The fourth concept we must define, before explaining what synchronic materialism entails, is that of the *superstructure* of society. There is debate among Marxist scholars concerning what is included in the superstructure. At a minimum, the superstructure includes the legal and political institutions of a society. When interpreted more expansively, religion, art, and the dominant ideas (or "ideology") of a society could be described as superstructural phenomena. Cohen, for example, argues that "the superstructure consists of legal, political, religious and other non-economic *institutions*."[10] Cohen excludes ideology from

---

10. Cohen, *Karl Marx's Theory of History*, 45.

the category of the superstructure. Other commentators, such as John McMurtry, recognize that Marx "sometimes uses the term 'superstructure' to refer to just legal and political institutions, and sometimes he uses it to apply more broadly to these as well as ideology and forms of social consciousness as a unitary whole."[11]

Whether one employs a narrow or broad understanding of the superstructure of society, it clearly includes things such as the criminal code, the constitution, and taxation laws. It is thus easy to see how slave societies have different superstructures than feudal societies, and the same is true for capitalist societies. In the latter, for example, particular rights are recognized by a constitution (e.g., freedom of expression, freedom of movement) that would not exist in feudal or slave societies. The primacy of the material entails that what occurs in the economic structure of a society shapes what happens at the superstructural level. If we want to understand why capitalist societies have different laws than slave or feudal societies, for example, we need to understand what is happening at the material level of life in such societies. The technology available at the time (e.g., early agricultural versus advanced industrial) will require different modes of production, and superstructures will arise to reinforce the relations of production needed to exploit the productive capability of that technology.

Synchronic materialism thus maintains the base of a society, that is, the whole set of its relations of production, shapes, and limits the superstructure of the society. Whether the laws of a society are those of slavery, feudalism, or capitalism is not determined by the ideas or beliefs people in those societies happen to maintain. Rather, the ideas and beliefs that people happen to maintain are determined by the level of productive technology of the society. Using the word "determine" runs the risk that Marx's account of synchronic materialism will collapse into a form of reductionism, where the superstructural phenomena of laws and ideas are inert. Allen Wood notes how Marx's conception of society is susceptible to this interpretation:

> The Marxian conception of society is sometimes described as "economic determinism." By this it is often meant that Marx's

---

11. John McMurtry, *The Structure of Marx's World-View* (Princeton, NJ: Princeton University Press, 1978), 100.

theory takes one aspect of social life (the "economic" aspect) to be the crucial one on which all others depend. Marx, according to this account, either reduces all of social life to economics, or he regards the rest of social life as an epiphenomenon of economics, or else as a series of effects proceeding entirely from "economic" causes. This interpretation of Marx, it seems to me, is fundamentally mistaken.[12]

If Wood is correct that economic determinism is a mistaken characterization of Marx's account of synchronic materialism, how can Marx argue for the primacy of the economic structure and yet avoid the charges of reductionism or relegating the noneconomic to the status of mere epiphenomenon? Marx seems to have in mind a two-way relationship, in that while superstructures need bases, bases also need superstructures—but the causal connection from bases to superstructures is the more dominant causal pathway. For example, Marx acknowledges that ideological forms of superstructural phenomena (on the broad understanding of that concept) can influence material relations. For example, Marx argues that "Protestantism, by changing almost all the traditional holidays into working days, played an important role in the genesis of capital."[13]

This shows that Marx believes both bases and superstructures can influence each other. Indeed, bases need superstructures. To ensure southern US enslavers retained effective control over the labor of African slaves, the owners needed a legal system that protected their ownership rights over the enslaved. Once that legal authority was challenged, their control became much more perilous. Synchronic materialism asserts the primacy of the material to explain why, when we take a snapshot of a society in time and find particular superstructural phenomena in existence (e.g., feudal laws, the divine right of kings, etc.). These superstructures reinforce the relationships of production that exist in that society at that particular time. To understand why revolutionary change occurs, and why superstructures are replaced with new ones, we must turn to *diachronic materialism*, which is Marx's fully developed account of historical materialism. It

---

12. Allen Wood, "The Marxian Critique of Justice," *Philosophy and Public Affairs* 1, no. 3 (1972): 244–82, 249–50.

13. Karl Marx, *Capital*, vol. 1 (Harmondsworth, UK: Penguin, 1976), 387n92.

is Marx's account of diachronic materialism that helps explain why particular relations of production come into existence in the first place, why they persist, and why they are (eventually) replaced with new relations of production.

Diachronic Materialism

In *Karl Marx's Theory of History*, Cohen presents Marx's account of diachronic materialism, which is how societies change over time, as consisting of two central theses, what he calls the *development thesis* and the *primacy thesis*. These theses maintain the following:

> *The development thesis*: Productive forces tend to develop throughout history.
>
> *The primacy thesis*: The nature of the production relations of a society is explained by the level of development of its productive forces.[14]

Cohen contends that Marx's development thesis is predicated upon two permanent facts about human nature and one fact about the human situation. The two facts about humans are that we are somewhat rational, and that we possess intelligence of a kind and degree that enables us to improve our situation. The fact about the historical situation of humanity is that our history has been one of scarcity. Together, these three facts vindicate the plausibility of the development thesis. Meeting our needs is difficult, so when improvements in technology are developed we will utilize them to meet our needs because we are rational. If the superstructure of a society impedes the development of that technology, that legal and political order will eventually be overthrown and replaced by a new superstructure that permits the new mode of production (e.g., technologies, like the loom) to be exploited.

The primacy thesis emphasizes the most important part of Marx's technology-driven account of human history: the relations of production that exist in a slave, feudal, or capitalist society are ultimately determined

---

14. Cohen, *Karl Marx's Theory of History*, 158.

by the level of development of its productive forces (e.g., means of production and labor). This insight is captured in perhaps the most important passage that addresses Marx's account of diachronic materialism, his famous "fettering" passage from *The Communist Manifesto*. This passage explains why Marx believed the French Revolution occurred, and from it we can also infer why (eventually) it will be followed by another revolution that will overthrow the capitalist mode of production.

> We see then that the means of production and of exchange, on whose foundation the bourgeoisie built itself up, were generated in feudal society. At a certain stage in the development of these means of production and of exchange, the conditions under which feudal society produced and exchanged, the feudal organization of agriculture and manufacturing industry, in one word, the feudal relations of property become no longer compatible with the already developed productive forces; they became so many fetters. They had to be burst asunder; they were burst asunder. Into their place stepped free competition, accompanied by a social and political constitution adapted to it, and by the economical and political sway of the bourgeois class.[15]

The feudal relations of production bound the laboring class to the property of their feudal lords in urban settings. Such an economic structure could not sustain the development of the new productive forces that were emerging in the early stages of the industrial revolution. To harness the power of the new manufacturing system, laborers were required to be amassed in the city, laborers who were free to sell their labor power to the factory owners rather than being bound to till the land of their feudal lords. Thus the existing feudal relations of production became fetters and were cast asunder. The new relations of production that replaced them were ones conducive to the emerging productive forces. Those conditions were the production relations of capitalism, a system where large pools of cheap labor can be amassed to exploit the new technologies created at the beginning of the Industrial Revolution. These new relations of production will remain in place until they themselves impede the development of the

---

15. McLellan, *Karl Marx*, 225–26.

productive forces. This is the central logic of Marx's account of revolution in diachronic materialism.

Exploitation and Alienation

In addition to Marx's scientific account of human history, there are also significant aspects of his writings that make normative moral arguments. Squaring these aspects of Marx's writings with this theory of history is often problematic. In this section we will cover Marx's account of exploitation and alienation, and then examine whether Marx's stance on morality is paradoxical given his account of historical materialism.

Before addressing the concepts of exploitation and alienation, which Marx believed were omnipresent in capitalism, it is helpful to clarify what capitalism is. Relying again on Cohen,[16] capitalism can be defined in two ways. First, we can define capitalism structurally, by reference to its dominant relationship of production. Capitalism is thus the system where the immediate producers (i.e., the proletariat) own their labor power but no other productive force (e.g., means of production, like raw materials or a factory). Second, Cohen contends that capitalism can be defined in a modal fashion by the purpose of capitalist production: to accumulate capital (that is, "self-expanding exchange value").[17]

In *Marx and Justice: The Radical Critique of Liberalism* Allen Buchanan claims that Marx's account of exploitation entails three distinct (but interrelated) accounts of exploitation:

1. A conception of exploitation in the *labor process* of capitalism.
2. A *transhistorical* conception of exploitation that applies not only to the labor process in capitalism but to the labor processes of all class-divided societies.
3. A *general conception* of exploitation that is not limited to phenomena within the labor process itself.[18]

---

16. Cohen, *Karl Marx's Theory of History*, 181.

17. Cohen, *Karl Marx's Theory of History*, 184.

18. Allen Buchanan, *Marx and Justice: The Radical Critique of Liberalism* (Totowa, NJ: Rowman & Littlefield, 1982), 36.

The account of exploitation in the labor process of capitalism relies on a distinction Marx makes between *necessary* and *surplus* wage labor. Suppose I am hired to work in a factory for ten hours, and what I produce in those ten hours yields a value equivalent to a hundred dollars. To meet my basic material needs for food, clothing, and shelter I require thirty dollars per workday, which will permit me to cover my rent, feed myself and my family, and so on. My employer pays me a subsistence wage of thirty dollars per ten-hour shift. This means that of the ten hours of labor I do per day, three hours are *necessary labor* (equivalent to the value of what I need to meet my basic material needs), and the remaining seven hours are *surplus wage labor*. That is, the value of what I create in the remaining seven hours is profit for the capitalist who employs me. I am not paid a wage equivalent to the value of what I produce (if I were, why would the capitalist employ me as they would make no profit?). This unequal exchange of my ten hours of value for a wage equivalent to three hours of labor is an unfair exchange. It constitutes an exploitative relationship, according to this first account of exploitation.

Marx's account of the exploitation that takes places in the labor process of capitalism presupposes the *labor theory of value*, an economic idea that is easily refuted as false. The labor theory of value posits that the value of some commodity is solely determined by the amount of labor it takes to create the product. So if it takes two hours of labor to create product A, and four hours of the same labor to create product B, then B must be double the value of product A. While this idea has some intuitive appeal, it does not hold up in the real world of capitalism, where many factors influence the value of a commodity. For example, something might be rare, or in demand, which could drive up its market value. Each year around the Christmas holidays, particular children's toys become hot commodities, and parents are willing to pay a much higher price for these toys. The price of such items often has little to do with the amount of labor it takes to create them. Indeed, after the rush of holiday purchasing, these very same toys are often available at heavily discounted prices. Supply and demand have an important influence over the market value of many commodities.

The transhistorical account of exploitation applies to all historical epochs, not just the capitalist system. Without the transhistorical conception of exploitation we could not make sense of Marx's claim in *The Communist Manifesto* that "the history of all hitherto existing society is the history of class struggle." Exploitation did not first emerge with capitalism; slaves were exploited in the system of slavery, and serfs were exploited in the feudal system. To make sense of these claims Marx must have a transhistorical account of exploitation. Buchanan contends that the following four conditions must be present for there to be exploitation according to Marx's transhistorical account:

1. The labor is *forced*;
2. A portion of it is *uncompensated* labor;
3. The worker produces a *surplus*;
4. The workers *do not themselves control their product*.[19]

These conditions are present in slavery, feudalism, and capitalism. In the slave society labor is forced in that coercion (whipping, mutilation, the use of slave collars, execution, etc.) is used by the enslaver class to ensure the enslaved undertake the labor the enslaver wanted completed. In the feudal system a "serf was legally tied to the landlord in a variety of ways, typically by being prohibited from migrating, marrying, practicing certain occupations, selling certain goods, participating in factor [e.g., where land and labor are sold] and product markets, or engaging in particular types of consumption without obtaining permission from his landlord."[20] In the capitalist system, before the institution of the poverty relief policies of the twentieth-century welfare state (e.g., workplace safety, unemployment and disability insurance, affordable housing, disability, health care, minimum wage, government pensions, etc.), workers were forced to sell their labor power, or to live in destitution relying on charitable handouts, or to simply starve.

The second and third components of the transhistorical conception of exploitation are that a portion of the labor of the producing class is *uncompensated* labor, and that a *surplus* is created. The enslaved person produces more than they need for their own survival, a surplus of which is taken by the enslaver. The serf also produces a surplus, and

---

19. Buchanan, *Marx and Justice*, 38.

20. Sheilagh Ogilvie and A. W. Carus, "Institutions and Economic Growth in Historical Perspective," in *Handbook of Economic Growth*, vol. 2, ed. Philippe Aghion and Steven N. Durlauf (Amsterdam: Elsevier, 2013), 403–513, 473.

those proceeds are appropriated by the feudal lord class (as uncompensated labor). The capitalist appropriates the surplus of the proletariat's labor, part of which is uncompensated as their wage is only part of the value of what is produced.

The fourth requirement of the transhistorical conception of exploitation is that the workers (slave, serf, or proletariat classes) do not themselves control their product. This is something that can only be achieved in a postcapitalist society, when the producers own the means of production and the motto "from each according to his ability, to each according to his needs" is realized.[21]

The third and final conception of Marxist exploitation is the general conception of exploitation which maintains:

1. To exploit someone is to *utilize* him or her as one would a tool.
2. This utilization is *harmful* to the person so utilized.
3. *The end* of such utilization is *one's own benefit*.[22]

The benefit of this general conception of exploitation, as Buchanan points out, is that it permits us to make sense of other examples of exploitation Marx invokes that do not involve the labor process or exploitation between classes. Members of the capitalist class might exploit other members of the capitalist class, such as when the petty bourgeoisie (small business owners) are pushed out of business by their larger competitors, who can afford to temporarily lower their prices to drive out competition.

Is Marx's theory of exploitation still relevant and compelling, at least when applied to the world's most developed economies of the twenty-first century? When Marx was writing about these topics in the late nineteenth century, most laborers lived on a subsistence wage, doing risky work with little to no protection against the risks of injury, being laid off, arbitrary dismissal, and discrimination. Laborers were expected to work much longer hours than now, and children were also recruited for work (including working in dangerous jobs, such as in coal mines). Critics will contend that the advent of the welfare state remedied the most compelling parts

---

21. Karl Marx, *Critique of the Gotha Programme* [1875], in Wootton, *Modern Political Thought*, 848–57, 851.

22. Buchanan, *Marx and Justice*, 38.

of the vulnerability present in early capitalist societies. Workers are no longer "forced to labor" as they were in nineteenth-century England. Furthermore, workers enjoy many luxuries that did not exist in the nineteenth century, such as ownership of automobiles, large-screen TVs, cell phones, and so forth. Similarly, many workers can afford the time to take holiday vacations to exotic travel destinations. Is it compelling to describe this class as exploited by the capitalist system? We will address the issues of class and the communist revolution in subsequent sections of this chapter when we consider how some scholars have attempted to update Marx's account of class and potential explanations of why the workers' revolution has not yet happened.

Alienation

In addition to Marx's critique of capitalism as a mode of production that exploits workers, Marx also argues that it is a system of alienation. Alienation is the experience of feeling estranged or isolated. For example, suppose in your childhood you were very close to a neighborhood friend. You spent most summer months playing outside together, but you moved away and lost all contact with this person over the past twenty years. One day you happen to pass this same person on the street, and you awkwardly smile and wave at them as you recognize their face as familiar. But now the relationship is one of alienation versus close friendship. Marx believes that different types of alienation occur in capitalism. In the *Economic and Philosophic Manuscript of 1844* Marx identifies four different types of alienation that occur in capitalism.[23]

First, the worker can be alienated from the product of labor. The worker on the assembly line of the original Ford motor car factory would not feel an intimate connection to the end product, for they would not own or use the car. The product of their labor belonged to someone else.

Second, the worker can feel alienated from the activity of labor. On the motor car assembly line, the worker simply hammers the hub cap onto the car wheels, over and over again. This specialized division of labor

---

23. Karl Marx, *Economic and Philosophic Manuscript of 1844*, in Wootton, *Modern Political Thought*, 766–72, 769.

permits the factory to efficiently make cars, but the worker does not have a sense of connection or meaning to the work they perform.

Third, the worker can be alienated from the human species. Marx contends that free, conscious activity is man's species-character, but this is not realized by the repetitive hammering of the hub cap onto the car wheels all day long on the assembly line. In capitalism, according to Lanny Ace Thompson, "Life has been reduced to an animal existence."[24] Thompson describes this aspect of Marx's account of alienation as follows:

> Human existence is social existence. Humans have consciousness and objectify it through labor. This consciousness is a social product in that it can only arise through the interaction of men. As we have seen, wage labor alienates man from his product and his labor. The abstraction, of human powers through money further alienates man from his species-being and from other men. Money itself becomes the social bond thus alienating man from man. Men no longer relate to each other on the basis of real qualities, but rather according to abstractions.[25]

The fourth way in which alienation occurs within capitalism is that we are estranged from nature itself. Marx does not provide many details about this final point, and it is not clear how it is distinct from the third type of alienation, which encompasses the idea that there is a specific type of social existence for our species that is compromised by the nature of the work in capitalism.

Having pieced together the essentials of Marx's account of both exploitation and alienation, we can explore the tension between these moral evaluative aspects of his writings and his attempted scientific account of human history. On the one hand, Marx's theory is presented as an account of how and why different superstructural phenomena arise in different historical epochs. This technological deterministic account explains why different legal institutions and forms of ideology (e.g., religion and morality) arise in different historical epochs. That is, those ideas help stabilize (by providing moral legitimacy to) the relations of production needed to

---

24. Lanny Ace Thompson, "The Development of Marx's Concept of Alienation: An Introduction," *Mid-American Review of Sociology* 4, no. 1 (1979): 23–38, 27.
25. Thompson, "The Development of Marx's Concept of Alienation," 28.

enable the productive forces to develop. But at the same time, Marx also expresses moral judgments that characterize capitalism as a system that exploits and alienates. If morality is simply ideology that legitimates the oppression of the ruling class, then how can Marx himself appeal to moral claims without such expressions simply being characterized as "ideology"? In other words, is Marx's stance on morality paradoxical? Can he claim that capitalism itself is unjust when his theory of historical materialism maintains that standards of justice are simply superstructural phenomena of a system designed to protect the ruling class?

In "The Controversy about Marx and Justice" Norman Geras provides an exhaustive analysis of the different stances scholars have taken on this issue, and the conflicting types of textual support one can find in Marx's writings for different interpretations of Marx on these issues. For the question of whether Marx condemned capitalism as unjust, Geras identifies four possible answers:

1. Marx did not view capitalism as "unjust" (as "justice" mirrors the "ruling ideas" and within capitalism the exchange of wage for labor is considered a just exchange).
2. Marx did think capitalism was unjust, hence why he condemned it as exploitation.
3. Marx believed capitalism was both just and unjust ("just" by its own internal standards, but objectively unjust).
4. Capitalism was neither just nor unjust (as the concept of justice was, for Marx, an archaic one that would be transcended in a future postcapitalist society).[26]

There is some textual support for all four of these positions, which has led scholars of Marx to argue for seemingly incompatible positions (e.g., Marx did or did not think capitalism was unjust). The third answer has the virtue of reconciling this apparent tension. One can say that sometimes Marx adopts the stance of the moral critic, when noting that capitalism is unjust. And when Marx adopts the stance of the historian explaining technological determinism, he is simply explaining that, according

---

26. Norman Geras, "The Controversy about Marx and Justice," *Philosophica* 33, no. 1 (1984): 33–86.

to how the capitalist system characterizes "justice," the exchange of labor for a wage is just. But the skeptic might wonder how Marx is capable of transcending the ideology of his time to make the moral judgments he does, as they are not simply part of the ideology of his time. This is the real challenge with the fourth answer: it presupposes that Marx, when he articulates his views on the moral failings of capitalism, is not advancing his own theory of justice but is instead functioning from a future evaluative perspective that has transcended justice (which is a legal concept, necessary in precommunist societies). The critic will question how it is possible for Marx to go beyond his own culture and its ideology, and if Marx can perform this epistemic feat, then why not assume others can as well (e.g., proponents of religion, liberalism, etc.)?

Class

Marx describes history in terms of class struggle, but what constitutes a class? How do we distinguish between a member of the proletariat and a member of the capitalist class? This is also a source of debate among Marxist scholars. Does class membership track some objective criteria, such as material circumstances (e.g., whether one's income is derived from selling one's labor versus owning the means of production)? Or is class membership determined by some subjective criterion, such as "class consciousness" and with whom we feel a sense of solidarity? Graham helpfully notes that it is useful to distinguish between the issue of "being a class" and "acting as a class."[27] The proletariat class (workers) can exist as a class, even though it does not (yet) act as a class. Indeed, such was the predicament, Marx believed, of the proletariat class in early capitalism.

The "oppressor" class in human history—enslaver, feudal lord, and capitalist—all survived off the surplus labor of others and possessed effective ownership over all (or most) of the productive forces. By contrast, slaves, serfs, and the proletariat labored to survive, producing a surplus that was appropriated by the ruling class.

In a capitalist society, the proletariat are the class of persons who must sell their labor power for survival. The worker exchanges their labor

---

27. Graham, *Karl Marx*, 21.

for a wage. At the time Marx was writing, the average wage for workers was one of subsistence, a feature that Marx believed was inherent to capitalism. Capitalism strives to maximize profit; otherwise a business will be beaten by their more successful (i.e., profit-driven) competitors. The most effective way to maximize profits is to try to extract the maximum amount of productivity from the worker for the minimal amount of cost. Thus Marx believed the situation of workers would worsen, not improve, over time.

In today's advanced capitalist societies the average worker enjoys a level of material prosperity and security that would have been unimaginable in the nineteenth century. Capitalism has increased material prosperity for all, not only the most affluent. Of course these improvements in wealth have not been equal, but they are improvements nonetheless. Many of these improvements were made because of class solidarity and action, such as the creation of trade unions and applying political pressure to introduce welfare-state provisions that limited market vulnerability.

Does Marx's account of class in capitalist society still have plausibility in the contemporary world? In *Karl Marx: Our Contemporary*, Graham offers an updated account of the proletariat class, in an attempt to respond to criticisms that Marx's account of class is antiquated. Graham defines the proletariat as follows:

> By proletariat is meant the modern class of wage- or salary-earning people whose lack of ownership of *sufficiently significant means of production* results in their having to offer their *labour power for sale*, for a *significant portion of their lives*, if they are to live at an *average, reasonable standard* of living in the prevailing historical circumstances without engaging in *specifically exceptional or dangerous alternative activities*, as well as people who are, in specifiable ways, *directly dependent* for their own livelihood on members of the proletariat as defined.[28]

The words in italics identify important aspects of this account of class worth noting. If a person earns money from selling their labor power, then, subject to a few provisos, they can be considered members of the

---

28. Graham, *Karl Marx*, 91 (italics added).

proletariat. Owning some means of production, such as some shares in the stock market, does not mean one is not a member of the proletariat if that person must continue to sell their labor power in order to live at an average, reasonable standard of living. However, if someone inherits a multimillion-dollar stock portfolio at age twenty-five, and thus could quit their wage-earning job of five years, then they are no longer a member of the proletariat, even though they had, in the past, been dependent on selling their labor to earn a living. Similarly, the professional athlete who gets paid a multimillion-dollar annual salary is not a member of the proletariat if they could exceed an average, reasonable standard of living off the income they have already received.

The provision regarding dangerous activities permits Graham to include drug dealers and prostitutes within the proletariat class, even though they might contravene other aspects of the criteria for class membership as a worker (e.g., a successful drug dealer might amass large amounts of wealth). Finally, the stipulation that a member of the proletariat also includes "people who are, in specifiable ways, *directly dependent* for their own livelihood on members of the proletariat as defined" means that children of the proletariat, for example, can be considered members of that class.

Marx portrayed the relationship between the proletariat and bourgeoisie as one of hostility and conflict. Eventually there would be a polarization, with members of the petty bourgeoisie being pushed into the same predicament as the proletariat. But has the class antagonism that Marx predicted occurred? The history of the twentieth century revealed that numerous other forms of conflict, besides economic, can pose formidable problems for human societies. The two world wars suggest that nationalism can trump class solidarity, as workers in Germany battled workers from the United Kingdom, France, the United States, and so forth. Religious conflict in Northern Ireland and racial conflict like apartheid in South Africa reveal a much more complex account of human conflict than that offered by Marx. While economics is no doubt important, the actual history of human societies and the collective action undertaken for various causes suggest that there are more factors at play than Marx presumed with respect to class consciousness and class conflict.

Rather than becoming, as Marx predicted, more militant over time, it appears that most workers, at least in the most affluent capitalist societies, are not interested in overthrowing capitalism. Does this mean Marx was wrong about the forces that drive human history, class antagonism, exploitation, and alienation? To fairly assess Marx's theories, it is perhaps best to separate out different elements. The viability of the technocratic determinism in Marx's theory of diachronic materialism, for example, might be very different than his theory of class or exploitation. The advent of welfare capitalism certainly suggests that capitalism was a more versatile mode of social production that Marx thought.

For example, in *Class Inequality and Political Order* Frank Parkin argues that capitalism has social mechanisms that can serve as a safety valve to deflate revolutionary aspirations.[29] These include:

1. Use or threat of physical force
2. Upward social mobility
3. Education system
4. Religion
5. Gambling

The growth of government, especially the police state (e.g., ability to use force as well as surveillance), has meant that the prospects of a proletariat uprising that overthrows the capitalist relations of production has faced more significant barriers than Marx envisioned in the late nineteenth century. The prospects of social mobility in capitalism, both perceived and real, can also deflate revolutionary tendencies as workers can be tempted to pursue the individual strategy of achieving a "rags to riches" story rather than being mobilized collectively to overthrow the capitalist system.

The education system can also deflate revolutionary aspirations by inculcating in children from a young age that one's expected life plan is to be an obedient worker. This can be coupled with patriotism and/or religion to foster the adaptive preferences needed to keep the workers content with the life prospects afforded them by capitalism. The education and support provided to children living in affluent and poorer neighborhoods can help reinforce compliant class expectations; the poor may be

---

29. Frank Parkin, *Class Inequality and Political Order* (New York: Praeger, 1971).

expected to finish school at a younger age and take up less skilled jobs, while the more affluent are encouraged to pursue postsecondary education, to develop the higher skills needed for a career.

Marxists have long espoused the sentiment that religion is the opium of the people. For Marx, religion is a form of ideology as it conceals the real nature of social and economic relationships. Rather than raising social consciousness about the inequality pervasive in the here and now of our earthly existence, religion instead focuses our attention on what happens in the next life. Being an obedient and hardworking proletariat is the message conveyed, rather than agitating workers toward revolution. Thus religion can be an effective tool to deflate revolutionary sentiments.

The last safety valve mechanism Parkin claims for capitalism is gambling. Like the "lottery" of upward social mobility, winning the lottery offers an individualistic solution to the ills of poverty and capitalism. Rather than pursuing collective action to overthrow capitalism, the worker need only buy a ticket and hope that the winning numbers come up. "Low-income individuals spend a larger share of their incomes on lottery tickets than those with higher income."[30]

The Communist Revolution

The French Revolution marked a turning point in the transition from the feudal system to the capitalist system, replacing the feudal lords as the oppressors with the newly emerging mercantile class of capitalists. Marx believed that eventually the capitalist system itself would also have a revolution, ushering in a postcapitalist era and the emancipation of the masses. This would be the communist revolution, a revolution Marx did not put a timeline on, nor did he offer expansive details concerning what communism would be like.

Capitalism emerged because it offered relations of production that could harness the newly emerging productive forces of the Industrial Revolution. But Marx believed the relations of production of capitalism

---

30. Jens Beckert and Mark Lutter, "Why the Poor Play the Lottery: Sociological Approaches to Explaining Class-based Lottery Play," *Sociology* 47, no. 6 (2012): 1152–70, 1153.

also had a lifespan. The high productivity of the industrial era meant that, for the first time ever, the material needs of humanity could be met. However, capitalism is not, according to Marx, a system committed to meeting those needs but rather to the accumulation of more capital for the ruling class. This meant that, despite having the technological capacity to meet the needs of all, the fate of the proletariat would be one of continued exploitation and alienation. This, coupled with the "boom and bust" of the capitalist economy, would lead to a tipping point when the class consciousness of the workers demands they rise up and take control over the means of production.

Marx explicitly states that he is not interested in providing a blueprint for the future postcapitalist society. However, there are some important features of it we can distill from what Marx does detail. In *The Critique of the Gotha Programme*, for example, Marx describes two stages of the transition from capitalism to communism. First, there is the transition to the "lower phase" of communism. During this phase society is governed by the *contribution principle*: you get back from society what you put in. This sentiment has appeal as it redresses the exploitation inherent in capitalism, where workers contribute much but receive little because the value of their surplus labor is appropriated by the ruling class. But the realization of the contribution principle is not the final destination for the emancipation of workers. Such a principle has inequitable consequences as the needs and abilities of people will vary. If I have a family of five to support and contribute as much as you, and you only have a family of two people to support, the contribution principle will leave me in a very vulnerable position compared to you. Furthermore, those who are unable to contribute very much (e.g., the infirm) will also be in a precarious position in a society governed by the contribution principle.

In the "higher phase" of communism the contribution principle is replaced by the motto of the communist society, which is "From each according to his ability, to each according to his needs." The appeal of this motto is that everyone will be expected to contribute to society to the best of their ability. There will not be a parasitic class that chooses to live off the surplus labor of others. So the first part of the motto captures the productive responsibilities expected in the postcapitalist society. Furthermore, "to each according to his needs" describes the distributive outcome of the communist ideal, that the needs of everyone will be taken care of.

Marx does not provide much detail about how our motivations change from the self-interest that governs in capitalism to the contribution principle in lower communism to the motto that governs the higher phase of communism. Marx did not believe human nature was fixed. Instead, humans are capable of responding to different types of motivations depending on the environmental circumstances they find themselves in. His faith in technological progress made him optimistic that, as technology progressed to a stage where the needs of all could be met, once the means of production were in the hands of the majority of the population (instead of the elite capitalist class), they would be motivated to fairly distribute the proceeds of social cooperation.

There are, however, a number of potential problems with this outlook. When Marx was writing in the nineteenth century, the ecological damage of resource extraction from economic growth was still mostly unknown. Climate change was also not a problem. But in the twenty-first century we have had to learn a hard lesson about the way technological advances that improve short-term predicaments (e.g., demands for energy) can cause significant long-term problems.

Furthermore, Marx's assumption about the high level of productivity communism can achieve also seems to be in tension with his assumption that the work we would perform in a postcapitalist society would be unalienated. Consider this famous passage from Marx's *The German Ideology* concerning what the normal daily life of a producer would be in communism: "hunt in the morning, fish in the afternoon, rear cattle in the evening, criticize after dinner, just as I have a mind, without ever becoming hunter, fisherman, cowherd, or critic."[31] This passage suggests we will not have to reduce our identity to just one specific type of occupation (such as mechanic, dishwasher, or teacher) in the communist society. Yet the high level of productivity capitalism yields is due, at least in part, to a division of specialized labor. Perhaps technological progress like automation and robotics will mean that many labor-intense human jobs will be replaced by machines. But until that time, it would seem implausible to believe we could make work more varied and enjoyable for people *and* be more productive.

---

31. McLellan, *Karl Marx*, 185.

Whatever one thinks about Marx's critique of capitalism and his outline of a postcapitalist society, there is no doubt he was a profound social thinker and important political theorist whom students should consider today. It would not be surprising if there were a twenty-first-century resurgence of interest in Marx, given the uncertainties and potential tribulations of capitalist economies and novel technological advances such as artificial intelligence, genome editing, and private spaceflight. If Marx's account of historical materialism has validity, then such new technology may transform existing relations of production if those relations prove to be a fetter to technological advancement.

CHAPTER 12

Conclusion

Political ideas and ideals have had a major influence on human history. The realm of antiquated ideas (e.g., the divine right of kings, patriarchy, racial supremacy, feudalism) can entrench the hierarchy and oppression that created substantive social, economic, and political inequalities. But political ideas and ideals can also inspire revolution (e.g., the French Revolution), greater inclusion (e.g., expansion of the right to vote), and experimentation in governance (e.g., liberalism and representative democracy as well as communism).

The classics in political philosophy, where intellectual giants helped shape and evolve these ideas, are critical to study today for a variety of reasons. At a minimum they can ignite our curiosity and interest. "What ideas helped shape where we are now?" "Are there any valuable lessons we can learn from the mistakes and successes of the past?" Our curiosity about the world, coupled with a recognition of the impact ideas often have, entices us to immerse ourselves in the study of the rich history of ideas that have populated the history of Western political philosophy.

Engaging with a diverse range of thinkers from the past, with the explicit pedagogical goal of revealing how those ideas can help us better understand and address the societal predicaments of today, also helps us develop our critical thinking. How do assumptions about human nature influence what we take to be the legitimate scope and functions of government? Can democracy be defended against Plato's critique that it simply panders to populism and the rule of the ignorant? What is human happiness? What are the pros and cons of championing tradition and stability over innovation and progressive change in political theory? How can we effectively abate the most problematic types of inequalities that persist in the world today? The thinkers of the past invite us to contemplate these profound questions and the tentative answers they have offered in response to them.

The intellectual task of engaging with and evaluating the arguments of past thinkers can also encourage *hope* for those of us studying political philosophy today. It reminds us that the cultural project of refining and evolving our political ideas and ideals is not a static project, but rather a constantly ongoing collective endeavor. Our minds and ideas are *plastic*, and thus each generation has the opportunity to leave its mark by pivoting, refining, and entrenching different political values and ideals. We may be today's current generation, but we will soon join the past. We have the responsibility of overseeing the future evolution of political concepts, ideas, and ideals. What do we want our contribution to the debates and discussions concerning how we ought to live our individual and collective lives to be?

This book has been intentionally designed to celebrate and refine three specific "intellectual virtues": (1) curiosity, (2) insight and nuanced understanding, and (3) optimism. The selection of thinkers, topics, and debates covered in this book has been made with these three intellectual virtues in mind. A humanistic education approach to the canon is one that transcends, indeed disrupts, the traditional view, which often presumes the somewhat static mindset that we should simply teach the same historical figures who were taught in the past, in the same manner.

The past was once the "present" and "future" of past generations. Historical political thinkers tried to diagnosis the problems of their own times, problems many of their contemporaries were oblivious to. For Plato, the problem with Athenian democracy was that political power was placed in the hands of the ignorant. Aristotle concerned himself with the primacy of moral and intellectual virtue, to ensure individuals and societies would flourish and minimize the risks of moral and epistemic vice. Hobbes perceived human nature, coupled with the appetite some of his contemporaries had to overthrow the monarchy, as a major danger that risked unleashing civil war and the devolution of society into anarchy. For Locke, the problem of his time was framed as one of ensuring the rights of self-ownership (life, liberty, and property) were protected. Inequality, and how to abate it, was the focus of Rousseau's political writings and democratic aspirations. The problem of inequality was also the central concern of the feminist thinkers Pizan, Wollstonecraft, and Cooper, as well as Black political thinkers like Douglass, Du Bois, King, and Fanon. Utilitarians sought to bring clarity to the issue of what government should be striving for (i.e., the maximization of happiness), while Karl Marx offered an account of human history that explained how technological progress shapes the relations of production and superstructure of different historical epochs, including capitalism and its exploitation and alienation of the proletariat.

The Unique Challenges of the Twenty-First Century

What are the most significant problems facing our societies in the twenty-first century? Can the ideas and arguments of past thinkers help us identify and overcome today's challenges? Of course, many of the problems of the past are *still* problems of today. While significant progress may have been made in certain parts of the world in terms of ameliorating the worst forms of patriarchy (e.g., denying females education and the opportunity to work and vote), racial inequality (e.g., slavery and racial segregation), and economic inequality (e.g., severe poverty), there is still work to be done in redressing the legacies of these historical inequalities. The #MeToo movement, for example, is a recent social media movement that brought greater attention to the persistence of sexual abuse and harassment. The pay gap between men and women and the gender composition of representative democratic legislatures remind us that the work of Pizan, Wollstonecraft, and Cooper must continue to inspire us to make further progress toward the ideal of equality between the sexes.

This chapter concludes by considering some of the major, and novel, twenty-first-century challenges facing humanity. These include climate change, genetic engineering, the COVID-19 pandemic, and artificial intelligence. Some of these problems are entirely new for human populations; others, such as pandemics, are not. The political philosophers of today must think imaginatively and innovatively to offer sage normative insights concerning how these predicaments can best be addressed to ensure the concerns of freedom, equality, justice, democracy, and human happiness are promoted versus diminished.

Climate Change

In the introduction I drew an analogy between political philosophy and medicine. First, success in both requires *diagnostic skill* to accurately identity pathology (in the case of medicine) and pressing societal ills (in the case of political philosophy). Second, both require *prescriptive skill*, the insight and foresight to know how best to prevent or remedy the problems/challenges (health-related or societal) identified by the first epistemic skill. Because climate change and its long-term impacts are not directly observable, it has generally not been treated as a pressing global problem that must be addressed.

But as with the history of political philosophy, studying the history of the world's environment and its species can help us better understand the significance and challenges of climate change. The environment can be precarious and even hostile. Food resources are typically scarce, and most living species are prey for some other species. Furthermore, microscopic organisms prey upon us by causing infectious diseases.

Most species that have ever lived—from ammonites to dinosaurs to dodo birds—have become extinct over the earth's history. While extinctions have occurred throughout time, scientists estimate that there have been five especially large mass extinction events over the past 500 million years.[1] "The body of evidence associated with mass extinctions lends much support to proximal kill mechanisms that include anoxia [oxygen deprivation], . . . and ocean acidification . . . coupled with changes in atmospheric greenhouse gases, notably CO_2, to name just a few."[2]

Humans are dependent on the earth's environment for survival. Marx's assumption that technology would continue to develop in ways that enable humans to exploit the world's resources to meet our material needs did not consider the serious ecological consequences of doing so for populations of billions of people. The reliance on fossil fuels has created a climate change crisis that requires urgent global action to prevent significant long-term harms. The home of future humanity will be warmer than it is today. NASA models estimate that, depending on the action taken to reduce greenhouse gases, the global temperature can be expected to rise between 2.5 and 4.5°C by the year 2100.[3] This warming is expected

---

1. David P. G. Bond and Stephen E. Grasby, "Editorial: Mass Extinction Causality," *Palaeogeography, Palaeoclimatology, Palaeoecology* 478 (2017): 1–2.
2. Bond and Grasby, "On the Causes of Mass Extinctions," 3–29, 3.
3. NASA, "Is It Too Late to Prevent Climate Change?," Global Climate Change: Vital Signs of the Planet, https://climate.nasa.gov/faq/16/is-it-too-late-to-prevent-climate-change/, accessed March 31, 2023.

to lead to increased extreme weather events and heat stress, as well as decreased air quality and global food security.

Bentham's "calculus of happiness" employs a type of cost-benefit analysis that can help clarify why abating the worst harms of climate change—through a combination of mitigation and adaptation—is so important. The calculus's criteria—like the "intensity of the pain" from severe climate change, the "certainty of those harms," "fecundity" (the likelihood that warmer temperatures will not only cause more heat-related deaths but increase deaths from other causes such as declines in food security as well as impose significant economic harms, especially on developing countries), and the "extent" of the impact (billions of people now living, as well as future generations)—easily reveal the folly of not taking the possible threats from climate change seriously.

Hobbes's insight into suboptimal joint decisions also reveals how challenging it is to achieve success in reducing greenhouse gases in the world. Climate change mitigation is a prisoner's dilemma.[4] There is no world government to force each country to meet its expected reduction in greenhouse gas emissions. Thus it is rational for each country not to go along with any global agreements to reduce greenhouse gas emissions, hoping that other countries will shoulder the entire burden (so they can free-ride off the sacrifices of others).

Many climate activists have engaged in different forms of civil disobedience and protest to raise public awareness about the severity of the problem and the lack of significant policy progress. Climate change is not something one can engage in direct civil disobedience about, so what forms of indirect civil disobedience are both effective and morally justified? For example, in 2022 climate activists threw soup across Van Gogh's famous *Sunflowers* painting in London's National Gallery. Is such a form of communication a morally justified one? While it is not violence against a specific person, potentially destroying (the painting was protected by glass) valuable art raises questions about the civility of such protest actions. Are such actions likely to convince climate change skeptics that they should support stronger collective action against climate change, or

---

4. Peter John Wood, "Climate Change and Game Theory," in "Ecological Economics Reviews," ed. Robert Costanza, Karin Limburg, and Ida Kubiszewski, special issue, *Annals of New York Academy of Sciences* 1219 (2011): 153–70, 168.

are they likely to further alienate people from the cause? Also, climate change is not something any one country can mitigate, and there is no world government or global law that could simply be changed to appease such protest. What are the scopes and limits of defensible protest in a complex case like climate change?

Furthermore, not all of the world's governments are democracies. The world's largest emitter of greenhouse gases is China, an authoritarian state. Historically China was not among the major contributors to greenhouse gas emissions. It has an interest in growing its economy and lifting millions of people out of poverty; it has also become the preferred location for global manufacturing. What is fair and feasible when it comes to shouldering (and enforcing compliance with) the burden of reducing greenhouse gas emissions? These are not easy questions to answer.

Biomedical Technologies

New biomedical technologies, such as genome sequencing and editing, offer the promise of personalized medicine and new therapies for genetic disorders. But the history of racial inequality reminds us about eugenics, when pseudoscience was invoked to justify policies and attitudes that were predicated on prejudice and assumptions of racial supremacy versus morally laudable aspirations that could be justified in a free and democratic society.

The philosopher Bertrand Russell defined eugenics as "the attempt to improve the biological character of a breed by deliberate methods adopted to that end."[5] Stated in this way one might contend that eugenics is morally neutral,[6] depending on both the "ends" and "means" in specific cases. An end such as the prevention of serious, early-onset genetic disorders via biomedical research is much more defensible than the ends of racial hygiene and ethnic cleansing. However, history teaches us that caution

---

5. Bertrand Russell, "Eugenics," in *Marriage and Morals* (New York: Liveright, 1929), 254–73, 254.

6. See Colin Farrelly, *Genetics and Ethics: An Introduction* (Polity, 2018) for a more expansive examination of this issue.

and scrutiny may still be warranted because, in the case of racial hygiene in Nazi Germany, medical professionals perceived themselves as custodians of national health.[7] The means historically pursued to achieve eugenic ends, such as involuntary sterilization, also constituted gross violations of reproductive freedom and human rights. The first eugenic sterilization law in the United States was enacted in 1907, and by World War II it is estimated that the resulting programs had sterilized approximately sixty thousand people in the United States. German Hereditary Health Courts under the Third Reich approved at least four hundred thousand sterilization operations within less than a decade.[8]

In addition to unjust "negative eugenics," or policies designed to prevent some people from reproducing, many eugenicists proposed "positive eugenics," or incentives for those deemed to have desirable heritable traits to reproduce. Paul Popenoe, who founded the American Institute of Family Relations in 1929 and championed exclusivist eugenic aspirations, had this to say about eugenics:

> Eugenics rests on two axioms so simple that a child can understand them. If a people is to survive, it must produce in each year, or each generation, enough children to take the places of those who die during that period. And if it is to avoid deterioration which would also prevent survival, it must encourage childbearing from the part of the population that is, in general, fit, rather than predominantly from the mentally diseased, the mentally deficient, and the physically defective.[9]

To avoid the mistakes of the past, we must take seriously the questions of which ends and means of biomedical research can be morally justified in a free and democratic society. Sound science *and* sound ethics were both missing during the eugenics movement of the late nineteenth and early twentieth centuries.

---

7. Sheila Faith Weiss, "The Race Hygiene Movement in Germany," *Osiris* 3 (1987): 193–236, 197.

8. Philip R. Reilly, "Eugenics and Involuntary Sterilization: 1907–2015," *Annual Review of Genomics and Human Genetics* 16 (2015): 351–68.

9. Paul Popenoe, "Education and Eugenics," *Journal of Educational Sociology* 8, no. 8 (1935): 451–58, 451.

In November 2018 the Chinese scientist He Jiankui shocked the world when he announced at a scientific conference that he had performed germ-line genome editing on healthy embryos to make the cells resistant to infection by HIV, and that the procedure had resulted in the birth of twin girls, Lulu and Nana. Performing such a procedure on embryos was controversial (resulting in Jiankui being sentenced to three years in prison)[10] because it was too experimental (more time is needed to study the safety and efficacy of genome editing) and because merely being susceptible to HIV is not a disease. Enhancing human biology through genetic engineering has been opposed by bioconservatives who believe its risks far outweigh any potential benefits.

In *The Case against Perfection: Ethics in the Age of Genetic Engineering*, Michael Sandel argues that a quest to perfect our biology "threatens to banish our appreciation of life as a gift, and to leave us with nothing to affirm or behold outside of our own will."[11] This echoes Michael Oakeshott's insight that conservatives prefer the "familiar to the unknown," "the tried to the untried." But is this a sage attitude to take toward biomedical interventions that may permit us to improve our biology, so that humans can live longer, healthier lives? What if we could enhance human cognition and perhaps even our moral behavior and human nature itself? These are vital questions in the twenty-first century, and among the most significant issues for the political philosophers of today to address. The ideas of the past may serve as a sage guide or antiquated constraint on determining how societies ought to regulate new biomedical technologies such as genome editing.

The COVID-19 Pandemic

In December 2019 the first cases of a new virus (SARS-CoV-2) were detected in China. The virus was rapidly spreading to other countries, and on March 11, 2020, the World Health Organization declared the

---

10. Dennis Normile, "Chinese Scientist Who Produced Genetically Altered Babies Sentenced to 3 Years in Jail," *Science*, December 30, 2019, https://www.science.org/content/article/chinese-scientist-who-produced-genetically-altered-babies-sentenced-3-years-jail.

11. Michael Sandel, *The Case against Perfection: Ethics in the Age of Genetic Engineering* (Cambridge, MA: Harvard University Press, 2007), 99–100.

outbreak a pandemic. While humanity had faced many pandemics in the past, and there were tried and tested public health measures that could mitigate the spread of infectious diseases—such as quarantine of infected persons, handwashing, and wearing appropriate face masks—many unprecedented public health measures were pursued during the COVID-19 pandemic. These included the prolonged closure of schools, businesses (e.g., restaurants, pubs, cinemas), and other nonessential services. When COVID-19 vaccines became available in 2021, many countries adopted "proof of vaccination" requirements for visitors from abroad wishing to travel, and for daily activities such as dining in restaurants and returning to in-class instruction at universities and colleges. The COVID-19 pandemic brought to the fore many of the concerns and issues addressed by the classics in Western political philosophy (e.g., right to self-ownership, duty to promote the greater good, the appropriate relationship between democratic governance and epistemic expertise).

Public health is "the science and art of preventing disease, prolonging life and promoting health through the organized efforts and informed choices of society, organizations, public and private, communities and individuals."[12] Like the consequentialist lens adopted by utilitarianism, public health prioritizes the health of a community over the well-being or welfare of any particular individual. For example, suppose I test positive for active tuberculosis, an infectious disease that killed approximately 1.6 million people in 2021.[13] The case for isolating me while I pose a risk of spread to others is very compelling because it would help prevent higher rates of disease and death for the population. Public health ethics prescribes that such limitations on my rights can be justified when the harm they prevent to population health justifies such restrictions.

There are of course limits to how stringent appeals to the "greater good" can be in cases of public health. Limiting my mobility rights and other freedoms for the duration of time I am likely to pose a risk of infection to others can be justified. But in the early stages of COVID-19 there

---

12. C. E. A. Winslow, "The Untilled Fields of Public Health," *Science* 51, no. 1306 (1920): 23–33, 23.

13. World Health Organization, "Tuberculosis," November 7, 2023, https://www.who.int/news-room/fact-sheets/detail/tuberculosis.

were not sufficient, and arguably even reliable, COVID-19 tests available, to see which members of the population were positive and infectious with COVID-19. Many infected persons were asymptomatic, which meant they did not present any symptoms of infection even though they could be contagious. Unlike quarantine of the infected, the large-scale lockdown measures many countries imposed in 2020, before vaccinations were available, treated the population as if they were positive and infectious for many months. Defenders of such policies argued such measures were necessary to reduce the risks of overburdening scarce and limited health-care resources if the virus spread rapidly through a naive population (a population with no natural immunity). Critics of such lockdown measures raised the kinds of concerns typically raised against utilitarianism—that such restrictions on people's freedom violated their basic liberties. Furthermore, the prolonged isolation of large sections of the population creates its own public health crises, as people's mental health is jeopardized, the education of children is compromised, regular medical checkups are disrupted, and so forth. Critics often pointed out that public health should be concerned with the overall health and well-being of the population, and not simply the risks of COVID-19 itself. The latter is a myopic public health lens.

Because of the uncertainly concerning the virulence and lethality of SARS-CoV-2, as well as its spread and how it could be transmitted, many precautionary public health measures were put in place to mitigate the spread of the virus. In the decades to come public health experts will no doubt continue to debate and learn from the mistakes and successes of the handling of the COVID-19 pandemic. The "intellectual virtues" are pertinent to public health decision-making. Getting credible information concerning both the specifics of a new infectious disease (e.g., how lethal it is, how it spreads) and the effectiveness of different potential mitigation measures (e.g., wearing face masks, social isolation, etc.) can help ascertain which public health measures are the most effective.

When faced with the risk of a new lethal disease, fear may compel some to invoke a Plato-like deference to "epistocracy." "Just follow the science!" some might contend. Others, appealing to Rousseau's procedural commitments of democratic governance, may contend that, while the input of scientists is important, the ultimate determination of which courses of action are best to pursue for the common good should "come from all, and apply to all." Alternatively, virtue epistemology can serve as a useful guide in reminding us how important epistemic virtues like humility, open-mindedness, and an adaptive intellect (trying new things rather than repeating failed strategies) can be when facing the risks of a new infectious disease we know very little about.

An "intersectional" lens on the harms and impact of both COVID-19 and public health mitigation measures (e.g., working remotely from home) can reveal how factors such as income, race, and gender can create different types of inequities. For some nonessential workers, working remotely from home for a prolonged period of time may have been feasible. But many occupations, especially lower-income but essential service providers such as cleaners in hospitals or warehouse workers, were exposed to higher risks of infection. Also, being isolated in smaller living conditions (e.g., a small apartment) is more challenging than in a large house with a backyard. Having young children at home doing remote learning while the parent(s) try to work could adversely impact both one's ability to be productive at work as well as one's mental health. A sudden increase in childcare responsibilities and household labor from lockdown will have different impacts on working fathers versus mothers. "The personal is political" still holds during a pandemic, and gender inequalities could be exacerbated by such measures.

Research on happiness and positive psychology, inspired by Aristotle's account of *eudaimonia*, might help individuals and communities develop the resilience needed to cope with the uncertainty and mental anguish of prolonged lockdowns. For example, while lockdown measures impose the hardships of isolation, if one is able to find meaning in such measures (e.g., to help protect the vulnerable in one's community) then such personal sacrifices may be more manageable. In "Collective Wellbeing and Posttraumatic Growth during COVID-19: How Positive Psychology Can Help Families, Schools, Workplaces, and Marginalized Communities" Waters et al. detail how a range of positive psychology interventions for families, workplaces, and therapists can help with collective well-being and posttraumatic growth.[14] For example, within families the lockdown

---

14. Lea Waters, Kim Cameron, S. Katherine Nelson-Coffey, Damien L. Crone, Margaret L. Kern, Tim Lomas, Lindsay Oades, Rhea L. Owens, James O. Pawelski,

measures could be a catalyst to promote more compassion for familial relationships, so that parents offer more support to their children because of the increased vulnerabilities of life under lockdown. New family practices, such as cultivating well-being by "eco-connections"—walking together in nature—could also be adopted in such adverse circumstances.

With respect to schools during the COVID-19 lockdowns, Waters et al. (2022) argue:

> COVID-19 has motivated many schools to have a dual purpose—that of promoting both learning and wellbeing. From a systems perspective, the larger *purpose* of schools to protect the wellbeing of their students in a pandemic creates a domino effect on teachers and school counselors who are encouraged to embed the use of PPIs [positive psychological interventions] into daily school life. . . . The importance of talking to students about the notion that they can not only survive the pandemic but can grow from the adversity it creates is a vital way of using wellbeing literacy . . . to support students at this time.[15]

Finally, Waters et al. emphasize how positive leaders in the workplace can demonstrate virtuous behavior during challenging situations such as the pandemic. Such leaders display gratitude, humility, forgiveness, and so on. They set positive examples for others in terms of how even turbulent times can be an opportunity to learn and display virtue. Resilient workplaces can also display *antifragility*, which means being in a state of improving through disorder, disruption, and uncertainty.[16] By applying insights from positive psychology to the adversity of the COVID-19 pandemic, one can identify and appreciate how resilient humanity can be, and how new opportunities for learning and development can occur from circumstances of adversity. This nicely illustrates how well-being entails

---

Tayyab Rashid, Meg A. Warren, Mathew A. White, and Paige Williams, "Collective Wellbeing and Posttraumatic Growth during COVID-19: How Positive Psychology Can Help Families, Schools, Workplaces, and Marginalized Communities," *Journal of Positive Psychology* 17, no. 6 (2022): 761–89.

15. Waters et al., "Collective Wellbeing," 767.

16. Nassim Nicholas Taleb, *Antifragile: Things That Gain through Disorder* (New York: Random House, 2012).

much more than the hedonic account of happiness advanced by utilitarians such as Jeremy Bentham.

Artificial Intelligence

The final twenty-first-century predicament we consider in this chapter is artificial intelligence. "In the past decade, Artificial Intelligence (AI) as a general-purpose tool has become a disruptive force globally."[17] Intelligence itself is an often-contested concept. Here is one influential characterization of intelligence:

> Intelligence is a very general mental capability that, among other things, involves the ability to reason, plan, solve problems, think abstractly, comprehend complex ideas, learn quickly and learn from experience. It is not merely book learning, a narrow academic skill, or test-taking smarts. Rather, it reflects a broader and deeper capability for comprehending our surroundings—"catching on," "making sense" of things, or "figuring out" what to do.[18]

If intelligence is understood generally as "problem-solving," then AI refers to problem-solving that is done by neither humans nor other animals. In 1950 Alan Turing first raised this issue in a famous paper in *Mind* titled "Computing Machinery and Intelligence."[19] Turing put forth what is now known as the Turing test to raise the question "Can machines think?" Turing believed this question was meaningless because, at least in the mid-twentieth-century usage of the terms, "machine" and "think" were too ambiguous. So he preferred to ask instead the question: "Are there imaginable digital computers that would do well in the imitation game?"

---

17. Silja Voeneky, Philipp Kellmeyer, Oliver Mueller, and Wolfram Burgard, introduction to *The Cambridge Handbook of Responsible Artificial Intelligence* (Cambridge: Cambridge University Press, 2020), 1.

18. Linda Gottfredson, "Mainstream Science on Intelligence: An Editorial with 52 Signatories, History, and Bibliography," *Intelligence* 24, no. 1 (1997): 13–23, 13.

19. A. M. Turing, "Computing Machinery and Intelligence," *Mind* 59, no. 236 (1950): 433–60.

The imitation game goes as follows: In one room there is an interrogator, who will raise questions to try to determine the identity of the two participants in the other room whom they cannot see or hear. In the other room there is one person and one machine, both of which respond to the interrogator's questions via a teleprinter communicating between the two rooms. If, when this imitation game is repeated many times, the human interrogator can only correctly identify who is human 50 percent of the time or less, then Turing contends we must say that there are digital computers that are indistinguishable from a human, at least by this method.

Computers have become significantly more powerful and complex in the decades since Turing's original essay in *Mind*. A number of key forces are driving the evolution of AI, including:

1. The exponential growth in computing performance;
2. Expanded datasets;
3. Advances in the implementation of machine learning techniques and algorithms (especially in the field of deep neural networks); and above all,
4. The rapid expansion of commercial interest and investment in AI.[20]

We will briefly consider three domains in which AI raises significant ethical and societal concerns: policing, war, and democracy itself.

In policing, for example, "a police agency might use predictive algorithms to forecast where crime is likely to occur in the future, or which persons might be at highest risk for crime victimization or perpetration."[21] But what might initially sound like a beneficial advancement—the more efficient deployment of strained policing resources—could, as Elizabeth Joh argues, amplify the biases and unfairness that already exist in racially biased police data collection. For example, if police are more likely to report incidents of suspicious behavior when patrolling predominantly nonwhite neighborhoods than when observing the same behaviors in predominantly white neighborhoods, then an AI system will simply

---

20. James Johnson, "Artificial Intelligence and Future Welfare: Implications for International Security," *Defense and Security Analysis* 35, no. 2 (2019): 147–69, 147.

21. Elizabeth E. Joh, "Artificial Intelligence and Policing: First Questions," *Seattle University Law Review* 41, no. 4 (2018): 1139–44, 1141.

replicate and amplify those same biases. AI is only as good as the intelligence of the human programmers, and if human epistemic vices are integrated into systems of artificial intelligence, we will simply be repeating and amplifying (rather than improving on) the shortcomings of our own cognition. Similar concerns have arisen over other AI technologies used in policing, such as automated facial analysis.

With respect to AI and the military, human civilizations have a long history of conflict and warfare. Intelligence in warfare offers a competitive advantage over potential foes. Technological advances in weaponry—from stones and wooden clubs, to swords, arrows, and muskets, and more recently to tanks, missiles, and nuclear weapons—have dramatically increased the potential lethality of warfare and determined the current dynamics of global power. AI could be a disruptive force in the way future wars are waged. Autonomous weapons and robotics may sound more like the science fiction portrayed in the movie *Terminator*, with unstoppable robots in relentless pursuit of their targets. But advances in AI are making science fiction–like scenarios a reality. AI drones can be deployed in military settings, removing the risks of injury and death to the military of the country deploying such technology (unlike when using human fighter pilots, for example). So one risk with such a technology is that, with the prospect of incurring casualties removed or at least reduced, the side deploying such technology might be more willing to engage or provoke military conflict, confident in the knowledge that doing so will not endanger the health of their own soldiers.

But there may also be benefits to relying on automated aerial vehicles over ones operated by humans. Humans are vulnerable to fatigue, stress, and other factors that can negatively impact their decision-making when undertaking complex and challenging military operatives. If AI drones removed or at least reduced these shortcomings of human decision-making, one might argue that such technologies could reduce some of the unnecessary carnage of warfare. "The ethics of AI must be studied in all circumstances on the basis of human values when fighting and in military ethics."[22]

AI may also have a significant impact on democracy itself. AI-created deep fakes and AI generated journalism threaten to distort our perception

---

22. Thibault de Swarte, Omar Boufous, and Paul Escalle, "Artificial Intelligence, Ethics, and Human Values: The Cases of Military Drones and Companion Robots," *Artificial Life and Robotics* 24 (2019): 291–96, 295.

of reality and news coverage. Most aspects of society are already interdependent with different forms of AI, whether it be data science or machine learning. In medicine, for example, machine-learning-aided tasks have already been widely used in clinical practice to make more accurate diagnoses of pathology than could be achieved by relying only on human intelligence. If, as I have conjectured at the beginning of this book, the dual task of the political philosopher/theorist is to (1) accurately diagnosis societal problems and (2) offer some prescriptions to remedy these problems, then perhaps there is a role for AI to play in the problem-solving of political philosophy.

Furthermore, following Plato's line of criticism against democracy, if justice entails "doing what we are best suited to do," and AI eventually surpasses humans in its ability to solve complex policy problems, then perhaps some will see an "Epistocracy 2.0" as an attractive future for humanity. Rather than appealing to rule by philosopher kings and queens, who would still suffer the epistemic shortcomings of humans, some might see appeal in the idea of rule by epistemically and morally superior AI. Rather than crafting public policies that respond to the self-interested and short-sighted preferences of the majority, AI could employ more reliable algorithms to make decisions that are more optimal to delivering on the common good. While there may be some appeal in such a utopian future, it also sounds like a dystopian future—one where political power is handed over to our robotic overlords (the "divine right of AI" instead of the divine right of kings). And how do we ensure that AI is working for the common good versus the wealthy and powerful?

Or consider the implications future advances in AI might have for Marx's account of historical materialism. Marx believed in technological determinism: productive forces that enable us to meet our needs more easily will continue to be developed, and when relations of production impede the development of productive forces, they will eventually be replaced by new relations of production, and a superstructure will come into being that reinforces the legitimacy of the new relations of production. Marx did not anticipate the coming of artificial intelligence, but it is certainly a powerful productive force. If existing relations of production impede the development of new technologies (they become a fetter) like androids, Marx's theory of history would predict that those relations of production will be cast asunder and replaced by new relations of production and a superstructure that solidifies the stability of those new relations. In other words, if Marx's account of history is correct (which of course is highly debatable), it would appear that AI is a juggernaut that cannot be stopped. Like the Industrial Revolution, the new technologies of AI will dramatically impact the way humans produce to meet their needs (perhaps this will be completely replaced by robotics in time) and how we relate to one another.

Finally, if androids and other AI systems advance in their problem-solving skills such that they surpass human intelligence, could and should they have some moral status? Would they count as "persons"? And if so, should they be included in Rousseau's account of the "general will" and perhaps given the right to vote? These are fascinating questions and issues political philosophers in the twenty-first century must grapple with.

In this book I have tried to ignite curiosity for the ideas of past political thinkers. We have canvassed a diverse array of philosophers, topics, and issues, including Plato's critique of democracy, the social contract and its critics, the issue of happiness, conservatism, Black political thought, feminism, and Marxism. Throughout the book I have tried to highlight "the good, the bad, and the ugly" of Western political thought. Doing so has, I believe, many pedagogical benefits. It reminds us that even the great minds of the past had their biases and cognitive limitations, and that when we engage these thinkers with curiosity, humility, and hope we may reduce the risks associated with either putting them on a pedestal as exemplars of moral and epistemic virtue or canceling them as antiquated relics of past eras because they do not share our modern moral sentiments.

To meet the challenges of the twenty-first century, the students of today should engage with the canon of the past. The specific (and limited) list of thinkers covered in this book is not meant to suggest that these and only these thinkers represent "the canon." Of course other thinkers could have been covered. But as a book designed to show why the past is important for thinking about the problems of today and tomorrow, I believe the ensemble of thinkers we have discussed here will serve well as an introduction to some of the central themes and debates in the history of political philosophy.

Index

African Americans: education, 163, 167–68, 195; entrepreneurship, 166–67; racial segregation, 217, 220–21; reparations for, 115–18; voting rights, 168, 216. *See also* racial inequality

America: Black conservatism in, 162–68; Black reparations for slavery in, 115–18; Civil War, 164, 166–67, 194, 216–18; counterculture in, 89; English colonization of, 87, 107–10; exceptionalism, 172; racial inequality in, 207, 209, 212–21; Reconstruction, 167, 216; Revolutionary War, 152, 156–59

anarchism, 80–91

Annas, Julia, 26, 32–33, 179

Aristotle: critique of, 71–73; on democracy, 63–64; *eudaimonia*, 2, 59–62, 301–2; on justice, 48–51; *Nicomachean Ethics*, 43, 52–53, 59–62; on political nature, 64–66; problematic views, 43–44, 62–63; virtue ethics, 44–59, 292

Armitage, David, 112

Arneil, Barbara, 109

artificial intelligence (AI), 303–7

Austin, John, 234

authoritarianism, 30–31, 132

basic materialism, 267

Belfour, Lawrie, 217–18

Bentham, Jeremy: calculus of happiness, 60, 235–40, 295, 303; consequentialism, 11, 45; democratic reform, 241, 254; *Introduction to the Principles of Morals and Legislation*, 235–40, 244; legal positivism, 234; *Plan of Parliamentary Reform*, 241, 254; and utilitarianism, 7, 234–42

Berlin, Isaiah, 139–40

Bertram, Christopher, 132n11

biomedical technologies, 296–98

Black conservatism, 162–67, 172–73

Black political thought: abolitionism, 206–12; anticolonial liberation, 225–31; civil disobedience, 219–25; feminism, 142, 194–98; intersectionality, 198–203, 205; racial inequality, 212–18, 292

Bou-Habib, Paul, 120

Boxill, Bernard, 115–17

Boyd, Robert, 88

Brennan, Jason, 41, 257–59

Brewer, Holly, 114, 118

Brink, David, 253

Brown-Grant, Rosalind, 180

Buccola, Nicholas, 210

Buchanan, Allen, 275, 277–78

Burke, Edmund: conservatism, 152–53, 157–58; on private property, 153–54; *Reflections on the Revolution in France*, 152, 169; *Thoughts on the Cause of Present Discontents*, 157

Canada, 12, 80, 102, 107, 170

capitalism: accumulation of capital, 105–6, 275, 283, 287; alienation in, 279–81; communism transition, 149–50, 286–88; exploitation in, 231, 264, 275–79, 281; and social mobility, 285–86

Carmichael, Stokely, 220, 224
China, 154, 173, 201n44, 264, 296, 298
Christine de Pizan: *Book of the City of Ladies*, 180; feminist critique by, 5, 142, 178–83, 292
civil disobedience, 219–26, 295–96
civil rights, 219–21
climate change, 16, 45, 90, 170, 174–75, 295–96
Coffee, Alan, 188
Cohen, G. A., 264, 268, 270, 273, 275
Cohen, Joshua, 93
colonialism: decolonization, 2, 7, 226–27, 231; Indigenous dispossession, 79, 87, 108–11; and inequality, 225–26, 230–31; political violence in, 98, 227–31; and social contract tradition, 7, 80, 87
common good, 21, 48, 83, 131, 136, 139
communism, 149–50, 270, 279, 286–88
Cone, James, 225
consent: express, 100–102; government by, 96; as racialized ideology, 113; and right to private property, 103–4; sexual contract, 103; social contract theory, 67, 99–103; tacit, 100–102
consequentialism, 11, 44–46, 233, 235, 249
conservatism: as disposition, 149–50, 174–75; importance of family, 159–60, 165–66, 170–71; moral domains, 150–51, 171; public policies, 168–75; status quo bias, 150–51, 153, 156, 161–63, 168–70, 174; welfare state opposition, 171–72. *See also* Black conservatism

Cooper, Anna: feminist critique by, 5, 142, 194–97, 225; on inequalities, 7, 11, 196–98, 292; on intersectionality, 198, 214; *A Voice from the South*, 194–95
Corcoran, Paul, 109–10
COVID-19 pandemic, 54, 298–302
Crenshaw, Kimberlé, 198–99
Csikszentmihalyi, Mihaly, 61–62

Dagger, Richard, 91
Dahl, Robert, 21, 144
decision-making: calculus of happiness in, 236–39; cost-benefit analysis (CBA), 11, 240; democratic, 90, 100, 132, 144; intellectual virtues, 53, 59; judicial, 56–59; virtue ethics, 56–57
democracy: competency testing, 257–59; conflict with justice, 23, 40, 219; constitutional, 39–40, 219; deliberative, 145–47; direct, 20, 22, 39–40, 255; and economic inequality, 134–35; education for, 40–41; and general will, 7, 125, 129, 131–32, 143; and happiness, 62, 65–66, 254–55; liberty principle, 246–50; majoritarian, 89–90; representative, 20–21, 39, 89–90, 131, 190–91; unanimous direct, 89–90
Dewey, John, 1, 8, 13–14, 17, 144
diachronic materialism, 267, 273–75, 285
Douglass, Frederick: condemnation of slavery, 2, 206–7, 209–12, 230; enslavement of, 163–64, 207–9; on inequalities, 7, 292; *My Bondage and My Freedom*, 210–12; *Narrative*, 207–10
Downs, Anthony, 64, 144–45

Du Bois, W. E. B.: *Dusk of Dawn*, 214; intersectionality, 214–15, 225; *Philadelphia Negro*, 212–13; political philosophy of, 5, 217; on racial inequality, 7, 212–18, 292; *Souls of Black Folk*, 216–17

Eisenstadt, Peter, 163
Elster, Jon, 39
Engels, Friedrich, 263
England: and American Revolution, 152, 156–59; Civil War in, 7, 10, 69–71, 83, 95; colonialism, 87, 107–10; Hundred Years War, 178; slave trade in, 113; utilitarianism in, 233; women in, 183, 186, 188
epistocracy, 219, 300, 306
equality: justice as, 48; political, 68, 79, 103, 112, 114, 122, 141; psychological resistance to change, 197–98; and same-sex marriage, 170–71; undermining of, 197–98. *See also* inequality
eudaimonia, 2, 59–62, 301–2
eugenics, 31, 296–97
exploitation: capitalism, 5, 231, 264, 275–81; colonial, 94, 231; general conception of, 275, 278; labor, 206, 275–79; and private property rights, 103; surplus, 277–78; transhistorical, 275–78

fairness: intellectual virtues, 53, 55; justice as, 50, 193–94, 261–62; as moral domain, 151
family: and conservatism, 159–60, 165–66, 170–71; division of labor in, 186, 189, 194; ethical life thesis, 160–61; gender inequality in, 7, 102, 161, 188–89; power relations in, 102–3, 187–89

Fanon, Frantz: anticolonial liberation theory, 7, 225–31; *Black Skin, White Masks*, 229–30; on inequalities, 292; political philosophy of, 5, 225; *The Wretched of the Earth*, 227, 230–31
Fashina, Oladipo, 229–30
feminism: Black American, 194–99; on consent-based theory, 102–3; on gender inequalities, 142, 161, 292; and intersectionality, 194, 198–203; personal is political, 178, 188–89, 301; in Plato's *Republic*, 32–33, 177
Fendler, Lynn, 3, 3n3
Filmer, Robert, 95–96
flow, 61–62
Fourier, Charles, 265
France: criminal punishment in, 201; feudal society in, 178; Free Army, 226; French Revolution, 10, 16, 124, 137–39, 142, 147, 152–53, 156–59, 183, 188, 263–65, 274, 286; inequality in, 7, 125, 141
fraternity, 142–43
freedom, 85, 129–30, 138–40, 188

gender inequality: domestic labor, 142, 161, 186, 194; educational, 103, 132, 141–42, 161, 177, 183–84, 186; family power relations, 102–3, 187–89; political representation, 190–91
general will, 7, 68, 125, 128–32, 139, 141, 143
genetics: differences in, 185; genetic engineering, 170, 293, 298; genome editing, 11; prevention of disorders, 296
George, Robert, 171
Geras, Norman, 281
Gilligan, Carol, 191–94
Gilroy, Paul, 206

Goldman, Emma, 5, 85–86
Graham, Jesse, 151
Graham, Keith, 267, 282–84
Gutmann, Amy, 146

Haidt, Jonathan, 151
Hampton, Jean, 69
Hanchard, Michael, 205
happiness: and democracy, 62, 65–66, 254–55; flow activities, 61–62; and highest of ends, 59–60; and lawfulness, 48–49; and utilitarianism, 233, 236–39, 243
Hayek, Friedrich, 155–56
Hegel, Georg, 159–62
Herbert, Gary, 72
historical materialism: basic materialism, 267; diachronic materialism, 267, 273–75; implications of AI, 306–7; Marx on, 264–72, 306–7; synchronic materialism, 267–72
Hobbes, Thomas: on absolute sovereignty, 67–72, 77–80, 87–88; on animal-human differences, 82–84; critique of Aristotle, 72–73; on felicity, 73–74; interest-based social contracts, 67–73, 78–79; *Leviathan*, 67, 70–71, 73, 82, 91; on state of nature, 73–79, 91
human nature: *amour propre/de soi*, 125–28, 136–38; common/private good, 83; and competition, 74–75, 82; and conflict, 81, 83–84; reciprocal cooperation, 73, 76–78, 86, 88

Imlay, Gilbert, 184
Indigenous peoples, 79–80, 87, 108–11, 196
individualism, 96–97, 113, 115, 142, 266
inequality: economic, 15, 134–36, 154; and intersectionality, 198–99; natural, 124–25; political, 68, 125; and private property rights, 153–54. *See also* equality; gender inequality; racial inequality
Inikori, Joseph, 207
intellectual virtues: curiosity, 15–16, 292; fairness, 53, 55; humility, 53, 301; nuanced understanding, 15–16, 292; open-mindedness, 53–55; optimism, 15, 17–18, 292; perseverance, 53, 56
intersectionality, 194, 198–203, 205
Ireland, 71, 215, 284
Italy, 215

Joh, Elizabeth, 304
Jost, J. T., 151
justice: competence principle, 258; conflict with democracy, 23, 40, 219; conventionalism, 26–27; distributive, 50–51, 260; as fairness, 50, 193–94, 261–62; immoralism, 26–28; individual, 29–35; instrumental value of, 28–29, 35; jury selection, 257–58; lawfulness, 48–50; legal realism, 56–57; misogyny in, 182–83; virtue of, 23–24, 27–31, 48

Kant, Immanuel, 159–60
Kekes, John, 150
Kelman, Steven, 260–61
King, Martin Luther, Jr., 219–26, 292
Kohlberg, Lawrence, 192–93
Kraut, Richard, 48
Krishnamurthy, Meena, 221
Kropotkin, Peter, 81–84, 86

labor: alienation in, 279–80; enslaved, 116, 165, 207, 270, 272, 277; exploitation of, 275–79; mixing of, 104–7, 115; productive forces, 269–70, 274–75; proletariat class, 282–83; surplus, 277–78, 282
labor theory of value, 276
Lenin, Vladimir, 264
Lewis, Angela, 166
liberalism: complicity with slavery, 112–15; limitation of state power, 5, 93, 103; and racism, 117–18; right to self-ownership, 96; social contract tradition, 102; and toleration, 119–20, 122
libertarianism, 155–56, 253–54
liberty: natural rights, 85, 95–96, 98, 113; positive versus negative, 138–40, 217; principle of, 246–51
Lloyd, Genevieve, 142
Lloyd Thomas, D. A., 100
Lober, Judith, 185
Locke, John: on consent, 99–102; on Indigenous peoples, 98, 108–10; and liberalism, 93–96, 102–3, 112, 117–19; on limited government, 67, 93, 95, 99, 103, 112; on religious toleration, 119–22; right-based social contracts, 68, 80, 93, 99, 101, 196; right to private property, 11, 87, 95–96, 103–12, 115; self-ownership, 95–99, 104–5, 113, 115, 292; on slavery, 93, 96, 112–18; on state of nature, 68, 85, 96–99; *Two Treatises of Government*, 67, 95

MacPherson, C. B., 105
Mansbridge, Jane, 190–91
Mao Zedong, 154, 264

Marx, Karl: on alienation, 279–80; on basic materialism, 267; on class, 282–85; *Communist Manifesto*, 263, 266, 274, 276; critique of capitalism, 2, 5, 7, 140, 263–64, 274–89; on diachronic materialism, 267, 273–75; on exploitation, 275–79; on historical materialism, 264–75, 289, 306–7; moral arguments of, 275, 280–82; primacy thesis, 273–74; productive forces, 269–70, 273–74; relations of production, 268–70, 273–74, 286–87; superstructure of society, 270–72; on synchronic materialism, 267–72; technological determinism, 273–74, 280–81, 287–89, 292, 294, 306
McMurtry, John, 271
Mill, James, 241, 254
Mill, John Stuart: democratic reform, 254–55; freedom of expression, 122, 251–54; informed preference test, 244–45; *On Liberty*, 246, 251, 254; liberty/harm principle, 246–51, 253–54; plural voting, 255–57; self-regarding actions, 247–48; utilitarianism, 7, 41, 242–52; *Utilitarianism*, 243–44
Miller, Joseph, 256
Mills, Charles, 112–14, 119, 177–78, 197, 205
Moloney, Pat, 87
moral virtues, 46–51

nature versus nurture, 2, 142, 183–86
Neuhouser, Frederick, 135
Nichols, Robert Lee, 80
Nisbet, Robert, 129
Nozick, Robert, 106–8, 155
Nussbaum, Martha, 14, 40–41

Oakeshott, Michael, 11, 149, 169–71, 175, 298
Ober, Josiah, 62, 64–65
Okin, Susan Moller, 188–89
Owen, Robert, 265–66

Parekh, Bhikhu, 94, 98
Parkin, Frank, 285–86
Parks, Rosa, 220
Pateman, Carole, 102–3, 187
patriarchy, 5, 13, 80, 177–78, 186, 189
personal is political, 178, 188–89, 301
Piaget, Jean, 192–93
Pinker, Steven, 84
Plato: *Apology*, 19, 36–37; critique of democracy, 6–7, 11, 22–23, 38–41, 153, 255, 292; *Crito*, 19, 37–38, 222–23; political philosophy of, 5, 19; *Republic*, 19, 23–35; on Socrates, 19, 22
Popenoe, Paul, 297
positive psychology, 60, 301–2
pre-commitment devices, 39–40
presentism, 3, 3n3
Price, Richard, 152
prisoner's dilemma, 75–77, 87, 295
private property rights, 104–11, 115, 153–54
Provine, D. M., 202
public health, 54, 248, 299–301
public health ethics, 299
punishment, 59, 96, 111, 192, 200–201, 234–36

racial inequality: immigration control, 201–3; incarceration, 200–201; intersectionality, 214–15; lack of attention to, 10, 13, 115, 177–78; lynchings, 221–22; nonviolent campaigns, 220–26

racial segregation, 116, 216, 220–21, 226–28
rational choice theory (RCT), 64–65, 144–45
Rawls, John, 193–94, 219–20, 228, 259–62
religion: exclusionary, 133–34; and slavery, 206–7; social contract tradition, 71–72; toleration, 119–22
Richerson, Peter J., 88
rights: civil, 219–21; democratic, 201; free speech, 253; Indigenous, 11, 98, 108–12; individual, 21, 39–40, 93, 98, 118, 211, 219; natural, 2, 7, 68, 81, 85, 95–98, 113–15, 234; primary goods, 193; private property, 104–11, 115, 153–54; same-sex couples, 171; self-ownership, 115, 123, 211, 292; traditional, 157; voting, 241; women's, 186–88
Rousseau, Jean-Jacques: *Discourse on the Origins of Inequality*, 68, 124–28, 136, 141; *Emile*, 123, 132, 141; on equality, 141–42, 292; on fraternity, 142–43; on freedom, 138–39; on liberty, 138–40; on private property, 103, 127; social contracts, 81, 123; on state censorship, 132–34; on will of all, 130
Rousseau, Jean-Jacques. *The Social Contract*: democratic governance, 67–68, 123, 127–29, 131, 131n10, 132, 136–40, 143; economic inequality, 134–36, 141; general will, 125, 128–32, 136, 143–44
Ruggles, David, 212

Saint-Simon, Henri de, 265
Sandel, Michael, 134–35, 298

Schmidt-Petri, Christoph, 245
Seligman, Martin, 60–61
Sharma, Nandita, 201–2
slavery: brutality of, 208–11; harmful legacy of, 116–18, 164, 215; hierarchical practices for, 114, 200, 206; and liberalism, 113, 115; reparations for, 115–18; and western civilization, 206–7
Smith, Brian, 111
social contract theory: and consent, 99, 101–2; and felicity, 72–73; interest-based, 67–73, 78–79; mutual advantage, 68–69; and political authority, 67, 79; right-based, 67–68, 93, 99; state of nature, 73–75
socialism: conservatives on, 172; hierarchical, 265; planned economy, 155; and redistribution, 171; utopian, 31, 265–66
Socrates, 19, 22–39
Solum, Lawrence, 56–58
Soviet Union, 139, 154, 264
Sowell, Thomas, 172
Spinner, Jeff, 158
Stalin, Joseph, 154, 264
state: censorship by, 121, 132–34, 253; conflict with autonomy, 89–90; violence by, 80, 83–86
Sterba, James, 173
Strauss, Leo, 4–5
Strossen, Nadine, 253
synchronic materialism, 267–72

Taylor, Michael, 86–87
Thomas Aquinas, Saint, 171, 234
Thompson, Dennis, 146
Thompson, Lanny Ace, 280
Tucker, A. W., 75
Tully, James, 109
Turing, Alan, 303–4
Turner, Piers Norris, 249

utilitarianism: consequentialism, 233, 235; critique of, 259–62; ethical predicaments in, 236–37, 242; freedom of expression, 252; happiness in, 233, 235–39, 243; on punishment, 234–36

violence, 80, 83–86, 224–31
virtue epistemology, 52–56
virtue ethics, 44–59, 300–301
virtue jurisprudence, 56–59
voting, 64–66, 144–45, 255–59

Waldron, Jeremy, 121
Wallerstein, Immanuel, 229
Walzer, Michael, 147
Washington, Booker T., 2, 5, 162–68, 172, 205
Waters, Lea, 301
Weber, Max, 86
Wedgwood, Ralph, 170
Weiss, Penny A., 177, 197–98
Whitman, James, 200
Wolff, Robert, 89–91
Wollstonecraft, Mary, 7, 142, 184–89, 292
women: domestic labor, 142, 161, 186, 194; educational inequality, 103, 132, 141–42, 161, 177, 183–84, 186; family power relationships, 102, 187–89; marriage expectations, 103, 183–84, 186–87, 189; political representation, 190–91; socialization of, 186–87, 189
Wood, Allen, 271–72

X, Malcolm, 224–25

Young, Charles, 49–50

Zagzebski, Linda, 52–53